THE PRINCE OF POETS

AND

MOST ILLUSTRIOUS OF PHILOSOPHERS

Concerning
Of Palla
Of Wis   Invention

"WHAT'S IN A NAME?"

"Motley's the only wear: It is my only suit.
. . . .
Invest me in my motley; give me leave
To speak my mind, and I will through and through
Cleanse the foul body of th' infected world
If they will patiently receive my medicine."
As You Like It, Act II., sc. vii.

"I have immortality in my pen, and bestow it on whom I will."
Return from Parnassus.

By

S. A. E. HICKSON

BRIG.-GEN., C.B., D.S.O. (R.E. RET.)

WITH SIXTEEN ILLUSTRATIONS

LONDON: GAY & HANCOCK, LTD.

MCMXXVI

PRINTED IN GREAT BRITAIN BY
BILLING AND SONS, LTD., GUILDFORD AND ESHER

THE PRINCE OF POETS

OR

"WHAT'S IN A NAME?"

THE PRINCE OF POETS
AND MOST ILLUSTRIOUS OF PHILOSOPHERS

Marble at St. Michael's Church, St. Albans, removed from its pedestal.

See p. 252.   *Frontispiece.*

ONE OF THE GREATEST OF MEN WHO HAD NO
NAME OF HIS OWN* BUT WHO MAY BE CALLED
BY A WHOLE LIBRARY OF NAMES:

GASCOIGNE—LANEHAM—IMMERITO—LYLY—BROKE—
GOSSON —WEBBE —PUTTENHAM—WATSON—LODGE—
DANIELL — GREENE —NASHE—PEELE —MARLOWE —
SPENSER—CERVANTES—MONTAIGNE—BACON—AND

SHAKESPEARE

FROM THE AGE OF TEN
HIS PEN WAS NEVER IDLE,
HIS MIND WAS NEVER WEARY,
HIS INDUSTRY WAS INDEFATIGABLE,
HIS UNIVERSAL GENIUS WAS UNPARALLELED,
HIS LOVE OF HUMANITY WAS IMMEASURABLE.

All that he wrote under the above names, and others,
will be found not to exceed the published works of Goethe
and many more. He was the first to use the Press
systematically for propaganda and, like the great painters,
he too had a school and trained pupils to assist him.

HERE IS THE LIFE OF A GREAT MAN.

" A combination and a form indeed,
Where every god did seem to set his seal
To give the world assurance of a man."
(*Hamlet*, Act III., sc. iv.)

---

* I have no name that is sufficiently mine.
(MONTAIGNE : Essay " Of Glory.")

LIST OF OTHER AUTHORS ON THIS SUBJECT WHICH MAY BE STUDIED WITH ADVANTAGE TO SUPPLY DETAILS WHICH MAY HERE SEEM LACKING.

MRS. HENRY POTT: Francis Bacon and his Secret Society.

W. F. C. WIGSTON: A New Study of Shakespeare.

W. F. C. WIGSTON: Francis Bacon: Poet, Prophet, Philosopher.

E. G. HARMAN: Francis Bacon and his Impersonations.

W. SMEDLEY: The Mystery of Francis Bacon.

GRANVILLE C. CUNINGHAM: Bacon's Secret Disclosed.

MME. DEVENTER V. KÜNOW (translated by MR. WILLARD PARKER): The Last of the Tudors.

SIR E. DURNING LAWRENCE: Bacon is Shakespeare.

ALFRED V. WEBER (Vienna Bacon Society): Der Wahre Shakespeare.

ALFRED V. WEBER: Bacon-Shakespeare-Cervantes.

PARKER WOODWARD'S Works.

MISS ALICIA LEITH'S Fly-Leaves.

Baconiana of the English Bacon Society; Baconiana of the American Bacon Society.

The Biliteral Cypher of Sir Francis Bacon: Deciphered by MRS. ELIZABETH WELLS GALLUP.

Sir Francis Bacon's (Word) Cipher Story: Deciphered by ORVILLE W. OWEN, M.D.

PREFACE

THIS new view of the character and early life of the author of the plays of William Shakespeare is put forward for the express purpose of challenging the strangely illogical view hitherto entertained of him.

That old view—gradually built up, as it seems, under a delusion—was that Shakespeare was a man lowly born, and country bred, who, without hereditary pretensions, without any perceptible education, and without living in real touch with the great spirits of his age, evolved, self-taught, an English vocabulary of new words from languages he may never have studied, and produced his great works without effort by virtue of innate genius, as a kind of *lusus naturæ*,* or freak of nature.

The view now put forward of Shakespeare's life and experience represents him as, on the contrary, high born, of a race distinguished for hereditary genius, perseverance, and force of will, through many generations: that his inborn gifts enjoyed exceptional advantages in careful nurture, education, and environment, to which he himself added painstaking and conscientious industry, and labour without parallel, steadily pursuing the exalted aims inspired in him in early youth, throughout a life of untold trial and mental suffering. It was thus he acquired his almost perfect power of expression and rhythmical beauty of diction, com-

* The " inspired idiot " of S. T. Coleridge.

bined with a philosophical soundness of judgment in the choice of matter, which culminated in inventions and achievements for the welfare and delight of man, that can only be described as phenomenal, through " The Plays of Shakespeare " and " The Great Instauration of Science," setting forth the value of induction, prophesying the new powers it must confer upon man—which we now see—and indicating their right use.

It has for some time been the fashion to decry Bacon as little short of a criminal, and to set up Shakespeare as a god. Neither was either. Both were one: a man like all men, liable to err, but one into whom God had breathed power, spirit, wit, will, eloquence, and knowledge of humanity and things, with love almost divine. The unity of the works in these two names is undeniable.

There may be errors in this attempt to draw a true picture of a man so very great. May its virtues give help and pleasure to many and overweigh its shortcomings. Our aim is nothing more than the scientific examination of a theory concerning the life and believed hereditary genius of Shakespeare which is more and more claiming recognition and held by many to be true, as disclosed by the cipher story.

It is assumed that the reader is acquainted with the researches of previous writers, such as those contained in the list given on p. ix; and he will find that the cipher story is quite consistent with what history, biography, and literature reveal when closely examined, whilst it fills in many gaps.

Certainly they who accept Gul: Shakspere as author of the famous plays which bear the name of William

Shakespeare have no right to complain of what is written here. For there is no proof whatever that the young rustic from Stratford could either read or write, or, as the historian Hallam says, that he had anything to do with the authorship of the plays.

They who thus accept, without proof or any reliable evidence, what is extremely improbable—nay, what is admitted more and more to be incredible—can believe anything. To them the *Deus in nobis* can inspire a man with a minute knowledge of facts of which he has neither been a witness nor read; they can at will contort anything, regardless of nature, mentality, psychology, environment, genealogy, or heredity, in none of which the believers in Gul: Shakspere are consistent. To them the poet needs no making; not only his inspiration but his scientific knowledge of composition, prosody, law, history, ethics, horticulture are all born in him. He has nothing to learn. He is a ready-made machine for writing poetry.

One thing is certain. Somebody has been gulled.

INTRODUCTION

A CERTAIN Japanese friend of the writer, on being recalled to his native land in 1914, placed in his hands a box of papers containing notes on, and extracts from, a multitude of works bearing on what he called the true life of Shakespeare. He said that he felt convinced that this was the same man as he who was known to his contemporaries in public life as Francis Bacon, but that he considered it outside his province as a stranger to present a point of view which—to his own great astonishment and no small amusement—seems repugnant to the mass of that great man's fellow-countrymen. So he left his notes unreservedly at my disposal with these words: "Speaking as a foreigner," said he, "and as an unbiassed Asiatic student of European literature, I am persuaded that no unprejudiced man can fail, on close scrutiny, to perceive that there was one master mind behind, and dominating, the whole literature of Europe during the last quarter of the sixteenth and first half of the seventeenth century. Moreover, this great master must emphatically have had from his earliest youth a very exceptional education and very peculiar opportunities of coming into touch with the great men of his time, both at home and in foreign countries. Indeed, if you pause to think, you will admit that reason must lead any thoughtful man, approaching the matter as a novice, to anticipate and expect that such a man as Shakespeare had such rare opportunities as a matter of course. To me, as a foreigner, your King Henry VIII. and Queen Elizabeth stand out, as we should say, amongst nature's prodigies—almost freaks. Both started well, but they shine as exceptions to the rule. Strong natures such as theirs not uncommonly rebel against the customs with which the art of man seeks to bind his fellows for the common good. As your own English idiom says very aptly: 'They kick over the traces.' Henry VIII. and Queen Elizabeth were, I am convinced,* Shakespeare's immediate ancestors. All three were contradictions. The struggle between nature and custom is the predominant theme running as an undercurrent alike in the plays of Shakespeare and in the philosophy of Bacon. The same mind pervades both. Both go direct to nature, and both show how nature, defying custom, works miracles by what thus seem to us contradictions. Nature, that is, reveals new phenomena, discoveries, and powers often by methods of her own, regardless of man's bonds, customs, predilections, and habits. Shakespeare was in this way nature's own child—a phenomenon, a miracle. Ask yourself this: Will future generations love Queen Elizabeth the more or the less for being the mother of Shakespeare ? Only one answer is possible. Do you yourselves cease to sing the psalms and praises of the great David of your Bible because he fell in love with Bathsheba, the mother of Solomon? or to extol the name and deeds of Nelson because he committed himself with Lady Hamilton ? So, too, will men forget Queen Elizabeth's departure from the customs of man. When great men shuffle off this mortal coil the sins of

* Or let us say, " were quite within the range of possibility " Shakespeare's ancestors.

the flesh are sometimes also forgiven in those who leave
behind them a spirit of real helpfulness to man, arising
out of their experience. True, only the truly great
can thus be forgiven; but surely who more than she,
to whom you and all the world owe so much, as to the
mother of Shakespeare?"

These were the words with which Mr. Bhutshenshu
bade me good-bye as he placed his notes in my hands.
He insisted, and I with some reluctance agreed, that his
name should be suppressed as only inspirer of any
publication that might result. The points of view
here expressed are the result of his researches. He is
the true author of this book. He is no more.* It
may be that here and there my fancy has carried me
up on stronger wings than even he would approve.
My aim is to examine rather than assert. I ask,
therefore, those who differ from the conclusion here
offered to look upon my book as a work of imagination
and to read it as a fanciful story—a fairy tale of the
Fairy Queen. They will at least concede that I have
made out a case for a Shakespeare reasonably well
educated in a rare environment with a more full, interesting, wonderful, and yet more probable record of
endeavour and achievement, than anything that can be
made out of the biography of Shakspere of Stratford.
Yet this new and to my mind true Shakespeare had
all that sweetness and amiability of character which
those who believe in Shakspere of Stratford fancy that
he must have had.

For those who take a more serious view of my work

* Mr. Bhutshenshu is an invention, introduced for the purpose of setting forth the possible view of a far-off stranger—
the author's *alter ego*.

I have endeavoured to give such references as will enable them to verify Mr. Bhutshenshu's researches, which, in writing, I have brought up to date. The genius, wit, and ability of Queen Elizabeth, her wonderful courage, her curious innate wisdom, and her taste for writing in verse, no less than her terrifying and flinty harshness and extraordinary power of dissimulation, come out most excellently well in Mr. Fred Chamberlain's recent work entitled, "The Sayings of Queen Elizabeth." The following extract from his book shows also the native tendency of the great Queen's mind, for euphuistic metaphor and antithesis,* long before "Euphues, or the Anatomy of Wit" was written, but when she was almost the same age (twenty-one) as Shakespeare-Bacon was (eighteen), at the time that that work was published,—(compare the dedication to Lady Elizabeth Vaux, p. 222): "August—I walk many times into the pleasant fields of the Holy Scriptures, where I pluck up the goodlisome herbes of sentences by pruning, eat them up by reading, chew them by musing, and lay them up at length in the high seat of memorie, by gathering them together, that so, having tasted their sweetness, I may the less perceive the bitterness of this miserable life."† These words, written, it appears, whilst the Queen was imprisoned at *Woodstock* after being in the Tower (1554), reflect the euphuistic mind of Bacon-Shakespeare exactly; as do the verses to

* She had probably read Lord Berners's translation of Guevara's "Marcus Aurelius," 1539. (It was again translated by T. North, brother of her friend Lord Roger North, in 1557, the year before she came to the throne, and was received by their father, Lord Edward North, at Charter House.)

† F. Chamberlain, "The Sayings of Queen Elizabeth," p. 8.

" Fortune "* which follow, and both had very possibly
been seen by him at Woodstock in 1575. Her literary
power of expression in letters and prose is altogether
beyond the ordinary; her wit like none so much as
Shakespeare's.

Mr. Chamberlain admits that he himself might be
called " an Elizabeth maniac " in the introduction to
his book (p. xi), and I most heartily sympathise with
him, though regarding the great Queen from a somewhat different, and even yet higher standpoint, as
nature's child. For she was essentially characteristic, or, to use M. Jusserand's expression, "representative " of her age. Now the license and Machiavellian
dissimulation, current at her Court and at all the Courts
of Europe of her time, cannot be denied. They were
in England the legacy of the Wars of the Roses and times
of Richard III. Yet she had a very real ambition to
serve her country and kind. In her we see nature
mighty and irresistible, wrestling with custom, the
human with the divine, the will with the law, wit with
folly, strength with infirmity, just as in the plays of
Shakespeare, and as I have sought to trace it, in his
own life and character, so full of contradictions. Thus
in one of the very beautiful Latin, Greek, French, and
Italian prayers of Queen Elizabeth, which Mr. Chamberlain gives, we find the following, written almost as
having Ascham's admonition on her mind:† " I confess
without hypocrisy, that I do not deserve to be honoured
and served, but for ever should be abandoned and

---

* These verses are said to have been written with charcoal on
a shutter at Woodstock by the Queen when deprived of pen and
ink. F. Chamberlain, " Sayings of Queen Elizabeth," p. 8.
　　† See p. xxv, below.

covered with disgrace. Nevertheless thou knowest that I am sorry and grieved that I have human infirmities. Alas, my God, do not judge me according to my deeds, for they are polluted, but, recollecting thy fatherly mercy, I confess and own as true that I have offended thee in many ways. Have thou pity for me, and forgive me according to thy promises, for thou art my Father and knowest my transgressions and my sins, black and bloody, are constantly before me to terrify me."* I confess that to me the impression of the real greatness of mind and sharp wit of Queen Elizabeth, that Mr. Chamberlain's "sayings" give, increases a thousandfold the soundness of the reasons for believing that she may have been the mother of Shakespeare, as by nature the most likely woman. Mr. Chamberlain himself says of his book, "So these sayings are tied about her neck. They tell the truth. They prove her great and small. . . . They prove her a saint and a murderess. They prove her truthful and a liar. They prove her sincere and a hypocrite. They prove her Catholic and Protestant. They prove her with only *one* principle—to make her country great! . . . She had *no* policy, as her words themselves show, except to do whatever seemed necessary at the moment." This is severe, but Mr. Chamberlain's "sayings" seem just. Yet strong as "nature erring" was in Queen Elizabeth, she conceived, I repeat, in early years the noblest ambition, but tossed about by her variable nature as a woman—a stranger to domestic affection swift to act, and often bewildered—her muse, like Shakespeare's, at times deserted her. With infinitely greater burdens to bear than the generality she, too

* F. Chamberlain, "Sayings of Queen Elizabeth."

was not always or in all respects true to her better self, or able quite to tame nature by habit. Mr. Chamberlain attacks Mr. Froude for minor omissions and inaccuracies, but does not show him to be substantially wrong historically: the one holds up to view the greatness of Queen Elizabeth's nature, the other her weakness. Her native cleverness no one denies. Her Napoleonic insight astonishes. And she, too, could be cruel.

It is, nevertheless, the true greatness of this wonderful Queen which I also, in common with nearly all Englishmen, in her own time and now, have at heart. In her youth she had herself found solace in learning as a source of strength, amid immense difficulties and terrific trials; and she loved to encourage learning, and the culture of genius, in the young, in its most practical form and application. I feel, therefore, that it is impossible to do her higher honour than by saying that, in her nature and greatness, I see intimately reflected the yet greater genius of *Shakespeare*, as it developed from early youth, I believe, under her guidance, counterbalanced by the gentle and pious nurture of the Bacons. My aim is not controversy, but to put before the public a point of view, evidently quite within range of possibility, for mature consideration: that it was the combined favourable circumstances of birth, environment, and experience, which together, one and all, contributed to produce the greatest seer of all time, whose aim was the Art of Direction on the right way to the right place, even more than Induction and scientific power, which was, however, to be the chief instrument and prop in finding and keeping it.

This conclusion has not been reached without a very

close examination of the works of George Gascoigne or Gascon; the letter of Robert Laneham or Langham; the essays of Michael Eyquem (Higham) de Montaigne, who suggests his descent from "a House well known in England" (see his essay on Glory, and Weever's "Funeral Monuments"). Also "Euphues, or the Anatomy of Wit," which first made our new English; Ascham's "Schoolmaster"; and the anonymous "Shepherd's Calendar," with its illuminating gloss, the professed work of the new poet; Webbe's "Discourse on Poetry"; Puttenham's "Art of English Poesie"; and similar works, English and foreign, not omitting "Don Quixote," have been analysed with a detail which would be tedious in a general summary such as the present work offers.

DIVÆ ELIZABETHÆ

QUEEN ELIZABETH AND DAVID—SHAKESPEARE AND SOLOMON

(A Letter Concealed for Two Hundred Years.)

NOTES

1. The letter of Sir Roger Ascham entitled *Divæ Elizabethæ*,* said to have been first printed from the manuscript in 1761, is not the least remarkable document in the literature of the sixteenth century touching on this matter. It is dated October 30, 1566, two years before Ascham's death, and when Bacon-Shakespeare was five years old. "The Schoolmaster" had been begun in 1563, and by this letter he apparently intended to offer this book on education to the Queen, but thought better, as he therein deliberately and boldly compares her "life and state" to that of King David, saying:

"Most noble Princess, and my best Lady and Mistress, I—oft thinking of this race of David's life, of his former miseries, of his later felicities, of God's dealing with him at all points to bring happiness to his present time, and safety to his posterity—have had for many causes, many like thoughts even of the life and state of your Majesty." He reminds her how God blessed King David and "he heard from God's own

* James Bennet, "The Works of Roger Ascham," 1761.

xxiii

mouth: ' *Thine owne seed shall sit in thy seat,*'* which is the greatest comfort that come to a great Prince." He then reviews the two books of Samuel, the second of which contains " the life of David, the image of a good Prince, a fair picture of a flourishing state and happy time, when God was always in mind and his former benefits, his former deliveries from danger of death never utterly forgotten, . . . and in the end, had this joyful blessing from God's own mouth by Nathan's message, which all true English hearts daily do pray, that God will send the same unto your Majesty: ' *Excitabo semen tuum postea, quod egredietur de utero tuo, et regnum seminis tui perpetuo firmabo* ' (' I will set up thy seed after thee, which shall proceed out of thy bowels, and I will establish his Kingdom ')." Had the courtly Ascham forgotten that he was addressing a professed Virgin Queen, who could expect no seed ? or did he, too, know " things that it is not for all men to know " ? His conclusion of the state and life of David, which seemed to remind him so much of Her Majesty, is certainly not wanting in frankness, Bathsheba being the mother of Solomon.†

Thus he proceeds: " But David was wrapt in a stranger case and kind of misery; for when God had showed him his greatest favour, and had given him the highest benefits that man in earth could receive, yet God suffered him to fall into the deepest pit of wickedness, to commit the cruellest murder, the

---

* Solomon, son of Bathsheba, was from another of nature's unions. Was not Shakespeare similarly the son of Queen Elizabeth ? See p. 15.

† Francis Bacon was born January 22, 1561, four months after the death of Amy Robsart, Leicester's wife.

shamefullest adultery that ever did man upon earth.
Whereinto he did not stumble by ignorance, nor slide
by weakness, nor only fall by wilfulness, but went to
it advisedly, purposing all practises, and finding out all
fetches, that mischief could imagine, to bring mischief
to pass. Yet though David had shaken from him
God's fear, yet God had not taken from David his
Grace. For, when God did knock, David did open;
when Nathan said boldly, ' *Tu fecisti malum coram
Domino* ' (' Thou hast done evil in the sight of the Lord '),
David answered humbly, ' *Ipse peccavi Domino* ' (' I
have sinned before the Lord '); and so out of this foul
matter is gathered the fairest example and best lesson,
both for prince and private man, that is in all Scripture. . . . And therefore was I very willing to offer
this book to your Majesty, wherein, as in a fair glass,
your Majesty shall see and acknowledge, by God's
dealing with David, even very many like dealings of
God with your Majesty . . . and in the end have as David
had—that is, most prosperity and surest felicity for
you, yours, and your posterity." The sin of David
was at least a strange one to hold up as an example
to a Virgin Queen, to whom, moreover, the prospect of
posterity would not appeal. Was poor Amy Robsart
the Uriah, and Shakespeare the modern Solomon ?
Ascham's parallel almost passes belief—a parallel
without parallel.

2. For the sake of distinction I have throughout called
the recognised actor and theatre proprietor by the name
of " Shakspere of Stratford," and have confined the
use of the name of " Shakespeare " to the authorship
of the plays. There is said to be no such name as
" Shakespeare " in the records of Stratford-on-Avon, in

which the spelling takes various other forms, such as Shaxpere, Shackspere, Shaksper, and even Chacspere. To quote an expert: " Though Shakespeare, as the poet had it printed in the title-page and dedication of his poems, is indubitably a Teutonic or Saxon compound, yet ' Shakspere ' in the signature of his will is Gaelic— derived from *seac*, or *shag*, dry, shrunken, withered, and *pier*, a leg or shank—similarly to Cruickshank. . . . In the marriage licence of the actor and Anne Hathaway, preserved in the Consistorial Court of Worcester, and first discovered and published in 1836, the name assumed a new variety and is twice written as ' Shagspere.' "* There is no register showing that the actual marriage took place, and Worcester is a long way from Stratford (forty miles). I also use Shakespeare-Bacon or Bacon-Shakespeare or Shakespeare-Immerito, etc., as signify-ing the same nameless and unnamed man who, under various motleys, wrote, as many believe, beside the plays, much and many things hitherto attributed to others.

3. The student of this problem must bear ever in his mind the definite description of his method of dissimula-tion in writing feigned history, given by John Barclay in the " Argenis," that he will write " a fable as a history " in such a manner that " he shall err as well that will have it all to be a true relation of things really done, as he that takes it to be wholly fained," not merely by giving the characters imaginary names, but also by inserting " many inventions which cannot pos-sibly agree with those I intend to point out." He thus makes it clear that he has in fact real personages in his

* Charles Mackay, " Glossary of Obscure Words and Phrases," 1887.

mind whose real names he purposely conceals, and leaves it to the reader to find them out; and men, " while they read . . . shall meet with themselves, and as in a looking-glass shall see the face and merit of their own fame."*

* John Barclay, " Argenis," translated into English by Sir Robert Le Grys.   London, 1629, with a key, published by His Majesty's command (*i.e.*, King Charles I.), p. 131.

See also "Bacon's Secret Disclosed," by Granville C. Cuningham.

CONTENTS

LIST OF ILLUSTRATIONS

ERRATA

Page 85, line 8: *For* " 1578 at Richmond " *read* " 1579."

Page 223. *The footnote should read:* " But the bee takes a middle course: it gathers its material from the flowers of the garden and the field, but transforms and digests it by a power of its own, etc."

Page 313, 5 lines from bottom : " General Hickson has said that Ariel " *should read* " General Hickson suggests that Ariel."

THE PRINCE OF POETS

CHAPTER I

BACON THE BELLRINGER

THE discovery that Shakespeare was very possibly a
royal Prince and heir to the throne of England offers a
new point of view which is worth examining. It seems
startling at first, but is not inconsistent with history.
Above all, it is in complete accordance with the character of the famous plays. They take just the form
natural to a Prince-poet. As Shakespeare, he sings
with evident pride of the history and deeds of his own
ancestors, giving them all from Edward I. to Henry
VIII., though not all under the same name, and Henry
VII. alone *in prose*, under the name of Bacon. Indeed,
the address to the reader of the " Vie Naturelle," published in France in 1631, records that the famous ancestors of Bacon " left so many marks of their greatness
in history that honour and dignity seem at all times to
have been the spoil of his family . . . (and) he saw himself destined one day to hold the helm of the Kingdom
in his hand."* This contemporary published fact is
entirely in accordance with what the cipher, and literature closely examined, clearly reveal.

Now the main issue of this discovery is really something colossal. It goes far beyond the mere controversy

* Granville C. Cuningham, " Bacon's Secret Disclosed,"
p. 50.

I

whether Bacon wrote the plays published under the
name of William Shakespeare, which is so completely
captivating and more and more powerfully engrossing
men's minds. The importance of the discovery lies
in the fact that it brings into a fierce light once more
the comprehensive unity and vast significance of the
scientific methods and aims of this great master. I
reveals Shakespeare in Bacon as a man so great, with a
mind so well balanced, that he could write both the
philosophical and profound " Great Instauration of
Science " as well as the famous and witty works of art
the immortal plays showing how men's passions affec
their actions in the use of power. Both appeared
at the same time. Together they symbolise the
" marriage of science and art " which he talks about—
of the scientific instrument of induction, and that ar
of direction on which Bacon laid so much stress.

For though he who is called Bacon was not himsel
the inventor of induction, it was he, above all, who per
ceived this to be the only sure method of endowing
human life with new discoveries and powers. He was
as he said, the bellringer, calling others to hear. H
hoped as none other that, with the aid of time, these
inventions might enable man " in some degree to subdu
and overcome the necessities and miseries of humanity
. . . Yet evermore," he said, " it must be remembere
that the least part of knowledge passed to man by thi
so large charter of God must be subject to that use fo
which God granted it—that is, *for the benefit of the sta
and society of man,*"* and so " cleanse the foul body o
th' infected world."†   It was thus to give right direc

* Bacon, " Valerius Terminus."
† Shakespeare, " As you Like It," Act II., sc. vii.

tion to men in the use of their powers that he laboured above all.

Such, briefly, were the aims of the wonderful child of fortune and misfortune known during life under the motleys of Francis Bacon and William Shakespeare. It is the all-embracing completeness and unity of his work as a whole which so animate the minds of men to-day.

For this discovery is the result of researches that are being carried out quite independently—not singly— and not only in this country, but in America, France, Germany, Austria, Holland, our own colonies, and in certain centres throughout the entire globe. They must therefore before long sift through to the wider rank of thinking man, and overcome his natural prejudice against the attack on a long-cherished idol. For all men naturally cling to their preconceptions. Such careful research work as that of Madame von Künow can but excite interest through her book entitled: "Francis Bacon, the Last of the Tudors," more especially seeing that it emanates from the classical German centre of Weimar,* and has been translated into English by Mr. Willard Parker, the President of the Bacon Society of America. Again, Herr Weber of the Bacon-Shakespeare Society of Vienna has published two important books entitled, "The True Shakespeare" and "Bacon-Shakespeare-Cervantes." He proclaims him the greatest genius the world has known, and declares that England is concealing the truth. In France, too, General Cartier, having checked the bi-

* Though based on research in the British Museum, Record Office, etc., and in consultation with such men as the late Sir Henry Irving.

literal cipher story, being a cipher expert, is forming a Bacon Society of France; and in Holland Dr. Speckman is making remarkable discoveries.

This gradual progress of the revelation of Bacon's work is entirely in accordance with Shakespeare-Bacon's conception of the revelation of truth with time, and his deliberate plan. He hoped that little by little the light which he was kindling would spread and embrace all the world. So it is doing. Yet one question always remained open in his mind: How to persuade men to use his new powers in the right direction —that is, to alleviate, not to inflict misery? His mirror of man, the great plays of Shakespeare; the obstinate wanderings of Don Quixote up and down in search of self-glory, etc., were examples of his endeavour to give direction, by showing how man's passions and preconceptions deceive his senses and mislead his reason unless controlled by habit, creating errors destructive of all well-being, in "Natural Histories" and plays.

He thus saw plainly the dangers of scientific invention in wrong hands, through misapplication and misdirection.

The recent war has brought nothing home to us more forcibly than the truth of this presentiment. As Sir Oliver Lodge recently pointed out, science and art have increased man's powers of destruction to an extent fearful to contemplate. Terrible are the facilities provided by modern inventions for suddenly dealing death and destruction and untold misery on millions of men. Thus this new revelation gives us something very tangible indeed to reflect upon. This misapplication of power was the chief danger against which our Shake-

speare-Bacon concentrated his main efforts. " This,"
he cries, " is the very thing I am labouring at and preparing with all my might ": " to find an art of indication
and direction "*—to keep man in the right way to subdue
human misery.† It was on the culture of the individual mind that he placed his faith. His mirror has
not yet proved fully efficacious. The individual minds
of men everywhere have not yet acquired sufficient force
of character to abstain from envy and national greed.
Men do not see clearly how patiently to resist the temptations and eliminate the terror of war, and to rely on
reason and time to accommodate their differences as the
more divine and noble solution; nor do they see clearly
how to use the new civilising powers to their full advantage, though they seem now to be concentrating on it.

Nevertheless the great bell of the now world-famed
Shakespeare continues to peal, calling louder than ever.
His plays are heard to-day all over the world, even in the
countries of our recent enemies—more, it is said, than
at home. May they be well understood. He is appeal-
ing ever to a wider humanity from a wider horizon.
His light is spreading, as he hoped, further and further
with its cry for unity: " Evermore it must be remembered that the least part of knowledge is subject to the
use for which God hath granted it, which is the benefit
and relief of the state and society of man."

This was the very keynote of the bell by which Bacon
in the name of Shakespeare hoped to tune all nations
to a common idea: the use of scientific power for the
welfare of man, not for national and individual greed.
Such was the aim of that new philosophy of which

* " De Aug.," Book V., chap. ii.
† " Plan of Great Instauration."

Bacon himself claimed only to be the bellringer, calling upon others to hear and help. The marriage of art and science, on which it was based, has now produced many of those invaluable discoveries which it was foreseen must result from logical induction. The mind of man has in many ways proved thus a match for the nature of things, and many new civilising powers have been conferred upon him. How vast, for example, are our powers of broadcasting propaganda, and educating the young, if only we applied them always religiously in the right direction. Shakespeare-Bacon saw that this is the weak point. Power can be had, but if direction be wanting, as the Great War shows, it is worse than useless.

So, again, we have lived to see the truth of the teaching of both Shakespeare and Bacon verified in another wonderful way. Both maintain that art *almost can change* nature.* In two cases the very nature and aims of a whole nation have been changed by education and propaganda within a single generation, within living memory. Germany achieved it disastrously under the influence of Prussia, forsaking peaceful philosophy, art, science, and manufacturing skill for Pan-Germanism and resort to force; taking direction to the wrong place in neglect of the teachings of Don Quixote. The motives of Japan seem sounder. Civilisation and art will, it is hoped, find a wiser solution in the Pacific Ocean, and avoid the hateful misdirection of power.

* Bacon, " De Aug.," Book II., chap. ii.
Shakespeare, " Winter's Tale," Act IV., sc. iii.; "Hamlet," Act III., sc. iv., l. 168:

" For use almost can change the stamp of nature."

Shakespeare-Bacon hoped that, as the mind of man became a match for the nature of things, through science, man would see how to use his knowledge more and more for civilising and humane purposes. Science has at last made all men neighbours. It has, however, not yet taught them, as he hoped, to be always " governed by sound reason and religion."*

It remains still for human art to use its new powers consistently " for the benefit of the state and society of man " by study, observation, conference, and above all, by inductive reasoning. For induction is the only competent substitute for war: the threshing out of particulars and, after eliminating errors, arranging them in logical order, each part supporting the other as incontestable fact beneficially instead of each man blindly worshipping his own idols and preconceptions. It is this very principle of induction that gives Parliament, with its committees and reports, its intrinsic power, and Bacon-Shakespeare was a member of it for twenty-five years. It is this that has made those Parliaments spread like Shakespeare himself—from England all over the world; and what else is it that is now inviting leagues and committees of *experts* of all nations to come to a unanimous and acceptable opinion on questions of all kinds in mutual conference ?

How vast are our powers now of thus gathering and marshalling particulars, in a short space, from all over the world ! Events happening in one country, or discoveries made anywhere, now pass in the same hour ' up and down " and all over the world. Particulars are thus more easily collected and disseminated. Broadcasting is at work by wireless. Soon individuals

* " Nov. Org.," Aph. CXXIX.

will be able to converse across the world.   What greater powers—we ask, surprised—can Bacon have dreamed of when he penned his great prophecy and unfolded it in the pages of his " New Atlantis "; or when he sent forth his great plays in the name of Shakespeare; or Don Quixote, in the name of Cervantes, to reflect his observations of human life, and to hold them up to all mankind in his great mirror as a first indication to man of the scientifically right, as compared with the wrong, direction ?   Time is now revealing to us his work as a whole, as he knew that it would reveal him and his true name.   We see and realise it with wonder; and the new powers amaze us.   Yet the great problem always remains: How to ensure their right use and get the full advantage from these powers.

Nothing, however, is more patient than Time. Truth clings to obscurity till science and the art of man force it into the light.   Such was Shakespeare-Bacon's favourite emblem.   Since, however, truth once brought into open daylight never dies but persists, the waves of intelligence which research is now sending out in respect of his work, growing larger, must presently intersect and unite all the world in a common scientific purpose. Reason—such was Shakespeare-Bacon's faith—must eventually lead man to perceive how immeasurably the new powers can, if rightly used, alleviate human misery.   The powers are there.   The culture of the individual mind in their use and adaptation is still wanting.   It is upon this, above all, that concentration is needed.

The bell of the great master of science and art is still ringing—Shakespeare, the myriad-minded and myriad-named !   It matters not whether we call him also Bacon or by any other of his many pseudonyms. "A rose by any other name would smell as sweet." Time's scythe is satisfied. The honour which he foresaw would be his is at hand, and will "make him heir to all Eternity!" Bacon is the ringer: Shakespeare is the bell, with sonorous measures calling on mankind to listen, and see set before their eyes the hurt which human nature erring can inflict upon itself through unreflecting passions, unrestrained by custom, habit, and good form. The mind of man must inevitably move forward on the lines he indicated. Art and science will endow him ever with new powers in the course of time. It rests with him to see those powers used, only for that end for which God granted them and Jesus died—*i.e.*, for the salvation and the benefaction of the state and the society of man.

It was thus that Shakespeare hoped to "cleanse the foul body of th' infected world,"* words so closely kin to those of our Communion Service, that our sinful bodies may be made clean.

*   *   *   *   *

To sum up. According to the new light, Shakespeare and Bacon are mere motleys woven by the same concealed Prince-poet, the lawful son of Queen Elizabeth: by nature the great son of a great mother, begotten under strange and almost inexpressible conditions. Neither, it well may be, were faultless to the human eye. Yet to none does mankind owe more, so paradoxical are nature's methods. No man ever had a more concrete and practical aim than this great Shakespeare-Bacon. In a Latin paper found tucked away in his desk after his death he has made known his hopes to

* "As You Like It," Act II., sc. vii.

posterity, just as in his will he left his true name and memory for future ages to discover. Mr. Spedding has very aptly translated his eloquent words as follows:

" Above all, if a man could succeed in kindling a light in nature—a light which should in its very rising touch and illuminate all the border regions that confine upon the circle of our present knowledge, and so spreading further and further, should presently disclose and bring into sight all that is most hidden and secret in the world, that man (I thought) would be the benefactor indeed of the human race."

If these were the hopes of Shakespeare, what man's hopes have been more gloriously fulfilled ? Concealed behind his motleys he relied on secrecy during life, content that time should reveal his true name and memory and bring it into the sun's light in ages to come. He definitely put aside living self-glory in those immortal words:

> " Let fame, that all hunt after in their lives,
> Live registered upon our brazen tombs,
> And then grace us in the disgrace of death;
> When, spite of cormorant devouring Time,
> Th' endeavour of this present breath may buy
> That honour which shall bate his scythe's keene edge
> And make us heirs of all eternity."
>
> (" Love's Labour's Lost," Act I., sc. i.)

" The hour's now come,"* says the same author;

* (" Tempest," Act I., sc. ii.):

PRO.: For thou must now know further.
MIR.: You have often
 Begun to tell me what I am; but stopp'd,
 And left me to a bootless inquisition,
 CONcluding, "Stay, not yet."
PRO.: The hour's now come.

" this very minute bids thee ope thine ear: obey and be attentive!" The magic art of Prospero aided by science, in Ariel on electric wings, is everywhere at work. Everywhere, too, is heard the voice of Shakespeare, Shakespeare, Shakespeare. His plays are everywhere, spreading his light further and further, till at last the full meaning and extent of his wondrous work shall be disclosed, and Ben Jonson's riddle be solved—written on his sixtieth birthday:

"Thou stand'st as if a mystery thou didst."

* * * * *

Such being the revelation which is now more and more forcing its attention on the public, it will be of interest to sketch the grounds upon which it is founded—*i.e.*, the ancestry, life, philosophy, and art of Shakespeare regarded as the son of Queen Elizabeth and one with Francis Bacon—a true Pan-Shakespeare, Bacon, Spenser, Cervantes, Marlowe, Lyly, Peele, etc., all in one.

May not, perhaps, the Bacon Societies now coming into being in all countries of the whole world be the beginning of a movement which may yet unite all men in one common idea, so nobly expressed: the use of knowledge and power subject to the end for which God granted it, which is the benefit of the state and society of man—a spiritual rather than artificial league of nations—to dispose of quarrels by Induction rather than War.

CHAPTER II

SHAKESPEARE'S HEREDITARY GENIUS

As I have already indicated, the main plot of all the plays of Shakespeare deals with kings and queens, princes, reigning dukes, courts, palaces, and parliament. In the comedies of Ben Jonson, however, the plot turns more frequently upon the scenes of middle-class life,* as it was in Old Jewry and round Moorgate, and the more plebeian parts of the city. In short, the prologue to Jonson's first comedy makes it clear that he purposely abstained from beating the big drum and wrote for the class which lived, like himself, now in St. Bartholomew's Close, now in Cripplegate, etc.; whereas the distinguished author of the plays of Shakespeare frequented Courts and palaces and the society in high life which he painted and held up to nature—a concealed Prince.

Unfortunately, except the well-known terra-cotta bust at Gorhambury, no quite authentic portrait of Francis Bacon exists to show us that intellectual "eminency" which Dr. Rawley says marked even "his first and childish years," but a child portrait at Gorhambury shows just the eyes twinkling with "towardness of wit" and profoundly apprehensive brow he describes. Not less striking is the beautiful Hilyard miniature of Francis at eighteen, in which we

* " And persons such as comedy should choose,
   When she would show an image of the times."
       (JONSON: " Every Man in his Humour.")

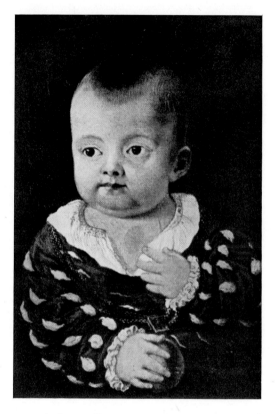

A CHILD PORTRAIT AT GORHAMBURY

Possibly Francis Bacon.

"A Child that guided Dotards."
Cymbeline, Act I., Sc. i., line 50.

Facing p. 12.

see the face of Shakespeare reflected in Queen Elizabeth. The alertness of Euphues, the erect Elizabethan carriage, the witty eye, the stiffly starched and princely ruff (just as described by Laneham), all bear witness to his true identity, whilst round the portrait—struck, no doubt, himself by the intellect of his sitter—the words " Si tabula daretur digna animum mallem " have been written by the artist—" Would that I could draw a picture worthy of his mind !" They are words which strangely resemble a line contained in the verses written against the Droeshout portrait of Shakespeare in the Folio, " O, could he but have drawn his wit."

Indeed, the assumption that Shakespeare was the son of Queen Elizabeth at once endows him with an ancestry as distinguished for literary talent as any that can be found. It includes even two influxions of the blood of the famous literary French royal house, one of which Isabella,* wife of Edward II., gave Edward III. his brains; the other, Katherine, gave Henry VI. his literary taste, so fatally unbalanced in him by the commanding vigour of the Plantagenets, owing to the early death of his father, Henry V., so that of him Shakespeare says: " Whose bookish rule hath pulled fair England down."† But the blood of Katherine of Valois flowed also in valiant young Edmund Tudor, and passed through him, and the highly intellectual, vigorous, well-disciplined, and devotional Margaret Beaufort, great-granddaughter of John of Gaunt, to Henry VII., Henry VIII., and Queen Elizabeth, and through her

---

* " Thy gentle Queen, sole sister to Valois."

(MARLOWE: " Edward II.")

† " Henry VI.," Part II., Act I., sc. i., last line.

—according to the present revelation—into the very veins of Shakespeare. Thus on him, according to the new light, genius descended intelligibly through a long line of famous ancestors by an heredity as marked for literary talent as it is lacking in distinction in the case of Shakspere of Stratford.

That ancestry has, moreover, this other distinctive feature: that, in the seven generations, running from old John of Gaunt, time-honoured Lancaster, the fourth son of Edward III., to Queen Elizabeth, there were no fewer than four marriages by free and natural choice, contrary to royal custom and constitutional practice. Further-more, each of these marriages brought fresh literary taste and connections to the royal blood. Thus John of Gaunt's third wife, by his free and indeed illegitimate choice, was the surpassingly beautiful and accomplished Katherine Swynford, widow of Sir Otes Swynford, sister of the wife of the poet Geoffrey Chaucer, and daughter of Sir Payne de Roet of Hainault. The great-grand-daughter of these two, Margaret Beaufort, was the most famous, pious, and generous patroness of our universi-ties, and of learning at large. " The genius of litera-ture hovered round the great-granddaughter of the friend of Chaucer,"* and she it was who married Edmund Tudor, the son of Katherine de Valois of the royal house and most literary family of France, being the widow of Henry V., after whose death Katherine, in turn, had married by free choice Owen Tudor, a gentleman of her late husband's Court, but of high lineage, boasting two royal descents. The issue of this marriage of Edmund Tudor, created Earl of Richmond, with Margaret Beaufort, "who had in a manner all

* " Life of Margaret Beaufort," by Caroline Halsted.

HENRY VIII

Facing p. 14.

that was praiseable in a woman,"* was King Henry VII., who married the gentle Elizabeth of York,† the daughter of Edward IV., who, by his own free choice, without even the knowledge of Parliament, had married Elizabeth Woodville, daughter of Luxemburg Jaqueline. It was her brother, Earl Rivers, who helped Caxton‡ to set up his first printing press in London, and introduced him at Court; and a translation of his from the French was the first book printed in England.§ The issue of this marriage was King Henry VIII., who, of his own free choice, married Anne Boleyn, the mother of Queen Elizabeth. Finally, in the light of the revelation which we are considering, the presumed union of Queen Elizabeth with the Earl of Leicester was one, again, of those natural and instinctive marriages of free choice which, clandestine as it was, did by one of nature's most incomprehensible decrees, produce, I believe, the man who was to become the wonder of the world, the founder of the new philosophy, and the reformer of the ways of man in respect of science and art, as well as the finger-post to the right use of their offspring—inventions both mechanical and poetical, new discoveries and powers.

Even this cursory glance at the ancestry and hereditary predecessors of Queen Elizabeth shows that there breathed in the genius of her royal veins the valour and virile wisdom of the Plantagenets, the distinguished

* Fisher's funeral sermon. (Caroline Halsted.)

† Margaret Beaufort, Countess of Richmond, loved her daughter-in-law, Elizabeth.

‡ Margaret Beaufort as Countess of Richmond likewise patronised Caxton's successor, Wynkyn de Worde, who printed her books and translations.

§ "Dictes and Sayings of the Philosophers," 1477.

literary taste of the French house of Valois, the indomitable will of the Tudors, the devout learning of Margaret
Beaufort, and the wit of Anne Boleyn.   All these characteristics, modified in some respects by the benign
nurture of the Bacons, are found highly developed in
Francis Bacon and peer forth no less, beautifully
adorned, in the plays of William Shakespeare; whilst
the fundamental ideas of the two on art, what it is, and
what it can do, will be found to be, as I shall show,*
identical down to the very words which they use.

Very really remarkable is the galaxy of variously
talented brave and surpassingly beautiful, accomplished
and witty, learned, affectionate, and devout women,
which throngs round the ancestry of Shakespeare,
in the light in which we are here studying him: Eleanor
of Castile, Isabella of France, Philippa of Hainault,
Katherine Swynford, Margaret Beaufort, Katherine
de Valois, Elizabeth Woodville, Elizabeth of York,
Anne Boleyn, and Queen Elizabeth.   These form a real
constellation of living women, such as it is easy to see
that the Prince of poets not only studied, but, which we
feel, that he must constantly have had in his mind from
youth, to a degree which heredity and consanguinity
can alone inspire, leading him to compare these ideals
with others that he saw around him, till experience
enabled him to paint female character, perfect and
noble, shrewd yet divine and gifted, as no other.
Highest amongst them all stands the " Venerable
Margaret," England's foremost patroness of learning
and its most pious devotee: " The progenitrix of a long
and glorious race, the benefactress of generations yet
unborn—the noble-minded but unassuming—the pious,

* See Chapter XVIII., p. 277.

the admirable, the illustrious Margaret Beaufort."* Here, indeed, is an ancestress worthy of Shakespeare. The wealthiest of heiresses, she was courted at the age of nine, married at fifteen, mother of a future king and a widow at sixteen. Her early life was one of vicissitude and profound trial faced with resolution. She died a devotee of learning, veritably directed to those ends for which God granted it, the benefit and relief of man. It was to her, more than all, that her Tudor descendants owed that faith in knowledge, as the true source of power which raised England's civilising power so high and which, in one word, gave us Shakespeare.

This opinion, and all that I have written of Bacon-Shakespeare's ancestry, is strengthened on reading the life of Henry VII., written by Bacon-Shakespeare himself (the only history not written as a play). It is confirmed on comparing the Shakespeare plays of " Richard III." and " Henry VI."

The character which Bacon draws of Henry VII.† reminds the reader forthwith of Shakespeare, saying: " He was fair and well spoken with *singular sweetness and blandishment of words*, studious rather than learned, with a devotional cast of countenance, for he was marvellously religious both in affection and observance." These, according to his pen, were the characteristics developed in the young Henry at Pembroke Castle by Sir William Herbert, the direct ancestor of the two incomparable brothers Pembroke to whom the First Folio of the plays is dedicated; and he calls him the " Solomon of England " on account of the treasure

* " Life of Margaret Beaufort," by Caroline Halsted.
† " Life of Henry VII.," by Bacon.

he laid up.   Bacon-Shakespeare also amongst many
things relates the story how, when Henry VI. saw him
as a boy at Eton, he prophesied that " This is the lad
who shall possess that for which we now strive," which
Shakespeare has immortalised:

KING HENRY: My Lord of Somerset, what youth is that
                        Of whom you seem to have so tender care ?
SOMERSET: My liege, it is young Henry, Earl of Richmond.
KING HENRY: Come hither, England's hope.   If secret powers
                        Suggest but truth to my divining thoughts,
                        This pretty lad will prove our country's bliss;
                        His looks are full of peaceful majesty."

                                        ("Henry VI.," Part III., Act IV., sc. vi.)

Bacon-Shakespeare, too, dwells on the noble character
of Margaret Beaufort and how much Henry VII.
owed her.

Indeed, the education of her grandson, Henry VIII.,*
also was personally superintended by the illustrious
Margaret Beaufort, his grandmother, "a pattern of the
best devotion of her times ";† and Erasmus, who tested
him very carefully when a young man, was greatly
struck both by the facility with which he absorbed new

---

* Henry VIII.'s mother, Elizabeth of York, was in every
way kindred in spirit to her beloved mother-in-law, Margaret
Beaufort, the venerable Countess of Richmond.   She, too, was
gentle by nature.   She, too, had passed a life of vicissitude
and trial with patient and dignified resignation in times of
singular cruelty, in which deception, craft, and dissimulation
prevailed to an extent which alone is sufficient to explain the
mutual distrust and Machiavellian aspect of conduct, still
current in Shakespeare-Bacon days, and so skilfully rendered
in " Richard III." and the Essays.

† Fuller's " Ch. Hist.," Cent. 16, Lib. 7.   See " Life of
Margaret Beaufort," by Caroline Halsted.

MARGARET BEAUFORT

Countess of Richmond and Derby, wife of Edmund Tudor and mother of Henry VII.

National Portrait Gallery.   *Facing p.* 18.

ideas, and yet more by his literary talent in giving the best turn to a sentence in expressing his meaning. Roger Ascham is even yet more eloquent on the literary genius of Queen Elizabeth. He styles her a star amongst women of learning, and holds her up as an example for the young men to emulate. He also makes a strong point of her love of any subject which naturally calls forth eloquence, and of her contempt for mere affectation in words; and it is noticeable that Bacon himself makes a very strong point of this in the "Advancement of Learning." In addition to the above, Bacon had in the Earl of Leicester a father who was the son of the Duke of Northumberland, said by Hume to have been the ablest man of his time after Henry VIII. So that our Shakespeare had in fact—on the present assumption—the two ablest men in England as his grandfathers. Nor can there be any doubt that the Earl of Leicester catered largely for those to whose hands the education of the young Francis was entrusted. Thus Arthur Golding, who was also connected by marriage with the Earl of Oxford—Burghley's son-in-law—dedicated his translation of Ovid's "Metamorphoses" to the Earl of Leicester, and dated it from Cecil House in the Strand, the house of Lord Burghley. Laneham and George Gascoigne were both protégés of the Earl, and above all these other translators; Sir Thomas North was the brother of Roger, Lord North,* the greatest friend both of Queen Elizabeth and the Earl of Leicester; and when Sir Thomas published his "Lives of Plutarch," the Earl of Leicester himself† wrote to

* Roger, Lord North, married the widow of Henry Dudley, brother of the Earl of Leicester.

† "Cal. of Hatfield MS.," part ii., p. 339, August 21, 1580.

Lord Burghley to ask him to promote the book.   Thus
it was the Earl of Leicester's patronage that encouraged
these translators, all of whom were in that same Court
circle in which the Bacons moved, and on whose
works admittedly so many Shakespearean plays are
based, and from them so many famous passages extracted.   Returning once more to Roger Ascham, his
" Schoolmaster " contains to an astonishing extent the
elements of Bacon's philosophy, and the history of
this book tells its own tale.   It was written during
Bacon's youth.   Francis was born on January 22,
1561.   Ascham relates* that it was on December 10,
1563, at Windsor, at dinner, that certain Privy Council-
lors, including W. Cecil, Lord Burghley, raised the
question as to the best method of teaching, when he,
Ascham, asserted that young children were sooner
" allured by love than driven by beating to attain good
learning."   He was then called away to the Queen,
with whom he was found later by Sir Richard Sackville,
who, taking him aside to a window, begged him to
teach his son.   A little later he pressed him to write a
book " concerning the right order of teaching, and
honesty of living, for the good bringing up of children."
" I, beginning some further excuse, *suddenly was called
to come to the Queen.*   The night following I slept little,
my head was so full of this our former talk, and I so
mindful somewhat to satisfy the honest request of so
dear a friend."

Sir Roger Ascham died in 1568, and his book was not
published till 1571, but a prefatory letter, already
referred to as " Divæ Elizabethæ," has been found,
intended apparently to dedicate it to the Queen, and

* James Bennet, " Works of Roger Ascham," 1761, p. 193.

dated October 30, 1566.* The book is entitled "The Schoolmaster, a plaine and perfite way of teaching children to understand, write, and speake, the Latin Tonge, but specially purposed for the private bringing up of Youth in Gentlemen and Noblemens' houses, etc."

Now, seeing that Ascham was at this time reading with the Queen "the noble oration of Demosthenes against Æschines," that the request to write this book on the education of the young emanated from a Privy Councillor and was made in the Queen's privy chamber, and that the book was dedicated to the Queen at the time when Francis Bacon (her presumed son) was growing up (1566) and five years old, there can be little doubt that it contains, as its contents indicate, the very principles upon which the genius of the future Shakespeare was nurtured and trained, and comparison with Montaigne's "Essays" confirms this. Two interesting examples—showing how easily Baconian literature can be traced to it—point the same way. Thus the first important work attributed to Francis was entitled, "Euphues, or the Anatomy of Wit," which is said to have made the new English and stands in the name of John Lyly. Ascham, in his book, dwelt upon this very quality—"Euphues"—as being the first essential in a child for learning according to the teaching of Plato, describing it as "goodness of wit and readiness of will to learn," a quality in which Bacon or Shakespeare must have been highly efficient. Indeed, Matthew Arnold in "Culture and Anarchy" translates it as "sweetness and light," the very character of Shake-

* See p. xxiii, "Divæ Elizabethæ." James Bennet, "English Works of R. Ascham," p. 179. Both Ascham and Quintilian commend exuberance of style in youth.

peare. So, too, Ascham expresses that same contempt for " certain books of chivalry . . . made in monasteries by idle monks* and wanton charrons," by which a man might well be led to "manslaughter and bawdrie," just as we find them condemned by Nashe and in " Don Quixote."

This book, on the education of the young and noble, was, moreover, written at a time when all the world was expectant. Would not the Queen publicly marry the Earl of Leicester and acknowledge him as her husband—and Francis as her son? Was it the doubtful circumstances accompanying the death of the gentle and neglected Amy Robsart, the first wife of the Earl, that stood in the way? What a tragedy! What a precedent! What a lesson and study for the brilliant genius of the young Shakespeare to contemplate !† Fortunately he knew nothing of it till he was fifteen. Long before that the great ideas that he had formed for the regeneration of the world had taken too deep a root in his mind to be shaken, as we may see in the Gabriel Harvey correspondence. He was resolved, as he tells us already in " Euphues," that the sovereignty of the reason in him should overcome the delights of the affections and self; and he seems never to have allowed himself to falter, in this respect, whatsoever his errors may have been. Small wonder that he learnt to see in human nature the soul of man darkly struggling to

* " Neither was I much unlike these Abbaie-lubbers."

(ARBER: "Euphues," p. iii.)

Nashe uses the same expression in " The Unfortunate Traveller."

† " Thence comes it that my name receives a brand."

(Sonnet CXI.)

thread its way through a *labyrinth* of errors woven by the ignorance and artifices of generations of earlier men groping likewise in the dark. His triumph has still to come. Time brings all secrets to the sun's light and will even now bestow upon him—

> " That honour which shall bate his scythe's keene edge
> And make us heirs of all eternity."
>
> ("Love's Labour's Lost," Act I., sc. i.)

It is the duty of art—that is, the mind of man—to perfect and exalt nature. This is primarily the task of the individual. Science confers increasingly new powers to help him, but his own integrity, industry, and trustfulness come first. Given these, then, by broadcasting, by means of the new powers of science, making knowledge common, and acknowledging a common end, we may yet, in days yet more enlightened, see more light, and a fund provided, not for the armament of man against man, but for the beautifying of our cities and surroundings, the improvement of health and the joy of all. Individual discipline, however, as Shakespeare and Bacon taught, the cultivation of good forms, customs, habits, and ends in the individual, directed by religion and common purpose as Christ taught, can alone prevail, can alone teach the application of the new powers rightly, and so provide beneficial laws. The more enlightened the individual the more enlightened his parliament. Scientific art provides the means. Human character must discern the method, giving patience and time their due.

CHAPTER III

SHAKESPEARE'S MOTHER AND FATHER

MISTRESS at last of England and herself, the bright, enlightened, shrewd, and majestical Queen Bess entered London from Hatfield, in 1558, by way of Charter House, where she stayed several days with Lord North before making her formal entry into the city. Lord North had two sons. The elder, Roger, who succeeded him in the title, and lived at Kirtling Castle near Cambridge, became the most confidential friend both of the Earl of Leicester and the Queen. But of greater significance is the fact that his younger brother, Sir Thomas North, was, as already mentioned, the translator from the Spanish of Guevara's " Marcus Aurelius," which is said to have inspired " Euphues, or the Anatomy of Wit," the book that, as already said, " first made our new English "; and, from the French, of " Plutarch's Lives," the bedrock of several of Shakespeare's plays and Bacon's essays on the Cæsars. So closely connected with Court and Queen were the men associated with the early training and education of Shakespeare-Bacon, for the Earl of Leicester was the patron of Sir Thomas North, and to him is also dedicated Arthur Golding's translation of Ovid's " Metamorphoses," published when Francis was seven years old, from which Shakespeare has stolen more than one line.

As yet the Earl of Leicester was still Lord Robert

Dudley. He had, however, often met Princess Elizabeth at the Court of Edward VI., whither he was not infrequently taken as a lad by his father, the intriguing but capable Duke of Northumberland, who married his eldest son, Guilford Dudley, to Lady Jane Grey. On the death of Edward VI. the Duke attempted to put this guileless lady on the throne, for which he, Guilford and Lady Jane, lost their heads, whilst Robert, the future Earl of Leicester, was imprisoned in the Tower (1554). Thither, also, that same year came Princess Elizabeth. Smart in dress and handsome in appearance, he is said to have been born on the same day and year that she was, and though the date of his birth is uncertain, he seems to have captivated her natural affections.* Thus, on her accession, though already a married man, he at once came to her side as Queen, escorted her round all the pageants of London arranged in her honour, mounted on a white charger, and was by her made Master of Horse. For the next two years—that is, the two years immediately preceding the birth of Francis in 1561—he is said hardly to have left the Queen's side.

The young lives of few sovereigns have been so clouded as that of the great Queen Bess. Few young princesses have presented a more pathetic figure. Such strange experiences seem fitly to presage a wonderful event. Her own mother, Anne Boleyn, was executed three years after her birth. She then had a succession of four stepmothers, of whom one also lost her head. All

* " I only show him favour because of his goodness to me when I was in trouble during the reign of my sister " (F. Chamberlain, " Sayings of Queen Elizabeth "). The question is, how far did her favours go?

loved her, for she was of a sweet, gentle, and amiable
disposition, curiously devoted to learning, yet of the
highest spirit, a spirit never broken by her tormentors
and prison; while the questionable courtship of herself
by Admiral Seymour was an experience which goes far
to account for her later-rumoured suspicious, moral
obliquity and that of her Court.   For her there was
never any happy private family life, so necessary for the
strengthening of character by good habits.   And was
she not herself set aside as illegitimate ?   The happiest
days of her early youth were those spent at Hatfield,*
reading with her dear brother Edward.   It is worth
while to compare the bright intelligence of her child
portrait, more especially with the intellectual Gorhambury bust of young Francis.   The tutor of young Edward
at this time was Sir Anthony Cooke, whose daughters,
Mildred and Anne, thus became her frequent companions.   These two ladies married Sir William Cecil
and Sir Nicholas Bacon, and the Queen felt more at
home in their family circle than in any other.   Almost
the first act of her reign was to appoint Sir William Cecil,
afterwards Lord Burghley, her Lord Treasurer, and Sir
Nicholas Bacon her Lord Keeper of the great seal;
and as an instance of that ready wit, which Shakespeare
her son inherited, she said of Lord Burghley—who
suffered from gout—that she employed him, not for his
bad legs but for his good head.   So, too, she said of Sir
Nicholas Bacon, who was corpulent, that his soul
lodged well.   On these very wise grounds she placed
the affairs of the Church mainly in his hands, so long as
he lived, both he, and Lady Bacon especially, being

* Once the seat of Katherine de Valois, widow of Henry V.,
after whose death she married Owen Tudor.

strict Calvinists, inclined to the puritanical, which indeed at one time nearly landed him in trouble, for the Queen herself favoured episcopacy. Nevertheless, the earnest piety of the Bacons had a powerful effect on Francis. It strengthened in him the moral fibre of that noble Tudor ambition which shines so brightly in them all in spite of faults, begotten by vanity of the pomp and adulation which is apt to warp nature in courtiers and kings. It taught him, as Francis Bacon, to shrink from this danger in such a manner that—thanks to nature, thus fortified and helped by the Bacons—the Tudor, Valois, and Plantagenet qualities came out in him as Shakespeare with that inestimable brilliancy which has won the admiration of the entire world. So wonderful and unfailing are his balance of mind, his perfect taste, his exquisite imagination, governed and controlled by the most profound judgment.

Sir Nicholas Bacon died early in 1579, when Lord Burghley took his place as the guardian of Francis, and the Queen relied more and more on Dr. John Whitgift in Church matters. He preached before her first in 1567, and was then made a royal chaplain, and Master of Trinity College, Cambridge, the college of the Queen's father, King Henry VIII. Francis Bacon, whom we think of ever as also Shakespeare, was sent to this college in 1573, and placed under Whitgift, the royal chaplain, as his tutor, though the college of Sir Nicholas Bacon was Corpus Christi. Moreover, Robert, Earl of Essex, said to be the brother of Francis, was sent to the same college in 1577, just before Whitgift left, on being created Bishop of Worcester. As Archbishop the Queen visited him at least once, and sometimes twice a year. He became, as it

were, her confessor, and to him she would reveal *the ver_
secrets of her soul*. He, as well as Sir Nicholas Baco:
and Lord Burghley, must have known well enough, toc
the secret of his delightful pupil's birth. Such clos
traits of character and face under such patronag
betray themselves, and nothing is more certain an‹
incapable of challenge than that the three principa
advisers of the great Queen—Nicholas Bacon, Williar
Cecil, afterwards Lord Burghley, and John Whitgift–
were the three men to whom, above all, was entruste‹
the education and care of the world's most preciou
genius, whom we hold to be William Shakespear‹
then known to the world as Francis Bacon. Eve
Stow's " Annales," by Howes,* with its appendix b
Sir George Buck, Master of Revels, will be found to hav
been written under a promise to the " renouned Whi'
gift, afterwards Archbishop of Canterbury, a Prelate ‹
first magnitude of sanctity, learning, patience, an
humility," as Dr. Rawley says; whilst Holinshed wɛ
well known to the author of the " Shepherd's Calendar.

Outside these three, and in a very different categor}
stood the Earl of Leicester, a man very far from bein
generally beloved, and widely regarded with suspicio
as entertaining physicians skilled in the art of poisonin;
Dashing and handsome, he may be described as th
Queen's toy terrier,† beside Burghley, her *urs
major*. His function was to cater for the Queen
taste for the drama and good acting, and for the deligh⁺

---

* " Annales " of John Stow to the end of 1614.   Letter b
Edmund Howes, gentleman to Prince Charles.

† " I could not be without him once a day; he is like m
little dog " (F. Chamberlain, " Sayings of Queen Elizabeth
p. 200).

f her affections and her pleasures in general. He was made Pallaphilos of the grand revels at the Temple, held in the Queen's honour in 1560. He formed the first company of licensed actors, including Richard Burbage and John Laneham. He founded the first and original " theater " in 1574, and he organised the famous Kenilworth festivities in 1575. He accompanied the Queen also to Cambridge and Oxford in 1564 and 1566, where the authorship and acting of plays formed so conspicuous a part, the Queen herself discussing the plays, patting the authors—Edwards and Preston—on the back, and vociferously applauding the acting of the students. He was, too, as we have seen, the patron of the classic translators of Shakespeare-Bacon's youth—Gascoigne, Arthur Golding, and Sir Thomas North—with whom must be mentioned Robert Laneham, the Council doorkeeper. Though he rarely interfered in politics, he was a most regular attendant at the meetings of the Privy Council; and it is remarkable that in the Register of its acts, after date May 12, 1559, we find this note: " The Register from this date until May 28, 1562, is unfortunately lost, and the record after that date is imperfect." It is also missing from May 3, 1567, to May 24, 1570. Francis Bacon and Robert, Earl of Essex, were born within this period—1559 to 1570. Also, amongst the few earlier records remaining are accounts of several payments, on account of actors before the Queen, to Lord Robert Dudley. Thus did the great Queen herself, from the first day of her accession, breathe the spirit of the drama into the students of her universities; and, upon the stage, into the citizens of London, preparing the way for the glorious plays of her world-famous son. She has long been the wonder of women, and may yet become the wonder of the world.

The strange character of Queen Elizabeth has indeed been a puzzle for generations—almost as great a mystery as the life of the Prince of poets, so exceptionally renowned, whom we can never quite separate from Hamlet the "black Prince" of Robert Laneham.* The pages of history open out to us glimpses of a nature in her even more contradictory than that of Henry VIII Thus Lord Burghley—himself accounted the gravest and wisest counsellor of his time—draws for us the following admirable picture of her great capacity as a Queen in council, saying, "There never was so wise a woman for all respects as Queen Elizabeth. . . . No counsellor could tell her what she knew not before. . . When her counsellors had said all they could say, she would then frame a wise counsel beyond all theirs "†—and she knew well how to see that her will was observed as law. Indeed, even Lord Burghley found the impetuosity and contrariness of her haughty feminine majesty at times trying. What, we wonder, was the immediate cause of his writing, as follows, to Sir Francis Walsingham on July 18, 1578, when our young Francis was in France and Queen Marguerite of Navarre was still separated from her husband, while Sir Amyas Paulet was doing all he could to effect their reunion : Something seems to have made her peculiarly testy just as she was setting out for Audley End, where Gabriel Harvey was presented to her. Burghley then gives us a touching description of her less serene and more

* Laneham calls himself "the black Prince" in the first paragraph of his letter and signs himself "El Prencipe Negro."
† Nichols's "Progresses of Queen Elizabeth," vol. i.

uffled Majesty, saying, " How sharp her Majesty has been with some of us here as counsellors. Yet we all most dutifully bear with her offence, not despairing that, however she mislikes things at one time, at another he will alter her sharpness, especially when she is persuaded that we all mean truly for her safety, though she sometimes will not so understand."*

For a picture of the Queen's social side, and of the gossip and intrigue which pervaded her Court, we turn to the pages of Gilbert Talbot, who, writing early in 1573, says: " My Lord Leicester is very much with her Majesty, and she showeth the same great, good affection for him that she was wont; of late he hath endeavoured to please her more than heretofore." But that follows is ominous of the double dealings of the Earl. " There are now two sisters in the court that are very far in love with him, as they have been long— by Lady Sheffield and Frances Haworth (daughters Lord Howard of Effingham) . . . there is spies over him. . . . My Lord of Oxford is lately grown of great credit, and her Majesty delighteth more in his personage and his dancing and valiantness than any other. . . . Hatton is sick and the Queen goeth almost every day to see how he doth."† Talbot adds, " At all these love matches my Lord Treasurer winketh and will not meddle anyway." Wise man not to burn his fingers. He must have seen much that we wish he had set down, but, like each one of this masterly Queen's counsellors, had his own job and stuck to it, without going beyond, at his peril.

To conclude: droll beyond expression is Gilbert

* Nichols's " Progresses of Queen Elizabeth."
† Letters of Gilbert Talbot (Nichols's " Progresses ").

Talbot's following sketch of this witty, whimsical
outside all ordinary, child of weird experience, so much
a human being and so feared and great a Queen; he
says: " About viii of the clock I happened to walk
in the tilt-yard under the gallery where Her Majesty
useth to stand to see the running of the tilt, where
by chance she was, unready, and in her night shift
so, when she saw me after dinner, as she went to walk
she gave me a great phylypp on the forehead, and told
my Lord Chamberlayne who was next to her, how I had
seen her that morning, and how much ashamed thereof
she was."*

At all this gossip the sage Lord Treasurer, as *urs
major*, winked. He knew his job: the welfare of Eng
land, not her eccentric and unmanageable Majesty'
love affairs. Of the truth of this Theobalds has more
to tell: Theobalds, one of the most beautiful and short
lived of palaces. Who shall tell the scenes enacted
there ? So great was the gossip and mystery that sur
rounded it, that after the great Oliver's democratic
triumph, the pure puritanical mind, shocked at it
infamy, was not slow to dismantle it. Let us love
whatever remains for Shakespeare's sake, who, as Franc
Bacon, probably spent many a happy day there.

* Letters of Gilbert Talbot (Nichols's " Progresses,
vol. iii., p. 92).

CHAPTER IV

SHAKESPEARE'S JUVENILE ENVIRONMENT

THE age of chivalry was dead, and was in the course of being buried. In Italy the Renaissance had already revived the study of letters and style; and science as well as art was beginning to provide new matter. The higher culture was gradually drifting towards England. Erasmus had been given a chair at Cambridge. In Sir John Cheke England saw her first professor of Greek. Of Roger Ascham we shall see more later. He was hardly in his grave when the light of probably the greatest literary genius that the world has yet known shot suddenly up into the sky. There, in language of his own, it now " stands fixed," and seems destined to illuminate human life with its rays " till the world's dissolution."* The birth of Shakespeare was an era not only in English literature but in the literature of the world. He was a singular man—unique—a phenomenon, and worked a Revolution. He passed, indeed, through life as Francis Bacon, but as Shakespeare he says he hates his name.† Nevertheless, under that name he shuffled off this mortal coil and all the heart-aches and the thousand natural shocks that death is heir to, a mystery man, perhaps a concealed Prince, the unacknowledged son of Queen Elizabeth, and but the foster-son of Sir Nicholas and Lady Bacon—

* " Shepherd's Calendar " (Epilogue).
† " Romeo and Juliet," Act II., sc. ii.

England's Solomon. This at least is the view which
while it increases our debt to the wonderful Queen Eliza
beth a thousandfold, and makes us ponder the more o
nature's working, is increasingly held by many—
namely, that Shakespeare was, as said, a Prince-poe
singing of the deeds of kings and princes. For th
cipher tells this same story; and indeed all the ciphe
does is to fill in one or two blanks in the story, as
can quite clearly be traced in history and literature
whether we consult his public life, his acknowledge
writings, or, still more, his pseudonymous writing
Thus Dr. Rawley, the author of the only contemporar
biography of Francis Bacon (if we except the "V
Naturelle," which is of doubtful authority), and wh
was Bacon's private chaplain, says that he was bor
on January 22, 1561, at "York House or York Place
Now Dr. Rawley must have known perfectly we
what all the world knew, that York Place was th
old name of Whitehall Palace, of which the play
Henry VIII. says:

> "'Tis now the King's and called Whitehall."
>
> (Act IV., sc. i.)

On the other hand, York House was at this time the we
known name of the town residence of the Lord Keepe
Sir Nicholas Bacon. What possible object could D
Rawley have had in quite unnecessarily alluding
York Place? Thus mystery confronts the student
his very birth, and we are ever reminded of that lir
of Ben Jonson, already quoted, when, in celebratir
the sixtieth birthday of Sir Francis Bacon, Lo
Verulam, in this very house, he wrote of him:

> "Thou stand'st as if a mystery thou didst!"

In short, taken in conjunction with other things, one can certainly but wonder whether Dr. Rawley is intentionally drawing attention to the birth of Bacon as having taken place at *Whitehall*—not York House. For he dwells also with very marked emphasis on the special interest taken by the Queen in the education and eminence of apprehension of the young Francis. Far more so than on the influence of Lady Bacon. Such maternal pride in the surprising genius of her disowned son would be natural. Flinty-hearted as she grew, she would love to confer with and cross-question her wonderful offspring, when not yet altogether hardened. Whatever the truth as to the place of his birth, it is certain that he appeared before the world as the son of Sir Nicholas and Lady Bacon, who lived at York House in the Strand, and who became his foster-parents from the moment he was born, whilst his real, his Queen-mother, who had elected to die known as the Virgin Queen, lived at Whitehall. Under such mysterious conditions did this wonderful Pan appear, destined to become known some day as the industrious and indefatigably painstaking author of propaganda printed under many names, with the sage aim of impressing the same doctrines, the same practical methods, and the same lofty aim, whether as Laneham, Gascoigne, Immerito, Lyly, Spenser, Marlowe, Peele, Green, Nashe, Ben Jonson, Beaumont, Fletcher, Webbe, Puttenham, Arthur Broke, John Barclay, Cervantes, Montaigne, Sorel, or others. For what he wrote under the name of each in most cases can hardly amount, in ink, to the paper splashed over by any leader writer in a week. He borrowed their names at times to conceal his own, and, like a great master, employed them as his pupils.

The great seer was baptised at St. Martin's in the Fields, between which church and the river, York House stood—that is, in the Strand, as may be seen from the water-gate, built later by the Duke of Buckingham, close by the modern Charing Cross railway station, still standing.

Where his earliest years were mainly spent is uncertain; a good deal, it may be, at Islington, of which more hereafter. Meanwhile, in 1563, when he was two years old, and in the same year that Roger Ascham, at the suggestion of a privy councillor, began to write his book on the education of young noblemen, Sir Nicholas Bacon began to build himself a new country seat at Gorhambury, a few years after his brother-in-law, Lord Burghley, had begun work on splendid Theobalds at Cheshunt. These two places are in Hertfordshire, fifteen miles apart, in amongst the Queen's favourite country and summer residences round which she gravitated year after year in her progresses between 1565 and 1578, not to say later. In this neighbourhood Francis Bacon grew up to maturity during the same period. There we are to believe that the juvenile genius for the drama was nurtured in him, whose master mind became renowned and known to all the world as that of Shakespeare. For there, secretly, his wonderful Queen-mother watched, supervised, and inspired his education in those things which delighted her most, confiding his more serious training to the pious Bacons and selected tutors. Did she not tell the students at Cambridge that she was not yet so old, but she might hope, like Alexander, to accomplish some great work? Alexander, too, was Shakespeare-Bacon's favourite hero

So, like mother, like son;—and did he and they not seek to hellenise the world ?

Gorhambury lies under the shadow of St. Albans, and is five miles to the west of Hatfield, of memories so dear to the Queen. Theobalds was nine miles east of Hatfield, close to Enfield, within easy reach of Hertford Castle. Moreover, fifteen miles, or an easy morning ride, yet further east, lay Romford in Essex, where Sir Anthony Cook lived at Gidea Hall, he being the father of the ladies Burghley and Bacon, and a dear friend of the Queen. The accounts alike of Gorhambury and Theobalds show that their style was most carefully calculated to inspire the inmates and residents with naturally imbibed taste, alike for classical literature and art, as well as for the more modern sciences. Here, in the midst and neighbourhood of palaces and courts, his education—jealously presided over from year to year by his bright, capricious, queer but capable, and ambitious Queen-mother — the early Muse, the Rose of Shakespeare, grew up and budded in its perfection.

Pennant, who visited Gorhambury in 1780, gives the following interesting account of this country home of Shakespeare-Bacon: " The building consists of two parts discordant in their manner, yet in various respects of a classical taste. On the outside of the part which forms the approaches is the piazza or porticus with a range of pillars of the Tuscan order in front, where the philosophic inhabitants walked and held their learned discourse; and within side is a court with another piazza, the one being intended for enjoying the shade, the other to catch, during winter, the comfortable warmth of the sun. The walls of the piazza are painted *al fresco*, with the adventures of Ulysses, by Von Koepen."* According to Nichols,† who betrays curious interest in the frequency of the Queen's visits to Gorhambury, the outer piazza was the gallery, 120 feet long and 18 feet wide, at the end of which were two apartments, one on each side, with a statue of Henry VIII., and otherwise suitably decorated, which Sir Nicholas added for the accommodation of the Queen-mother; and it was doubtless in this piazza that Puttenham, who was probably Shakespeare-Bacon himself, relates having seen Sir Nicholas studying Quintilian. This may even be the gallery where the author of "Leicester's Commonwealth" and his friends deliberated. The following further touches are significant of the nature of the environment of the budding sage, our latent Shakespeare.

"A little banqueting house adorned with great curiosity, having the liberal arts beautifully depicted on its walls, stood in the orchard, the pictures which adorned it being of such men as had excelled in each; and under them verses expressive of the benefits derived from the study of them, as grammar, arithmetic, logic, music, rhetoric, geology, and astrology." Thus:‡

ON MUSIC.
"Sorrow I soothe, relieve the troubled heart,
And by sweet sound exhilarate mankind.
Arion, Terpander, Orpheus."

---

* "In awful hand she (Pallas) shakes her shining spear."
("Odyssey," Book I.)

† See Nichols's "Progresses of Queen Elizabeth," vol. ii. p. 56, giving a print of Gorhambury.

‡ Nichols's "Progresses of Queen Elizabeth," vol. ii., p. 60.

But illuminating above all, in respect of my purpose, are the remarkable verses in the " Orchard," referring to some Orpheus who abode there, and whose heavenly art so soothed the rugged nature of the place:

" Of yore how frightful did this place appear,
How howled wild beasts and satyrs frolicked here !
When, luckily for me, *this Orpheus* came
Whose *heavenly art* has soothed my rugged frame.
For withered stocks gave these fair spreading trees,
And raised a shade that deities might please.
Labours like these my Orpheus here employ;
Oh, may we both each other long enjoy."*

There was but one laborious Orpheus whose heavenly art made Gorhambury his abode. What more convincing hint that Francis Bacon was the poet, the greatest Orpheus of all times, the renowned Shakespeare, to whom, as we shall see, the Queen-mother, in the " Hermit's Tale," gave the following wise injunction: " Knight, prosecute thy purpose, it is noble, learning by me not to fear, and of thyself to take pains, remembering *nothing notable is won without difficulty*. Hercules had by *his labour* his renown, his ruin by love." Thus on all sides was the fertile, happy mind of the young prodigy made to love art and science, verse and philosophy; surrounded by both, as well as by zealous servants of her gracious Mother-Majesty, all eager to inspire the phenomenal spirit of the wonderful child, who so worshipped her himself, that he could write and feel that " it was the want of his worth that made his service unacceptable, no impossibility of her will."† Yet our young Shakespeare at that time had no idea of his true relationship to the Queen. Was it

* As translated in Nichols's " Progresses."
† " Play of the Hermit."

her maternal instinct, showing through her majestic grace to him as the son of her Lord Keeper, which even already inspired him ?

Such was the domicile of the growing sage under the roof of his foster-parents. We turn now to the splendid mansion of his guardian and ostensible uncle, Lord Burghley, the Lord Treasurer. This grew in magnificence, at the instigation of the Queen, until it became the most splendid palace in England. It stood, as I have shown, within an easy ride of the Lord Keeper at Gorhambury on one side, and of Sir Anthony Cook at Gidea Hall on the other. Here the Lord Treasurer excited no small jealousy by his jolly splendour, of which the following extract from the " Homes of the Cecils," by Fox Davies, gives this glowing account: " All visitors extol its magnificence, its numerous buildings and galleries, its artistic paintings of all the most important and remarkable towns in Christendom, its ceilings with signs of the zodiac* and stars proper for each, even furnished with mechanism to give motion to the sun, walls decorated with trees to imitate nature, and birds also." The gardens were equally splendid, with mirrors and fountains and summer-houses, great variety of trees and plants, water and boats and labyrinths, requiring much labour, costly, beautiful, and pleasant—a maze garden and a pheasant garden. Of all this glory naught remains. The ruthless hand of the Puritan in 1651 dismantled these relics of royal vanity and scenes of mumming and masking, in which the young Shakespeare must have figured frequently as Francis Bacon, son of the Lord Keeper. As Fuller

* See plates of " Shepherd's Calendar " (Immerito), and " Francesco's Fortunes," by R. Green, for signs of the Zodiac.

eloquently laments: " Our fathers saw it built, we behold it unbuilt, and whether our children shall see it rebuilt He only knows who hath written, ' There is a time to cast away stones and a time to gather stones together.' "   What joyous days must young Shakespeare have spent there watching the pageants and plays, even taking a hand in them, and learning early his craft.   For there the Queen-mother, our angelic Fairy Queen, would spend weeks together, year after year, within easy hail of Gorhambury and of all whom inwardly she loved most dearly.   There in summer the virgin mother would often keep her Court.   She even received ambassadors there.   There " she hath been seen in as great royalty, and served as bountifully and magnificently as at any other time and place, and all at his Lordship's charge, with rich shows, pleasant devices, and all manner of sports that could be devised, to the great delight of Her Majesty and her whole train, with great thanks from all who partook of it."*

The Earl of Leicester, Sir Nicholas Bacon, Lord Burghley, the Earls of Oxford, Southampton, Rutland, Sir Francis Walsingham, Sir John Norreys, Sir Walter Raleigh, Sir Francis Drake, the Duke of Norfolk, the Earl of Derby, the Norths, the Earl of Northampton, and, above all, the Earls of Pembroke and Hunsden— we seem to see them all—this brilliant galaxy of princes, queens, lords and ladies—all peacocking, strutting, and playing their parts there, before the very eyes of the young Francis, naturally transforming his comprehensive mind into that of Shakespeare, the great dramatist, who reflects them in his mirror for us,

* Peck's " Desiderata," chap. xviii., p. 25.

and passes so many stately, royal and noble, sage, princely, and commanding personages before our eyes.

Yet not a single picture of Theobalds remains, so ruthless were the puritanical hands. Not a record of the splendid masques and entertainments has been handed down. All that we seem to have are Thorpe's plan and survey of the park and house made in 1611; the Parliamentary survey of 1650; and " a list of the Roomes and lodgings in the two courts of Theobalds, May 22nd, 1583." From these, through Nichols's " Progresses," Lyssons, and Fox Davies's " Homes of the Cecils," we learn one further item of interest. The reception rooms were on the ground-floor; the guests generally on the first and second floors, while " the third storey was occupied principally by a gallery for the Queen's Majesty. At the south end in the tower and above Lord Hunsden was the Earl of Leicester."*

Thus was the Earl honoured here also, his private quarters alone on the same floor as the Queen's, and separated from her only by a gallery and the royal maids of honour, the sage *ursa major*, Lord Treasurer Burghley, Her Majesty's host, winking at these love matters. Otherwise he might quite easily have lost his head. Thanks to his wisdom, he both kept his head and rendered good service to his country.

* Nichols's " Progresses of Queen Elizabeth," vol. ii., p. 403.

CHAPTER V

SHAKESPEARE'S JUVENILE ENVIRONMENT—
Continued

KENILWORTH—THE GREAT TRANSLATORS.

SUCH was the skilful nature of the environment which the great Queen built up for her own entertainment during the summer months, and the maternal care she manifested for the nurture and education of the new Solomon, the heir, who, "from the sacred ashes of her honour"* was to "star-like rise as great in fame as she was." His fame is rising still as the veil is lifted, and the unity and efficacy of his plays and philosophy shine out with increasing brilliancy. New scientific inventions and new powers everywhere! Nature ever more closely interpreted. His plays in all countries! A King's speech at Wembley heard all over the world.

Theobalds, of course, exceeded Gorhambury altogether in the magnificence of its royal splendour; but in both classical taste, poetry, and pictures were predominant in the decorations, while the recognition of the sciences and reason, mathematics, logic, ethics, and politics is noteworthy. This was not the first generation of Tudors which have made a careful study of education. Thanks to the wise and venerable Margaret, they seem to have understood it better than we do; and it was about to achieve its most notable and glorious triumph in a nature in which genius, the will

* " Henry VIII.," last scene.

43

to learn, the wish to learn, and the power both to learn and to achieve, were paramount beyond all parallel: sweetness and light—Euphues! The Queen seems to have visited both Gorhambury and Theobalds whilst building, and to have given either of her favoured statesmen to understand that she wished them both to be prepared for her reception. To her Lord Keeper Sir Nicholas Bacon she observed: " You have made your house too little for your lordship."* Hence the wing which he added for her reception; though, as the Lord Keeper wittily observed, the truth was that " Your Majesty has made me too big for my house." As regards Theobalds, Burghley himself states that " it was begun by me in mean measure, but increased by occasion of Her Majesty's often coming; whom to please I never would omit to strain myself to more charges than building it. And yet not without some special direction of Her Majesty, upon fault found with the small measure of her chamber, which was in good measure for me, I was forced to enlarge a room for a larger chamber!"

There was, however, yet another famous castle highly favoured by the Queen, and to which she paid four visits during the adolescence of the growing Shakespeare, which must have much impressed him. Kenilworth! Endless pageants, interludes, and festivities were arranged there by the ambitious Earl of Leicester for the delight of Her Majesty and that of the rising sun whom we believe to have been their mutual heir. Here the interest is historic, and cannot fail to have attracted the inquiring mind of the young Bacon Shakespeare, as can be recognised in the plays. For Kenilworth was, above all, for four hundred years a

* Nichols's " Progresses of Queen Elizabeth," vol. ii., p. 56

castle of the Crown, held in long succession by members
of the royal family under the title of Earl of Leicester,
to which later was joined that of Lancaster. It was,
indeed, founded in 1135 by Geoffrey de Clinton, but
appropriated to the Crown in 1165 by Henry II., who
was no lover of private castles.* The castle was,
however, held against him for his rebellious son, when
Robert, Earl of Leicester, Hugh, Earl of Chester, and
many others sought the aid of the King of France
against him. So, too, Henry III. granted possession
of it to Simon de Montfort, Earl of *Leicester*, and his
wife Eleanor, and in turn it was held against the King,
enduring a six months' siege from June 25, 1266, to
December 21, 1266, the garrison coming out " so pale
and meagre " as to cause wonder that men in so
wretched a state could make a defence so noble.† The
castle then passed to Edmund, Earl of *Leicester and
Lancaster*, who, in 1279, held a famous tournament
here, attended by Roger Mortimer, Earl of March.
Later, after receiving the ill-fated King Edward II.
as a prisoner,‡ it passed in turn—through the heirs of
the above Edmund—to Blanche, the first wife of that
very John of Gaunt whom the mature Shakespeare,
his own descendant, now before us as Francis Bacon,
immortalised in the ever memorable line:

> " Old John of Gaunt, time-honoured Lancaster."

John of Gaunt and Blanche handed their royal
castle on to their like famous son and heir Henry,

---

* See " The Castle of Kenilworth," by the Rev. E. H.
Knowles, 1872.   † *Ibid.*
‡ See Marlowe's " Edward II.":
> " Your Majesty must go Killingworth."
>   (Act IV., sc. vi.)

known as Bolingbroke and Duke of Lancaster, who
seized the throne and reigned as Henry IV., and was
made no less famous, in years after, by the as yet boy
Prince-poet Shakespeare, who was now visiting the
castle with his mother. It then remained a castle of
the Crown till 1563, distinguished as the home and
habitation of royal earls. Then came a change. The
curiously quaint and imperturbable, the unconventional and impenetrable Queen Bess bestowed this
ancient castle of the Crown upon a favourite, a subject
of but mean descent, whom with her own royal hand
she raised to the proud title and estate of an earl
This castle, which for centuries had flown its proud
flag under a royal title, passed thus to Sir Robert
Dudley, the grandson of that Dudley who had, with
Empson, flourished by extortion. He is accounted of
mean estate but of great value, in the play of " The
Hermit " presented at Woodstock in 1575, to which
we shall come later. He never stood high in the love
or estimation of his country, yet must have been a man
of some taste and ability, seeing the great and admitted
power of his father, the Duke of Northumberland
Ambition without scruple was the curse of both. His
father and grandfather both lost their heads on the
block; and even Queen Elizabeth, when his patent of
nobility as earl was first put before her, observed that
he was a traitor in three descents. Nevertheless, true
to her chameleon-like variableness, having first presented
him with a royal castle, she thought fit the following
year (1564) to give him also a royal title, and made
him Earl of Leicester in succession to a long line of
royal earls. Clearly but one interpretation could be
put on this—namely, that she intended to make him her

royal consort; more especially as she paid her first visit to the new Earl at Kenilworth in 1566, and, keeping him always in hope, followed it up with other visits in 1568, 1572, and 1575, at which time the growing Shakespeare-Bacon, so bright, profound, alert, and lively, was respectively seven, eleven, and fourteen years of age.

Of the interior decoration of the castle we hear little, but some of the architectural remains are very beautiful. King John, Henry III., John of Gaunt, Henry V., and Henry VIII. all shared in its embellishment; the staterooms and Great Hall having been remodelled by John of Gaunt, who raised also a magnificent Tower and beautiful Lobby.* It was not till 1571 that Robert Dudley, Earl of Leicester, began the reconstruction of the whole, with apparently doubtful taste, reforming the southern range of staterooms, adding grand oriel windows and much else. But his efforts were directed also to the gardens and pleasaunce. For was not the Queen about to visit him (in 1572), and must not there be some display of his magnificence in her honour, and perhaps for the amusement of their son? For though we hear little of what passed on the occasion of this visit, "Laneham," whom we take to be Shakespeare-Bacon, that son and heir himself, gives a gorgeous description of it all in his letter of 1575. So a new garden after the French fashion was made, the tower turned into aviaries, and a new turreted gateway, approached by a long bridge, was added.

Thus from beginning to end the famous Kenilworth is reminiscent of scenes from history and Shakespeare. Nor ought mention to be omitted of one particular

* E. H. Knowles, "The Castle of Kenilworth."

incident in the play of " Henry V." which Shakespeare
locates in the Tower of London, but which is said
historically to have taken place at Kenilworth, mention
of which might, however, have told against his secrecy.
It was in Lent, 1441, while the King lay at Kenilworth,
that messengers arrived from the Dauphin with a
present of tennis balls for him to play with, " but the
King wrote of him that he would shortly send him
London balls with which he would break down the
roofs of the houses."* It is Stow who relates the
anecdote, which is only one more of the many Shakespearean incidents to be found in both Stow and
Holinshed, in whose histories—the former written
under a promise to Whitgift—Bacon's hand is to be
traced.   Thus in the play of " Henry V." we read:

KING: We are glad the Dauphin is so pleasant with us;
      His present and your pains we thank you for;
      When we have matched our racquets to these balls,
      We will in France, by God's grace, play a set.

     *   *   *   *   *

      And tell the pleasant prince this mock of his
      Hath turned his balls to gunstones; and his soul
      Shall stand sore-charged for the wasteful vengeance
      That shall fly with them.
                      (" Henry V.," Act I., sc. ii.)

This happened in reality at Kenilworth, it seems.

Let us now turn to the movements of the Queen and
her immortal son, in and amongst these scenes, which
for years together she perambulated in her progresses
during the summer months. So deeply interested in
these was Nichols, the famous author of the " Progresses," that he exclaims with surprise and emphatically that, when at St. Albans, the Queen must have

* Stow's " Annales," by Howes, p. 344.

stayed at Gorhambury close by. She can, indeed, hardly have omitted to visit her Lord Keeper, even if his foster-son had not been her real one, for he had special apartments at her disposal. So struck was Nichols with the curt way in which the progresses are recorded by Lord Burghley in his diary—the dates and length of her visits to St. Albans being omitted—that he made independent research, and shows, in an appendix, that the Queen was at Gorhambury on days altogether unrecorded, having signed documents there under the great seal, which the presence of the Lord Keeper rendered possible. This makes it certain that her gracious and maternal Majesty paid surreptitious visits to Gorhambury. Nor can there be but one reason for secrecy and the omission to record those visits—*i.e.*, her desire that their frequency should be unobserved, together with her natural maternal anxiety to see the son whose genius and eminency in learning the great men about the Court were gradually beginning to regard as phenomenal. Would she make him her successor, this born Prince of poets, this illustrious philosopher, this pioneer of historians? Who knew? Mystery prevailed, and none dared mention the question of the succession, but an Act of Parliament provided for the heirs of her natural body to succeed.*

Certain it is that Her Majesty was at either St. Albans or Gorhambury, and perhaps both, in the years 1568, 1572, 1573, 1574, 1575, 1576, 1577, covering the most important educational period of the early life of the young Solomon known as Francis Bacon, with whom she loved to confer, and whom to examine and cross-

* See Camden's "Annales," 1571, p. 143, and Leicester's Commonwealth."

4

question* we know was to her so great a delight. Such evidence was he of her own sharp instincts, so responsive was he to her enlightenment. Might not the day come when she could acknowledge him as her own flesh and blood? How the question must have rankled in her mind! What a chance was here, if only she could have seen a little more ahead, and announced herself to the world as the mother of Shakespeare—as which she will yet become known.

Taking the progress of 1568 first: this is a good instance of the mysterious nature of Lord Burghley's record of the progresses, to which Nichols draws attention. It will be seen that the dates are given of each halt up to St. Albans, where, and at the remaining places, the dates of arrival or departure cease. As shown below, on July 30 the Queen was at Hatfield which is itself but five miles from Gorhambury. On what day she arrived at, or left, St. Albans, which adjoins Gorhambury, is not stated; nor is any record given of the length of her visits to this and the following places. The entry runs thus:

July 4th.—Greenwich.
 ,,   6th.—Charter House, *i.e.*, Howard's Place in
             London (Duke of Norfolk).
 ,,   14th, 15th.—Havering Bowre.
 ,,   19th.—Copt Hall.   (The Queen also visited
             Gidea Hall, Sir Anthony Cook.)
 ,,   25th.—Enfield.
 ,,   30th.—Hatfield (here the dates stop).
August   .—At St. Albans.
             At Whaddon (Lord Grey de Wilton).
             At Eston.
             At Grafton, Bysseter.
             Rycot, Newbury, Reading, etc.†
N.B.—The visit paid to Kenilworth this year is not recorded

---

* Rawley's " Life of Francis Bacon."
† Nichols's " Progresses of Queen Elizabeth," vol. i., p. 25

Now this year 1568 must have been a red-letter year in the life of Shakespeare, as indeed it was, unconsciously, the dawn of English literature, by the appearance of the first fluent translations and adaptations of classic and Italian Renaissance, poetry, philosophy, and history. In these it was George Gascoigne, Arthur Golding, and Sir Thomas North, all protégés of the Earl of Leicester, Queen Elizabeth, and members of the Bacon circle, who played so great a part. Ariosto, Bandello, Euripedes, Guevara, Ovid, and Plutarch were all finding their way to expression in good English prose, blank verse, and rhyme, the Earl of Leicester being in many cases the patron, and the whole emanating from a knot of men familiar at Court.

Gorhambury had just been completed. Shakespeare-Bacon was seven years old. New arrangements had to be made for the prosecution of his education. The Queen, it will be noticed, went first to Gidea Hall, the home of her brother's old tutor, Sir Anthony Cook; then to Enfield and St. Albans, or practically Gorhambury—which accounts for the omission of dates—and from Gorhambury she went on to Whaddon Hall, twenty-five miles further, where lived Lord Grey de Wilton.* Now Lord Grey, a connection of the Queen, had made a friend of George Gascoigne, whose home and Ascham's was at Walthamstow, close to Enfield and Theobalds, and Gascoigne had not only just published his adaptation of "Phœnissa" of Euripedes called "Jocasta," concerning Œdipus, but this year (1568) presented a MS. copy of it to Roger, Lord

* Coventry MS. shows, it is said, that she also visited Kenilworth (E. H. Knowles, "The Castle of Kenilworth").

North, brother of Sir Thomas North, who in turn this same year issued his newly revised edition of his translation of Guevara's " Marcus Aurelius." This he significantly called " The Diall of Princes," and added to it " The Favoured Courtier." Truly, then, here is evidence of the nucleus of a Court literary coterie round young Shakespeare. For it is on Guevara that " Euphues "* is founded; and there are other manuscripts of Gascoigne amongst the Royal MSS. in the British Museum, including certain elegies,† " wherein the doubtful delights of man's life are displayed, written for the Queen's most excellent Majesty." So, too, the first edition of North's " Lives of the Noble Grecians," by Plutarch of Chæronea, is dedicated to " the most high and mighty Princess Elizabeth "; and the Earl of Leicester wrote to Lord Burghley to ask him to interest himself in it (Hatfield MS.). Even of yet greater interest in respect of our point is the manner in which Arthur Golding's translation of Ovid's " Metamorphoses " saw light. It was begun in 1563. The first two books were published in 1565, and the whole completed in 1567, when our Shakespeare was six years old. The dedicating letter is dated 1564, and is addressed by Golding‡ to the Earl of Leicester from Cecil House, the house of the Queen's Lord Treasurer which stood nearly opposite to York House in the Strand, the town house of Sir Nicholas. It is difficul

* " Euphues, or the Anatomy of Wit," published as by John Lyly.

† Notably Gascoigne's translations of " The Tale of th Hermit " with its frontispiece hand-painted in sepia.

‡ A. Golding was uncle to the Earl of Oxford, and the latte was son-in-law to Lord Burghley.

to know in reading Montaigne's " Essays "* how much of what is told there refers to the youthful education of Francis Bacon, the growing Shakespeare. But bearing in mind that in our time J. S. Mill learnt Greek at the early age of three years, it is easy to believe that this infant prodigy—as Montaigne relates of himself— loved nothing better at the age of seven than to get away into a corner and read Ovid. So, too, Dr. Rawley, quoting Ovid in his life of young Francis, says of him: " Et quod tentabam scribere versus erat "; and J. Lyly, in " Endymion," renders this sarcastically:

> " Quidquid conebar dicere versus erat,"†

and makes one of his characters say: " I feel all Ovid de arte Amandi." Certain it is that Shakespeare-Bacon never wearied of quoting Ovid, and that at least one famous passage of the " Metamorphoses " of A. Golding's translations has been transferred to the play of " The Tempest " almost verbatim from Golding's translation:

PROS.: " Ye elves of hills, brooks, standing lakes and groves,
    And ye that on the sands with printless foot
    Do chase the ebbing Neptune," etc.
                    (" Tempest," Act V., sc. i.)

" Ye Ayres and windes; ye Elves of hills, of Brooks, of woods,
    Of standing Lakes, and of the Night, approach ye every one."
                    (Ovid's " Metamorphoses.")

The stories of Philomene and Pyramus and Thisbe are also to be found in the " Metamorphoses."

* Many hold that Francis Bacon wrote the " Essays " of Montaigne, a friend of himself and Anthony Bacon, from whom he received a letter on his death-bed.   † See p. 228.

We seem to catch here a touching glimpse of the immense pains taken by the Queen and Earl of Leicester to stimulate a really natural love of all that is most beautiful in literature and nature in the infant Shakespeare, nature's own poet, born a Prince, not only, we believe, by blood and disowned as such, but also by nature King* of a Kingdom of which nothing could rob him; the great Emperor of Letters, over which he still presides to-day. This young Prince, our supposed Shakespeare, was seven years old the year after the date of publication of Golding's "Ovid." Golding was connected by marriage with the Earl of Oxford, for whom he acted as receiver. He lived, certainly in 1575, at Powles-Belchamp in Essex, within easy reach of Theobalds. He is mentioned in Laneham's letter,† and was in religion a zealous Calvinist of the very type beloved by Lady Anne Bacon. Besides translating Calvin's work on the books of Daniel and Job, so beloved by Bacon, he translated Theodore Beza's "Life of Calvin," Beza‡ being a personal friend and correspondent of Shakespeare-Bacon, and in 1575— *i.e.*, in the year of Kenilworth festivities—an adaptation of Beza's play, "The Tragedy of Abraham's Sacrifice," appeared in Golding's name.

Further, the later editions of Guevara's "Marcus Aurelius," by North, and Golding's "Ovid," 1587

---

* A Solomon, whom he loves to quote.

† This Golding may, however, be Goldingham; the passage reads, "Master Golding hā lent it him."

‡ Theodore Beza is also referred to by George Gascoigne in the 1575 edition of his works, which has the "Tempore pate occulta Veritas" emblem in the letter "to the Rev^d divines" which forms the preface. Bacon corresponded with him (see Spedding and J. Birch, "Memoirs").

edition, have the well-known double A, which is evidently nothing more than a monogram composed of the name Bacon as may be seen in the Minerva Britanna (see Fig. 3 below):

Fig 1
Fig 2
Fig 3
Note the Back-conies

being an A and an N with CO between. The B will be found by looking sideways, and the emblem has been much elaborated and given various forms, and carries also the deeper signification of a double alphabet.

Plutarch's "Lives," 1612 edition, has the same elaborate variation of this monogram—with Satyrs and Bowmen and Back-conies—as appears on the Shakespeare Folio, indicating by this imprint his unmistakable handiwork, even if only as editor. Similarly, the "Steel Glass," written in 1576, under the name of George Gascoigne, and the 1575 edition of his works have the same elegant emblem of Time with his scythe raising Truth from her obscurity that appears, slightly improved in its spacings, as the "New Atlantis," written under the name of Bacon. Thus carefully is the hand of the master emblematically signified on his works over and above the internal evidence they contain.

In that evidence it is not within the scope of this work to enter. My aim is confined to tracing the early life of the growing Shakespeare as based upon researches made elsewhere and by others. The reader must satisfy himself on points of detail. To me it belongs only to trace the unfolding of the beautiful bud which later blossomed into the lovely " Rose" that we name " Shakespeare," known as it is becoming to be known by many other names as well.* One little but all-important extract only it behoves us to give here. The prefatory lines to the " Steel Glass " are so indicative of the dual nature of the genius of Shakespeare-Bacon, of his equal power of reason and imagination, that it cannot be passed over. Bacon in a letter to Fulgentio, written forty years later, tells of a juvenile work he had written, called " The Greatest Birth of Time," and in these lines of the " Steel Glass " we see already in embryo his idea of the marriage of science and art that is so prominent a feature of his philosophy, in which he also details four logical or rational arts—namely, invention or enquiry, judgment, memory, and elocution or tradition.

The words I refer to in the Prologue to the " Steel Glass " of 1576, when Shakespeare-Bacon was fifteen years old, are:

> " But truth to tell, there is a kind of fame
> The which I seek with *science* to assault,
> And so to leave remembrance of my name,
> The walls whereof are wondrous hard to climb,
> And much too high for ladders made of *rhyme*.
> Then since I see that rhymes can never reach
> Unto the top of such a stately tower,
> By *reason's* help I mean to make some breach
> Which yet may help my feeble, fainting power,
> That so at last my muse may enter in,
> And *reason* rule where *rhyme* could never win."†

---

* " A rose by any other name would smell as sweet."

† Prologue to the " Steel Glass," Gascoigne, 1576, *vide* " Works," 1575 edition.

Who but Shakespeare-Bacon could have written thus? And, lo! at sixteen here we have already the marriage of science with art in embryo.

I have ventured so far on a somewhat long digression in order to show how very far the plays of Shakespeare are from being the work of a mere *lusus naturæ*, or inspired idiot. It grows plain that, as might be expected, the very opposite was the case. We see, in fact, the favourite maxim both of Bacon and Shakespeare verified, that poets are *made* as well as born. Thus here at Gorhambury the young soul of the growing age was put into the closest and most kindly possible touch, not only with nature free and noble, as a rising Orpheus, but with the most brilliant and able students, historians, philosophers, and versifiers of the land, from his very earliest childish years. Always, too, we see the great Queen, his concealed mother—whom he lived only to honour, and dared not say that he loved*— aiding and encouraging his talent, and the Earl of Leicester seeming to cater for meet tutors and companions for their astonishing heir, whilst pageants, plays, and masques rejoiced his eyes and spirits. Instead of being a mere errand boy, the young life of the true Shakespeare, the greatest and most profound, as well as the wittiest and most eloquent of philosophers and poets, shows in this light a fullness of occupation, an environment of men of the greatest learning, and an education more carefully considered, various, and enlightening, than have accompanied the nurture and evolution of the mind of but few men of rare genius.

* See John Lyly's " Endymion."

CHAPTER VI

SHAKESPEARE'S EDUCATION

THE sweet Orpheus of Gorhambury, the divine Shakespeare of the future, under the cloak of Francis Bacon, was thus surrounded by everything that could favour the natural growth of his heavenly art. Not only was he in the midst of nature helped by art, but in close touch with men of learning of every kind, philosophers, historians, classical translators, and poets—all courtiers under the patronage of the Queen and Earl of Leicester —Gascoigne, Golding, North, and later such men as Sir Francis Walsingham, Sir A. Paulet, Holinshed, Gabriel Harvey, and Bishop Hall, a Calvinistic friend of the Bacons, who in his satires attacked Shakespeare's " Venus and Adonis " and " Love's Labour's Lost " under the names of " Labeo " and " Gallio " (1597). Everything that could facilitate the refined culture of genius was there. Nothing in these early days was left undone to render life happy and learning attractive as a practical end and the natural companion of wisdom and power. Whilst the pious Lady Bacon inspired, the witty Queen-mother cross-questioned and encouraged. She loved much to confer with him, and the frequency of her visits testifies to her maternal solicitude.

For this, the real Shakespeare, was no plough-boy. He was a Prince—a Prince-poet, a royal throstle, singing of kings and queens; a real Orpheus—a honey-bee

QUEEN ELIZABETH

National Portrait Gallery.

FRANCIS BACON AT EIGHTEEN

Hilyard Miniature.

'Tis not her glass but you that flatter her,
And out of you she sees herself more proper,
Than any of her lineaments can show her.

Orville Owen Cipher, vol. v., p. 905.

who, as he hummed his glorious song, sucked honey from the very choicest flowers.* His judgment and intellect thus grew in perfect proportion with his brilliant imagination. A wise man will make more opportunities than he finds, he says. Accordingly this true Shakespeare added indefatigable industry,† drawing short only of impossibilities, in his devoted service and desire to delight the Queen. How very different from the vacant youth and environment of Shakspere of Stratford! On the one hand, the care bestowed on him by his strange Queen-mother could not fail to stimulate alike reason, ambition, wit, and fancy. On the other hand, the pious but bright home of the Bacons supplied the desirable restraining influence in resisting undue levity and directing the mind towards noble ends. Sir Nicholas Bacon, Lord Burghley, the Earl of Leicester, all the great men about Court recognised the unusual eminency of his young but apprehensive mind, which, as we now know, must have been phenomenal. All, moreover, knew, or must have guessed well enough, that this promising boy, in every sense a Prince, and whose grandfathers had been the two ablest men of their time, might at any moment become the recognised heir to the throne should her whimsical Majesty bring herself to acknowledge her marriage with the Earl. Such a fairy tale was the boy's life. So high did the Earl of Leicester stand, if not in the Queen's estima-

---

* " I have not left any flower whatsoever untasted."
     (Translation of Bandello's " Hamlet," 1608. See
          Shakespeare, library edition, 1875.)

† " Experience is by industry achieved,
     And perfected by the swift course of time."
          (" Two Gentlemen of Verona," Act I., sc. iii.)

tion, at least in her affections, even up to 1576, if no
later. Could she but overcome her distrust! Thu
in his youth all must have regarded the young lad—
the Shakespeare whom they knew as Bacon—so quic
and erudite, and, as Laneham the black Prince say*
such a favourite amongst the ladies, with very specia
attention, interest, and wonder; though people abou
Court are not wont to speak openly of royal scandal
and in those days did so at their peril. As a certai
Mr. Fisher learnt in attending Her Majesty fror
Warwick to Kenilworth in 1572, there are " such thing
as some for their truths and some for other cause
had been better untold, but as he did it counsel rashl
in heat, so by experience at leisure coldly he repented
. . . What these things mean is not for everyone t
know."*

What was it, we wonder, that at Kenilworth in 157
thus roused the curiosity of Mr. Fisher to indiscretion
and brought upon him a sudden descent of Her Majest
upon his house ?

I have already indicated how from 1568 to 1572 th
education of the juvenile brain of Shakespeare, know
then as Francis Bacon, was promoted by furnishin
him with companions and tutors skilled in foreig
languages and renowned for their translations and a
versifiers. He took, it seems, to knowledge as a duc
to water. His natural thirst for it was unquenchabl
his industry inexhaustible. Yet he was no boo
worm, and was familiar with field sports, delighting
nature free and untouched. He could discuss horses
hawks, and deer with the best country masters, ar

* Nichols's " Progresses of Queen Elizabeth," vol. i., p. 31
† Francis Osborne.

t was ever new matter, new experience he was
n search of, the acquisition of knowledge for use,
eing his aim and delight, but not the vaunting
f it.

There is, indeed, little room left for doubt as to the
principal influence of the Queen in directing his studies.
'or if we are to believe Ascham, there was a very
marked kinship between the instincts of the great
Queen and the son who was so far to outshine her.
Erasmus himself relates the natural skill which even
Henry VIII. (his assumed grandfather) showed as a
oung man in giving the best expression to a
ew thought. But what Ascham—who died when
Shakespeare-Bacon was six years old—relates of
Queen Elizabeth is little short of miraculous as
ght thrown on the true origin of Shakespeare.
He says:*

" She likes a style that grows naturally out of the
ubject-matter, free from barbarities, because it is
clear. She much admires metaphors when they are
ot too strained, and the use of antithesis when it is
warranted, and may be used with effect."†

Now these words were written before the young
Francis Bacon could speak, much less figure as Shakespeare, yet if " he " be substituted therein for " she,"
very word of it is as true of Shakespeare as of Bacon,
whether they be one or two. No writer delights the
reader more with apt metaphor, even though it is

* Letter to Sturmius, April, 1550.
† For example, writing to Mary, Queen of Scots, she says:
The bark of your fortune floats on a dangerous sea, where
many contrary winds blow " (F. Chamberlain, " Sayings of
Queen Elizabeth," p. 227.   But see, above all, the Introduction,
xviii, above).

sometimes so curiously mixed—none is more skilful in the use of antithesis, whether as Bacon or Shakespeare It was his inheritance.

Here surely is a very remarkable indication of hereditary genius. And it is certain that, such being the close affinity of instinct to start with, the taste for it would be immeasurably strengthened by that frequency of intercourse and conference with him and cross-questioning of him which, as Dr. Rawley relates the Queen allowed herself. Thus it occasions small surprise to find that Bacon himself, in his "Advancement of Learning," blames both Ascham and Erasmus for dwelling too much upon polish of words, and on the deifying of Cicero and Demosthenes, rather than on the importance of the subject-matter; and he very conspicuously condemns the study of style before matter saying: "For as subject of matter is better than beauty of words, so contrariwise vain matter is worse than vain words." And again: "The affectionate study of eloquence of speech," he says of the bookmen, "grew speedily to an excess, for men began to hunt more after words than matter."* Here was a species of literary obliquity, the vanity of which the Queen herself may well have impressed upon her brilliant son. In short, the advance from mere love of elegance in books and Renaissance adoration of classical style, to the love of substance and truth in nature, was in a measure anticipated by the instincts of the Queen, and by her handed down to the future philosopher-poet, the rising Orpheus who thus went direct to nature and learned very early the dislike and danger of plodding over books, for,

* "Advancement of Learning," Book I.

> " Study is like the heaven's glorious sun
>> That will not be deep-search'd with *saucy looks* :
> Small have continual plodders ever won
>> Save base authority from others' books.
> These earthly godfathers of heaven's lights
>> That give a name to every fixed star
> Have no more profit of their shining nights
>> Than those who walk and wot not what they are."*

Apart from the Queen's influence, the education of ne lad continued very much in spirit on the lines laid own by Roger Ascham, every care being taken to indle his love of learning by gentle treatment and ise suggestion.† In conduct as a ruler, indeed, Queen Elizabeth set up her father as her example, alike in his irtues and vices, and never was there greater chameleon ian Henry VIII. For the first twenty years of his eign no Prince was ever more popular or deemed more oble. Then he became a bluebeard. Power seemed drive him mad. He spared no man in his anger and o woman in his lust, says Hume. Yet he had been kilfully educated by Margaret Beaufort, his grand-other, till vanity and Court adulation eclipsed the onstancy of his better self; and he provided the best tors of that literary age for his children, Edward VI., ueen Mary, and Queen Elizabeth. In this, too, Queen lizabeth seems to have copied her father, so that it not too much to say that, assuming Shakespeare-acon to have been her son, he was the true child of family which had estimated the value of knowledge its highest for several generations. " Knowledge is

---

* " Love's Labour's Lost," Act I., sc. i.
† Nashe, in " The Anatomy of Absurdity," also mentions e influence of Ascham, "more especially his ' Schoolmaster,' '" a passage full of Baconian philosophy (see E. Harman).

power " may indeed be said to have been the Tudo[r]
maxim, and of them the man was now born who wa[s]
to teach the acquisition of knowledge, of new dis[-]
coveries and new powers as the principal agent o[f]
human progress, through truth by induction, as th[e]
foremost aid rightly directed in alleviating the miserie[s]
of humanity.*

Nevertheless, though maternal instinct and car[e]
provided the means in the first instance, the debt du[e]
to Sir Nicholas Bacon, beside Lady Bacon, as th[e]
philosophic guides of the rising star, must not b[e]
neglected. Roger Ascham had no doubt absorbed int[o]
his " Schoolmaster " most of the first principles [of]
education to be gleaned from Quintilian's " Instituti[o]
Oratoria " and the treatise "περί τῆς παίδων ἀγωγῆς "
(concerning the guidance or education of childre[n]
which is ascribed to Plutarch.† Thus Puttenhan[m]
who seems also to have been Bacon himself, tells us ve[ry]
pointedly in his " Art of English Poesie "—showi[ng]
how well he knew Gorhambury—that: " I have co[me]
to the Lord Keeper, Sir Nicholas Bacon, and foun[d]
him sitting in his Gallery alone, with the works [of]
Quintilian before him, indeed, he was a most eloque[nt]
man, and of rare learning and wisdom as ever I kne[w]
England to breed, and one that joyed as much [in]
learned men, and men of good wits."‡ We feel gratef[ul]
indeed to Puttenham for this feeling touch of u[n-]
reserved enthusiasm and affection concerning t[he]
philosophic and lovable nature of the foster-father

* Compare "Diary, Life and Letters " of O. L. Shafter, U.S.
† Plutarch, in this work, divides life into Contemplati[ve,]
Active, and Voluptuous. It was translated in 1535 by Sir
Elyot.
‡ Puttenham, " Art of English Poesie," Book III., chap.

our beloved Shakespeare, named after him—Bacon. We feel it all the more intensely when, in wondering what it was that Sir Nicholas was thus brooding over alone in his gallery with its Tuscan columns and frescoes of the travels of Ulysses by Von Koepen, we turn to the pages of Quintilian, and find the following astonishing passage:

"We are educating a man who will bring to human affairs a mind eminent by natural endowment, and, in particular, embracing the fairest qualities within its folds, a man *such as no previous age has known, sole and perfect on every side, thinking the best thoughts and expressing them in the best language.*"* Can it be that, as Sir Nicholas Bacon read these words written more than a thousand years even before his time, he realised that he had in his charge "Shakespeare," the man who, *par excellence*, was to outshine all others in beauty of thought and expression?

Quintilian continues: "The man whom I educate, I desire to be a sage of the Roman mould, one who will show forth the truly urbane man, not in private controversy, but in the deeds and in the actual conduct of affairs."† Here we see, again, that Elizabethan concentration on the subject-matter and practical ends of learning, and who more practical and urbane in his philosophy and life than Bacon? Even Macaulay admits it. We see it. Invention—invention everywhere, literary and mechanical invention, new discoveries and powers without end, which he hoped might in some degree alleviate the miseries of humanity;

* See "A Short History of Education," by J. W. Adamson.
† J. W. Adamson and Quintilian's "Institutio Oratoria."

5

by means of logical induction, each part truthfully
supporting the other.

It would be difficult indeed to find better words to
picture the place that Shakespeare now fills in the
world than those of Quintilian. This single touch tells
us more than all else too about the nature, of the kind
and learned statesman and Lord Keeper, one of her
props, to whom the sagacious, and from youth lonely
and unconventional Queen entrusted at the same time
the regulation of her realm and the education of the
immortal Shakespeare. Sir Nicholas must have pon-
dered much over these words of Quintilian, as little
by little he saw the child grow,* and, even as a boy
begin to show that wonderful power of expressing the
best thoughts in the best language which so distin-
guishes Shakespeare, and this to such a degree as to
surprise, delight, teach, and illuminate each generation
of the men of all countries, ever since, throughout the
whole wide world. Eloquent, indeed, is the further
tribute which Puttenham pays to Sir Nicholas, when—
coupling him with Shakespeare-Bacon's later guardian
Lord Burghley—he speaks of them as men "from
whose lippes I have seen to proceed more grave and
natural eloquence than from all the orators of Oxford
and Cambridge" (Arber's reprint, p. 152).

Turning now to the probable influence of Plutarch's
treatise "περί τῆς παίδων ἀγωγῆς" (first translated
in 1535) on the education of Shakespeare-Bacon,
it fits in with the recognised influence of Plutarch's
"Lives" on the plays of Shakespeare and, as I have
already shown, also the translator of the "Lives"—Sir
Thomas North belonged to the same Court set a

* Sir N. Bacon died in 1579, when Francis was seventeen.

the Bacons, and Francis Shakespeare-Bacon, without doubt, had a hand in re-editing them. " The perfectly happy men," says Plutarch in effect, in writing for children, " are those who can combine service to the state with the individual pursuit of philosophy. In the training of children and youths, morals, manners, fair and courteous speech, are of first importance. Bodily exercise, especially of a military kind, must not be omitted; when practised in youth it ensures a hale and tranquil old age."* Now, seeing the acknowledged connection between Plutarch's " Lives " and Shakespeare's plays, it is of particular point to read that "An English version " of Plutarch's " Treatise for the Guidance of Children " is embedded in *John Lyly's* " Euphues, or the Anatomy of Wit " (1579). The treatise was included by Philemon Holland in his English translations from *Plutarch* (1603). Montaigne repeats its insistence on the need for the " discipline of the understanding and of conduct."† " Euphues and his Ephœbus " is, in short, little more than a translation of Plutarch.‡ Thus Lyly, Montaigne, Bacon, and Shakespeare, all fed on Plutarch in youth, and have, quite independently, been shown by research to have been all pen-names of the same great " perfect-on-all-sides " universally and manlike-minded Shakespeare.

Wise, indeed, were both the guidance given to the mind of the young son by the Queen herself, and the choice she made of those in whose hands to place his education, insisting always on the importance of his

* Adamson, " Short History of Education."
† *Ibid.*
‡ The precepts of Polonius in " Hamlet " may be traced to Plutarch on " Education."

subject-matter and practical ends of knowledg
Nothing, indeed, could restrain this young Orpheu
from courting the muses. He must soar, he mus
climb, even if the cliffs he aspired to ascend seeme
inaccessible; and Gascoigne's " Instruction on Verse,
Webbe's " Discourse on English Poetry," and Putter
ham's " Art of English Poesie," are all studies
language, in all which, nevertheless, he insists, from th
first and always, on the need for *aliquid salis*—
something sound, savoury, and with grit, as the bas
to call forth the natural and spontaneous beauty
language.

Thus did the education of Shakespeare-Bacon con
tinue to progress between the years 1568 and 1572, o
lines unusually favourable for the stimulation of geniu
and in an environment no less so. The power of h
young pen was a divine and incontrollable forc
reaching at times a furor, too great even for Quee
Elizabeth or Lord Burghley to suppress, had the
wished to do so; and though the Queen excluded hi
from office, she kept him ever close to her side, ar
called him her " watch candle." At eleven years
age (1572) he was already wide awake and his mu
beginning to sing. At twelve he was deemed ripe f
the University. Meanwhile his stay amid nature
Gorhambury was no doubt varied by visits to Londo
to York House, and the Court there, and probably
Islington. Moreover, Gorhambury was but a mor
ing's ride from Richmond, where the Queen stay
much, and she loved riding. From there, unobserve
she could easily ride over to St. Albans. Literatu
had been the delight of her youth, and now she h
a son born to it.

Men of action, however, at this time still fought shy of books. A literary world was a new phenomenon. Printing, it must ever be remembered, was less than a century old when Shakespeare-Bacon (whether one or two) was born. Its import, and all it meant or was to mean, to the world was not yet fully understood. Even to-day, when new inventions are made, their full use and application as a civilising influence remains long unsolved. Thus, even in Bacon-Shakespeare's time, a hundred years after printing came, there were still no newspapers, no daily critics, no magazines. What took place in one part of the world, or even in one part of London, took long before it was known in another, and then only a garbled or contorted version was heard, as is circulated from mouth to mouth. He, however, was now born who was to be the first, and more than all, to realise and make use of the power of the Press, our Shakespeare-Bacon. His method of applying it, by the use of innumerable pseudonyms, is memorable. This is not the place to investigate his identity in them.* Suffice it to say here that by thus concealing his identity and using his pen—in the name of a large secret society and under many pseudonyms—he spread his practical and scientific propaganda, as well as his ideas as to the true use of invention, " for the benefit of the state and society of man," impersonally, and without self-glory, over the whole civilised world, writing even in foreign tongues and under foreign names. Calling himself the Bellringer, he thus sought to call all men together,

---

* The English, Vienna, New York, and other Bacon Societies, and their individual members, and many others such as E. Harman, have investigated this.

under one flag, the unity of one idea, making his one voice seem as the voices of many, all obsessed with the same idea, which may be found expressed in similar words—in Spanish, as those of Cervantes; in French, as Montaigne; in English, as Nashe in his " Anatomy of Absurdity." All, carefully examined, will be found fundamentally the same as in " Bacon " or " Shakespeare." Their unity speaks for itself. We see before us in all the MIND OF BACON as he tells us to seek: " *Mente videbor.*"

There was, however, another cause which in early days, even while yet a boy, impelled young Shakespeare-Bacon to shun publication in his own name and to conceal it under those of others, quite apart from his royal blood or princedom. The ancient prejudice against too much learning and bookishness, in men who aspired to place and power, was still intense, and dissimulation was in vogue everywhere. As I have said, a literary world was a new phenomenon. Young courtiers and men seeking state employment were looked upon askance if they dabbled openly in literature. This, as we know, was actually one reason pressed against Francis Bacon as an excuse against his holding office. It will help, therefore, much to a right understanding of the age and its conditions to venture on a brief digression showing the gradual evolution of genteel education from the days of the Middle Ages— which were now being left behind for ever. The immensity of the change from the age of chivalry to the age of literature fully accomplished in the sixteenth century is rarely realised.

The world was then just shaking off the last vestige of chivalry. Ascham in his " Schoolmaster " had drawn attention to the harm the romances of its degenerate days were doing, and this was later taken up vigorously by Shakespeare-Bacon in " Don Quixote." Now it must be remembered that no literature of any sort had entered into the education of young gentlemen in those preceding dark ages. Their education had been purely physical. " The ideal of chivalry prescribed a long and careful preparation for the degree of knighthood which was quite unlike the preparation of the scholar, because it was directed to capacity of a different kind. It sought to educate a man of action, the richer soldier and courtier, not the thinker or fluent speaker. . . . The appropriate school for this purpose was the feudal court and the lord's household. . . . To run, to leap, to ride, to practise open-air sports, and the use of toy weapons, to carry the heavy shield of the knight, and in his last years help the squire in arming and in giving personal attendance to his master, these formed his more strenuous occupation." Edward III. enacted " compulsory military service on all men between the ages of sixteen and sixty. . . .

" A series of Archery Acts, the earliest dating from the time of Edward III. and the latest passed in 1541 (Henry VIII.), directed that Englishmen of all ranks should exercise themselves in shooting, and that under heavy penalties they should refrain from such sports as tennis and bowls."* The change from this purely physical training of individual prowess under arms, of which chivalry and the protection of the weak was the central idea, to a more intellectual education, was gradual. Winchester and other schools were founded in the fourteenth century. Eton followed in the

* J. W. Adamson, " Short History of Education."

fifteenth century under the half-Valois and literary
King, Henry VI. Charterhouse, Merchant Taylors,
Shrewsbury, and others later. Printing itself only came
in 1477 in the reign of Edward IV. The tournament *à outrance* was then already dying out. The
great duel between Lord Anthony Scales and the Great
Bastard of France at Smithfield had rendered it ludicrous, though " Giltspur Street " still revives its
memory. Printing killed it. A book by the same
Lord Scales, afterwards Earl Rivers, was the first book*
printed in England. He also wrote verses on the eve
of his execution. The muses and letters, under the
influence of Margaret Beaufort, were only just forcing
themselves to the front. Henry VII. abolished feudal
armies. The feudal court was no longer the school.
Gascoigne's (*i.e.*, Bacon) " Steel Glass " shows this very
clearly, and how even the knights and lords crowded
more and more to London and civilised centres. Traditions die hard. Learned and cultured as Henry VIII.
was, it was on being the best archer and rider of his
time that he prided himself. Yet even he added music
and dancing and letters to his accomplishments, and
none realised earlier that as skill of arms died out other
healthy amusements must be found for the people.

It was left, however, to Queen Elizabeth to effect the
final change from Chivalry to Letters† as the guiding
spirit of her Court, giving also Edward VI. and even
Queen Mary their due. It was entirely she, the great
Fairy Queen, who personally encouraged love of the
classical drama and literature. It was for her edifica-

* " The Dictes and Sayings of Philosophers."
† See " English Novel in the Time of Shakespeare," J. J.
Jusserand.

tion that theatres were built to improve acting and study scenic effect; and, above all, it was she who insisted on sending her royal wards to the University. That man had little hope of entertainment or advancement at her Court who had no literary accomplishments, even if he could not write in verse or rhyme.

Nevertheless, the customs, habits, and traditions of chivalry persisted, even in the reign of Queen Elizabeth, so far that too much addiction to books was still regarded with distrust in the choice of rising statesmen and men of action. Thus though no young courtier could hope for preferment without learning, woe to him if his love of letters carried him so far as to put his name to a book as its author. Concealment of identity in authorship was, in short, not peculiar to Francis Bacon or Shakespeare. Amongst courtiers it was the common custom, to which there were but a few exceptions, such as Sir Thomas More, Sir Walter Raleigh, etc.—men, however, who had an established reputation as men of action. Action and quickness of wit, with knowledge and love of men, and of books only without bookishness, was the commanding characteristic demanded of the aspiring courtier.

Moreover, liberty of the Press was as yet unknown, whilst its danger as a means of spreading disaffection was well known. Did not the Earl of Essex himself cause the Shakespeare plays to be acted with a view to exciting the people to rebellion ? Thus Shakespeare's life was on the very verge of peril, and as Bacon he felt, above all, that he must have liberty—as free a charter as the wind to blow on whom he pleased. Much that he had to say would, he knew, be regarded as rank heresy, and must endanger his life. There was thus but one course open to him: birth, custom, safety, and, as time went on, the nobler desire of self-effacement all enjoined on him and compelled him to find shelter and comfort in concealment. He began and ended his life a concealed Prince and " *a concealed poet.*" " Under my cloak a fig for the King," says this supposed author of " Don Quixote "; and Shakespeare the true man walked thus through life " under a cloak," a mystery, a phenomenon, clothed from first to last in motley—*in umbrâ*. As Laneham, already we are told, he figured as " the black Prince "; as Hamlet we read of his " inky coat."

Such were the circumstances and conditions under which the world passed from Chivalry to Letters.

Shakespeare-Bacon was the man destined to complete this reform. Hitherto man had walked darkly seeking after knowledge but not knowing how to find it He proclaimed and propounded the way, and showed man the immense value and importance even then of direction. The new philosophy was to be the means of making new discoveries and inventions and so of furnishing man with new powers, and rightly applying them. This was to be effected through the marriage of science and art. Invention was no longer to be fortuitous. All the civilised world must know the new method: but even then how to ensure its right use " for the *benefit* of the state and society of man." All the world must study this too. It must be propagated under the names of Shakespeare, Cervantes, Montaigne and a host of others, forming an army, an international society of reformers under pseudonyms.

Thus resigning fame until such hour as Cormorant devouring Time, should think fit to divulge his true name and raise him up from his voluntary obscurity his young Orpheus of Gorhambury, dedicating his life and heavenly art to mankind, and resigning fame, became, during that life, a man of many colours or motleys, call him Shakespeare, Bacon, or what you will. He accordingly adopted as his ruling maxim the motto, "Tempore patet occulta veritas," with the device of Time raising up Truth from her concealment, and this same device is to be found on all the following works:

> George Gascoigne's Works (1575 edition), "Steel Glass" (1576).
> John Lyly's "Love's Metamorphosis" (1601).
> John Weaver's "Mirror of Martyrs" (1601).
> Francis Bacon's "New Atlantis" (1627).

What more transcendently wonderful than what this concealed Prince, poet, and philosopher, thus waiting on Time, attained by his own efforts, unaided and irrespective of rank and high birth? If no fairy tale can compare with it, no dream could be more strange. We see a man by nature indescribably sweet, a very Solomon born a Prince, but ignorant of it till on the verge of manhood, who, by virtue of his own genius and industry, became the world's paragon of poets and philosophers. He was educated as a subject like the heroes of so many of his stories,* in the home of a trusted minister. There, unconscious of his royal blood, but inheriting literary genius and ambition, he grew up to him, not at an earthly crown and glory, but at the noblest of all human ambitions, "the endowment of human life with new discoveries and powers." Conceived in sin but nurtured with care, he worked to redeem the memory of his mother by the brilliancy of his own achievements, compelling the world to acknow-

* See, for example, Barclay's "Argenis."

ledge in his birth a debt which might permit men to
condone the *unnatural* circumstances of his birth,
for which he was not responsible.* When—

> " The foul crimes, done in my days of nature,
>   Are burnt and purged away."
>
> ("Hamlet," Act I., sc. v.)

For—

> " Crimes, like lands, are not inherited."
> ("Timon of Athens," Act V., sc. iv.)

Boasting, by right, the noblest ancestry, he was reared
ignorant of it. The force of his own intellect and the
purity of his aims alone raised him as Bacon to the
highest position in the State which a subject could
occupy, and in secret as Shakespeare to the highest
pinnacle of universal admiration in all the world.
He became a highly honoured Member of Parliament
where he stood ever for clemency and reason rather than
for severity and force. Wherever he was, his amiability
the sweetness of his nature and profound wisdom
made him beloved and respected. He rose to be Eng
land's Chancellor, her supreme Law-Lord. For a time
he was even Regent of the kingdom he was born to rule
—and he fell condemned without a real trial—con
demned by a general verdict on charges he had never
admitted, and for bribery which, in truth, he had never
committed, although, according to the custom, he had
accepted gifts not affecting his judgment and verdict.†
He, by right a king, was condemned by countrymen

* What does Shakespeare delight more in depicting than
"unnatural" acts,

> "Put on by cunning and forc'd cause"?
> ("Hamlet," Act V., the end.)

† See Robertson's "Philosophical Works of Francis Bacon.'

whom he, above all, and his forefathers for generations had strained every nerve to serve. What greater tragedy ? What irony of fate ! Well might he liken his fate to that of Œdipus and admire St. Paul's perfection: " That he would wish to be an *anathema* from Christ, for the salvation of his brethren, it shows much of a Divine nature and a kind of conformity with Christ himselfe."* Thus did this great man solace himself in adversity.

* Bacon's " Essay of Goodness and Goodness of Nature."

CHAPTER VII

SHAKESPEARE IN 1572

THE muse of the yet youthful Shakespeare-Bacon, tha
most industrious of honey - bees, was now not onl'
beginning to sing, but already eager that her voic
should be heard. This first and earliest inspiration c
his early youth—his Rose, or muse—never left him
or he it. It was probably breathed into his childis.
ears and wondering soul by sweet Lady Anne Bacon, an
was already goading, urging, and pressing him, youn
as he was, into action. Reform, the benefaction c
human life, the alleviation of human misery—whe
their seeds have been successfully sown within th
first few incorrupt years of life—have always been th
most powerful of all incentives to stir the healthy min
of vigorous genius to dare. We are dealing wit
perhaps the rarest known mind of this kind, a min
endowed with practically all the gifts that Ascham i
his " Schoolmaster " includes under Euphues—*i.e*
" goodness of wit, and readiness of will to learn; soun
in body and mind; whole, full, and able as to all it
qualities; a tongue not stammering, but plain an
ready to deliver the meaning of the mind; a voice no
soft, weak, piping, womanish, but audible, stron
and manlike; a countenance fair and comely;
personage tall and goodly, giving credit to learning
and authority to the person, thus disarming contemp

and precluding disfavour of it."—All of which Mr.
Matthew Arnold has summed up under " Sweetness
and Light." We see in our mind's eye such an alert,
witty, merry, yet prompt and zealous youth, fearless
and candid, and industrious beyond measure. He
was but eleven years old. Such, however, was his
eminency in learning already, that the following
year he was deemed ripe for the University, when
till but twelve, and found little there to increase
his knowledge.

In short, the year 1572 is marked by two important
events. First, this was the year of the first edition of
the " Posies " against the name of George Gascoigne
and sundry others gathered out of our English Orchards,
which is said to have been published surreptitiously
by certain young men during Gascoigne's absence in
Holland; and, secondly, for a public visit of the Queen
of three days to Gorhambury when on her way to her
third visit to Kenilworth.

It is possible that the one event was connected with
the other. The little volume of poems is entitled
" Hundreth sundrie flowers bound up in one small
poesie gathered partly (by translation) in the fine
outlandish fields of Euripedes, etc., partly by invention
out of our own fruitful Orchards in England."* It is of
particular interest as having appeared under conditions which show the first indication of the coming
into existence of a " crew of courtly makers, noblemen,
and *gentlemen* of *her Majesty's* own servants, who
have written excellently well, as it would appear, *if
their doings could be found out and made public.*"† Here

* London, 1572.
† Puttenham, " Art of English Poesie," p. 75, Arber's reprint.

we have not only direct evidence of the growth o
literary taste at Court, but also of the fact that author
ship was cultivated secretly by men who conceale
their names. It comes, moreover, from the pen o
Puttenham,* who can be no other than Shakespeare
Bacon himself, or his school, and amongst those thu
recorded as writing in secret are the Earl of Oxford, Si
Philip Sidney, Sir Walter Raleigh, Master Edwar
Dyer, Master Fulke Grevell, *Gascon* (*Gascoigne*), Britton
and *Turberville*, all well known and intimate friend
of Francis Bacon. Moreover, it will be seen that th
list actually includes the names of George Gascoign
and George Turberville, two of those concerned in th
publication of the " Book of Posies " under considera
tion, which the printer says were offered to him by tw
young gentlemen, G. T. (George Turberville) and H. W
(Henry Wotton),† who pretended not to wish to hav
it published. " All these words notwithstanding
fear very much that these two gentlemen were of on
assent to have it printed," says the printer. So printe
it was. The result was something like a conflagra
tion. For these " diverse discourses and verses in
vented upon sundrie occasion by sundrie gentlemen '
contained, written under the name of Dan.Bartholemew
attacks not only on the customs of the times, bu
" offensive for sundrie wanton speeches." Here wa
reform actually in being. The courtiers themselve

* Puttenham, " Art of English Poesie."
† See " Francis Bacon," by W. Steeves, p. 217.
Henry Wotton was a lifelong friend of Bacon, and osten
sibly his cousin and that of T. Meautys, his secretary. Verse
by Bacon were found amongst his papers after his death
and he is said to have composed the inscription on the monu
ment to Bacon in St. Michael's Church.

made fun of. It was clearly high time that this merry young Prince and heir to the throne thus employed, or implicated, should be got away from home; and the Queen's visit in July, 1572, heralded the entry the following year of the Gorhambury Orpheus, our budding Shakespeare, under the name of Francis Bacon at Trinity College, Cambridge, the college, as already said, of Henry VIII., where our poet was placed under the tutelage of the master and royal chaplain John Whitgift.

Thus the concealment of his name as a poet was not in the first place peculiar to Shakespeare-Bacon. It was the fashion of the day, and was adopted by him from his earliest youth primarily on this account, though other reasons conspired later. As Arber showed, now fifty years ago, in publishing his reprint of Tottill's "Miscellany," the poets of that period wrote " under a whole host of initials and pseudonyms, which are, but often vainly, supposed to attest the authorship of so many extant poetical pieces." They were content to be known only to one another in private. They proposed to write for the culture and amusement of the public, not for fame, as Shakespeare so splendidly shows in the first lines of " Love's Labour's Lost." Two years later Gascoigne admitted that " I was not unwilling the same should be imprinted " in 1572, and in 1575, probably under Court influence, he published a second edition of the " Posies," in which he assumed responsibility for the whole; whilst, on the contrary, in a third edition published eleven years after his death in 1587, the " Steel Glass " is inserted, *without pagination*, indicating a separate author. The pagination of all three editions baffles description, but appears

6

nevertheless to be a kind of madness with a secret
meaning.

In fact, by them we are able to establish that the
young Shakespeare was already acquainted with the
tales of Bandello, which included the novel of " Giulietta
and Romeo " and " Historie of Hamlet,"* and had been
translated into French by Boisteaux in 1559 and
increased by Belleforest. Putting this together with
Gascoigne's masque for the Montague wedding, on
the subject of the feud of the Montacutes and Capulets
and the line of Hall's satires (of which more later)—

" Should *Bandell's* throstle die without a song ?"

—lo and behold, we find that the " Romeus and Juliet "
attributed to the totally unknown Arthur Broke
was, there is reason to believe, an early work of our
young Prince-poet Shakespeare, even though the date
assigned to it is 1562, the probable real date being 1582
when another edition was registered but not published.
It is, moreover, written in the same measure as
Golding's " Ovid " and Gascoigne's " Complaint of
the Green Knight," being that very metre which
Gascoigne describes in his " Instructions " as " Poulter's
measure, which giveth 12 for one dozen and 14 for
another."

The following brief passage will illustrate the great
beauty of parts of this forgotten and long-buried gem
and can hardly fail to remind the conversant reader
both of the Hilyard miniature of Francis Bacon and

---

* This was not translated into *English* till 1608, from the
French of Belleforest, probably by Bacon himself. " English
Novel in the Time of Shakespeare " (see its Preface), J. J
Jusserand.

f the lines below the Droeshout portrait of Shakespeare
1 the First Folio:

" This Romeus was born so much in heaven's grace
  Of Fortune and of Nature so beloved that in his face,
  Beside the heavenly beauty glist'ning aye so bright
  And seemly grace that wonted to glad the seer's sight,
  A certain charm was *graved by Nature's* secret art,
  That virtue had to draw to it the love of many a heart."

        (" Romeus and Juliet," A. Broke, ll. 1067 to 1072.)

Is this in truth a description of young Shakespeare ?
seems wonderful that such a work has remained
dden. The explanation is that the real author may
ave suppressed it later himself. At the same time,
ke Golding's " Ovid " and Plutarch's " Lives," it
rnished the public with a possible source whence
e illiterate Shakspere of Stratford might have
thered his knowledge of Italian tales without knowing
alian, so completely was the great hoax engineered,
d the great " Gul " of Stratford ingeniously placed
gh upon his lofty pedestal. The masque* for the
ontague wedding was, in fact, written for performance
a lad of twelve years—very possibly our young poet
mself.

I have endeavoured thus to show the advanced stage
learning which the true Shakespeare had reached
eady at the age of eleven, without losing anything
the buoyancy of youth. As in his portraits, so in
youthful writings and life, there was a distinct trait

This masque is also in poulter's measure; thus we are told:
" And for a further proof he showed in his hat
  The token that the Montacutes do bear always for that
  They covet to be known from Capels, where they pass
  The ancient grutch which long ago twixt these two
      houses was."

of the rogue in him, a cutting garrulous wit, beside a
earnest purpose, the will and persistency of the Tudor
but immeasurably better balanced and directed—
child in whom the proudest mother might take th
greatest pride.   Did the Queen take him with her, whe
after her visit to Gorhambury in 1572, she proceeded i
her progress to Kenilworth ?   There is no doubt tha
her interest in his surprising accomplishments cause
her visits from this time forward to become mo
frequent.   She was at his home again in 1573, and
is said to have been for this special occasion tha
that wing and gallery was added to the house
Gorhambury,* which was reserved for Her Majesty
private accommodation.   What scenes of absorbir
interest may not have passed here, between nature
strange child, our capable Queen Bess, and that Shak
speare, then but a boy, a rising star, now so permanent
fixed in the admiration of all the world.

Queen Elizabeth paid in all four visits to Kenilworth
namely, in 1566, 1568, 1572, and 1575.   Little is kno
of the visit of 1566.   It is said that the Coventry M
shows the 1568 visit to have been a surprise visit of
secret nature, which accounts for the mysterious entr
of this year's progress as already given, all dates bei
omitted after St. Albans—that is, practically Gorha
bury—was reached; and no mention made there
Kenilworth.   In 1572, again, she went from Theoba
via Gorhambury to Kenilworth,† and seems to ha
followed the same route in 1575.   Now I have sho
how the young hand of Shakespeare is traceable
the works of Gascoigne.   So, too, signs are not wanti

* Nichols's " Progresses of Queen Elizabeth," vol. ii., p.
† Ibid., vol. i., p. 309.   See also vol. i., p. 602, Appendix

ıs generally admitted, that Shakespeare himself saw
he festivities both of 1575, which Gascoigne supervised
ıy appointment of Leicester, and those of 1572, when
Queen Elizabeth received there the French Ambassador
La Motte and rejected the overtures of the Duke of
Anjou, the French Prince known also as d'Alençon
(brother of Marguerite of Valois), whom she entertained
n 1578 at Richmond, " with so much kindness that
Leicester raged, being now quite frustrate of his long-
oped-for marriage " (Leicester's " Commonwealth ").

This was the shrewd, pock-marked, dark, and any-
hing but beautiful brother of the French King, whom
ur diplomatic Queen kept hanging on hope for so many
ears—the strange little being whom she christened her
renouille, or frog, and who accepted that title, and wrote
nder it the most ludicrous love-letters it is possible
o conceive.   Here is the true and real Bottom with the
ss's head of " Midsummer Night's Dream," to whom
itania (Queen Elizabeth) deeply enamoured of him says:

> " What angel wakes me from my flowery bed ?"
>
> *   *   *   *   *
>
> " I pray thee, gentle mortal, sing again ? . . .
> Mine ear is much enamoured of thy note;
> So is mine eye enthralled to thy shape;
> And thy fair virtue's force, perforce, doth move me
> On the first view, to say, to swear, I love thee."
>
> *   *   *   *   *
>
> (*Then to this ass-headed Bottom*),
>   " Thou art as wise as thou art beautiful."*

hus did Queen Elizabeth (politically) pretend† to be
fatuated of her French *grenouille*, and woo him,

---

* " Midsummer Night's Dream," Act III., sc. i.
† " The hopes I gave that I would marry Alençon were
~~g~~iven for the purpose of getting him out of the Netherland
~~St~~ates " (F. Chamberlain, " Sayings of Queen Elizabeth ").

in like manner as Titania, enchanted by a love philter
wooed the ass-headed Bottom. The scene in the play
is the very height of farcical comedy. Yet the truth
the true comedy, as actually enacted, is hardly les
extravagant. Few things in real life are more supremel
extravagant than the language in which this Frenc
Prince caused Simier, his representative, to approac
England's Queen, and himself addressed her—Simie
relating " how little repose your *grenouille* had las
night, doing nothing but sigh and weep *for eight hours*
till at last he made me rise and discourse of your divin
beauty."* Deeming this not enough, the next da
the Duke wrote himself to declare that " the tears fa
from his eyes continually. He is occupied withou
intermission in wiping them away. He can neve
feel easy except when, pen in hand, he is remindin
her Majesty of her grenouille." This is indee
anticipating, as these letters did not pass till later, whe
d'Alençon himself visited England, but that he
Bottom to the very life, and the source from whic
Shakespeare derived his inspiration, seem more tha
likely, and one can picture the witty mother and so
laughing heartily over these letters—for Queen Elizabet
publicly pretended to be as deeply enamoured of he
frog as he was of her, and said she could not bear
think of him swimming in the stagnant marshes of th
Low Countries. Even Gabriel Harvey, the dea
special, and singular friend to whom Shakespear
Immerito† confided all his woes, entered into the fu

---

* Cal. of Hatfield MS., August 28, 1579; August 29, 157
September 24, 1580. (The Queen was forty-six, d'Alenço
twenty-nine.)

† " Shepherd's Calendar," January gloss.

and knew well his interest in these great personages, writing: " The Queen Mother at the beginning or end of every conference; many bargains of Monsieur (as d'Alençon was called); Shymeirs (Simier) a noble gallant fellow."* Why does he bring these names in, in a letter on literature, except for the notoriety of what was happening and the interest of his young friend at Court therein.

To return, however, to earlier days. In 1572 the earlier overtures of the French duke were being less favourably regarded. Our young Prince-poet was but eleven years old. The Earl of Leicester was still in supreme favour, and there can be little doubt that the great Queen still hoped she might be able to recognise the young son whose genius was already beginning to astonish men. This royal castle of Kenilworth which she had presented to the upstart Earl, was it not to indicate him as her future Consort ? And had not the conspicuous and delightfully witty ability of the young Shakespeare—in disguise her own progeny—softened and touched a tender point in her maternal heart ? She had once expressed a wish,† like the great Alexander, to do some great thing, and leave behind her in token of her own goodwill to man. Here, had she dared, was her very wish fulfilled. If only she had been able to foresee the heights to which this son, whom she had borne, was to star-like rise, so that before his genius all men on earth should bow! Would she, even then, have dared to acknowledge him ? Or would the ghost of Amy Robsart have risen up before her, as that of Banquo did before Lady Macbeth ? Why did she

* Gab. Harvey, " Correspondence with Immerito."
† At Cambridge, 1564.

hover around Gorhambury? But that cuckoo-like she had laid her egg there. Why did she allow her name to be thus linked with that of Leicester? She was the daughter of King Henry VIII. and took him as her model. She spurned custom. Her father had his many wives, and she her many favourites, and but one inference is possible, as a certain Mr. Fisher saw, and said too much, and learnt at leisure to repent him.

Thus following her bent Her Majesty, in 1572, arrived at Warwick Castle on August 14: " That Monday her Majesty tarried at Warwick, and so all Tuesday. . . . On Wednesday she desired *to go to Kenilworth* . . . where she rested at the charge of the *Earl of Leicester* from Wednesday morning till Saturday night, having in the meantime such Princely sports as might be devised. On Saturday night (August 19th) very late her Majesty returned to Warwick."* It was on the following Monday that the aforesaid Mr. Fisher was suddenly visited; and learnt to repent coldly at leisure certain things spoken rashly in heat; for, as he found, " what these things mean is not for everyone to know." But Her Majesty that Saturday night (August 19) was lodged again in the castle of Warwick, and on the 21st after visiting Mr. Fisher, " her Majesty taking that pleasure in the sport she had at Kenilworth would thither again, where she rested till Saturday after (August 26th)." Fulke Greville was there too, the owner of Warwick Castle and largest land-owner of Warwick, with a property close by Stratford-on-Avon and, it is said, the Recorder of that town. He was one of Bacon's staunchest friends, and in London lived next door to him at Gray's Inn. On this occasion he took

* Nichols's " Progresses of Queen Elizabeth," vol. i., p. 318.

part in a gallant show of fireworks and an assault at arms led by the Earl of Oxford, another close friend of our Shakespeare-Bacon. All the Court and ministers were there. Was not he—the foster-son of the Lord Keeper—of course present too, to see these princely sports in honour of the Queen, his mother? But "what these things mean is not for everyone to know." The Queen on this occasion returned to London via Woodstock, precisely as she did after the yet more famous Princely festivities at Kenilworth in 1575. Moreover, twenty years later, when the Earl was dead, and every chance of the princely recognition of Francis had faded away, none more staunchly supported the claim of this Francis, our Shakespeare, to the Attorney-Generalship than Fulke Greville, Lord Brooke.

Was it, perhaps, at these Princely sports of 1572 at Kenilworth that Fulke Greville first saw our young Francis—Shakespeare? Was it he, we wonder, who later put Bacon into touch with Shakspere of Stratford, the actor and theatre proprietor? He was even yet more the friend of Sir Philip Sidney, whose life he wrote; and Sidney was by blood the first cousin of Shakespeare-Bacon; Mary Sidney, the mother of Philip Sidney, being the sister of the Earl of Leicester—that is, Mary Dudley by birth.

It was the wish of Queen Elizabeth's favourite hero, Alexander the Great, to hellenise the world. Did she dream that the wonderful child Francis, whom we know as Shakespeare, would do more to achieve this than any man before or since? Was it she who herself breathed that noble desire into him? Certain it is, as Dr. Rawley broadly hints, that her interest in him at this period —say from 1572 to 1576—was so marked as to invite

universal attention, and as she rejected the overtures of
the Duke of Anjou in 1572 so she again rejected them
in 1579-80, when the attractive physiognomy of her
wonderful son, as shown in the miniature of her own
Court painter, must have made her mother's heart yearn
to acknowledge him—but for the ghost of Banquo.

It is a significant fact that both Queen Elizabeth and
Lady Bacon were not in their right minds towards their
end, and that the principal plays of Shakespeare, the
great tragedies written after their death, turn so much
on madness, feigned and real.

It was in the year following this visit—*i.e.*, in 1573—
that Francis was sent, as already stated, to Henry
VIII.'s college at Cambridge (Trinity) and placed under
the Queen's dear friend Whitgift as his tutor. Of his
life at Cambridge history records little save what Dr.
Rawley relates of his more than ordinary proficiency
and difference from Aristotle.*

* J. M. Robertson's " Bacon," p. 2.

CHAPTER VIII

SHAKESPEARE AND THE PRINCELY PLEASURES OF KENILWORTH

LET the reader picture to himself an England, half of which was forestland full of game, with a Thames full of salmon; but no railways, no better roads than a cart track, no motors or even light carriages, people travelling mostly on horseback. There were no steam engines, no factories as we understand them, and still fewer civilised amusements. Orchards and strawberries grew in Holborn. London's first theatre was just being built. Interludes were played in inn yards. The morris dance was the chief delight of the country, other than sport and archery. Telegraphs, telephones, gramophones, motors, cinemas, wireless, flying—all were undreamt of, unless, perhaps, by Shakespeare-Bacon. As archery and compulsory training went out, games were, however, beginning to force themselves to the front, though long kept back by law as prejudicial to archery. Large tracts of forest remained as yet little touched by art. The whole population has been estimated by Hallam at under four millions, and much of the country was still wild and even savage. Thus we read in Stubbes's "Anatomie of Abuses" of 1583 of even a wild kind of Rugby football just coming in, of which Stubbes says: "As concerning football playing, I protest you, it may rather be called a friendly kind of fight than a play or recreation; a bloody and murthering practice, than a fellowly sport or pastime. For doth not everyone lye in wait for his adversary, seeking to overthrow him and to pitch him on his nose, though it be upon hard stones, etc., etc. . . . but whosoever scapeth away the best, goeth not scot free, but is either sore wounded, craised, and bruised, so as he dieth of it, or else scapeth very hardly."* What would Stubbes have thought of the Stadiums of to-day for 150,000 persons to witness this same game in these better regulated days ?

A young and acutely observant lad, suddenly transferred from the depths of the country to-day to London, and witnessing for the first time the wonderful sights of the Empire Exhibition at Wembley, or the gorgeous military displays at Olympia, the opera and our theatres would carry away with him much the same impression as young Laneham or Langham (for he spells his name both ways) recorded of the impression made on him by the Princely festivities of Kenilworth in 1575, calling and signing himself "the black Prince." As the presence of the King adds to the glamour of the show to-day, so did the presence of the greatly beloved Queen in that day. I say *young* Laneham or Langham advisedly, because in the Duchess of Portland's copy the age of the Minstrel of Islington is given unmistakably as XIV†—that is, *fourteen*—which in 1575 was Bacon's age, and the whole style and exuberance of his famous letters are manifestly boyish. In other copies it is given as xlv, which

* See "The Castle of Kenilworth," E. H. Knowles, p. 86.

† See Nichols's "Progresses of Queen Elizabeth," vol. i., p. 460. (I have not myself seen the Duchess of Portland's copy.)

might be read as forty-five; and this use of Roman numerals itself indicates concealment, whilst the description of the Minstrel of Islington is again a concealed and entertaining description of a young man of fourteen—that is, of the young Orpheus we know as Shakespeare himself, in the garb of the miniature of Francis Bacon by Hilyard. Look at the stiff setting of the ruffs of the smart young courtier there, and then turn to Laneham's description of him, remembering Bacon's notorious love of Islington, which, as said, he brings into his masque of the Prince of Purpool at Gray's Inn, and where he held a forty years' lease of Canonbury Tower,* still to be seen in the state he left it, with its handsome oak panelling and carvings, and inscriptions of the Kings of England in the top room of the Tower, " Fr——" being inserted between Queen Elizabeth and James I. Mark the sparkling, exuberant wit of a boy bubbling over with fun, rather than the staid humour of a Council doorkeeper who died in 1580, in which year the Privy Council granted, on April 1, 1580, " a warrant to the Treasurer of her Majesties Chamber to pay unto the wife of Robert Langham *late* keeper of the Council Chamber the sum of ten pounds for his paines taken in the provision of flowers etc, for the said Chamber for one whole year ending the feast of the Announciation of our Lady last past."† His mission, as the Act of the Privy Council shows, was to provide flowers, shovels, tongs, and bellows.‡ We hear nothing of any literary

* Canonbury Tower is now the seat of the Bacon Society.

† Acts of Privy Council. Langham was paid ten pounds a year salary from 1573, and the entries occur every April.

‡ Acts of Privy Council, vol. ix., April 15, 1576: A warrant to the treasurer of the chamber to pay Robert Langham, Keeper of the Council Chamber, the sum of £x in consideration of his

labour, such as he must have incurred who wrote this wonderful letter, and then was silent for ever—at least under this name. "A person very meet seemed he for the purpose of XIV years old," who made his hair "to shine like a mallard's wing by means of a sponge dipped in a little capon's grease," his beard smoothly shaven, and "with *ruff fair starched* sleeked and glistering like a pair of new shoes, marshalled in good order with a setting stick."* At every line we seem reminded of Hilyard's miniature and garrulous Euphues—metaphor, simile, and even antithesis abounding. He can be in earnest as well as jest too, and he betrays his master hand as an artist in a remarkable passage, on the subject of unity, or one-hood (as he calls it), in which he introduces Bacon's favourite motto, *Cor unum, una via.†*

We are at Kenilworth; with us is the young Shakespeare (known as Bacon) at the age of fourteen. To him the sights he has seen are wonderful. Of all, even at this early age, he is the most observant of men. Nothing escapes him; he can find something to notice or smile and jest at in every detail; above all, he attends "at my good Lady Sidney's chamber, a noble woman that I am as much bound to, as any poor man [*sic*] may be unto so gracious a Lady." Lady Sidney was the sister of the Earl of Leicester, and therefore his aunt by blood. Her daughter, the Countess of Pembroke, was the sister of Philip Sidney and mother of

---

paines taken and provision made of boughs, flowers, etc., for that office, and also xiijs and iiijd for a fire-shovel, pair of tongs, bellows, and fork for that chamber.

* Setting sticks of wood, silver, and even gold were used for setting the ruffs. (See the ruff of Hilyard's miniature.)

† E. H. Knowles, "Castle of Kenilworth," p. 111. Nicholas Bacon's heraldic motto was *Mediocra firma*.

those two incomparable brothers to whom the famous
first Folio of the plays is dedicated. He is present at
Kenilworth, as son of the Lord Keeper, and is as yet
ignorant of his royal birth, and his language in respect
of the Earl of Leicester is the more remarkable. Like
Euphues he adores the ladies, and says of the Earl of
Leicester: "As for the amplitude of his Lordship's
mind, albeit that I poor soul can in conceit no more
attain unto, than judge of a gem whereof I have no
skill: yea, though daily worn and resplendent in mine
eye, yet some of the virtues and properties thereof, in
quantity and quality so apparent as cannot be hidden,
but seen of all men, might I be bolder to report here
unto you: but as for the value, your jewellers in their
carrots let them cast, and they can.

" And first: who that considers unto the stately seat
Kenilworth Castle, the rare beauty of building that
his honour hath advanced; all of hard quarry stone:
every room so spacious, so well belighted, and so high
roofed within. So seemingly to sight, by due proportion without; a day time so glittering by glass;
night by continual brightness of candle fire and torch
light transparent through the lightsome winds, as it
were the Egyptian Pharos relucent unto all the Alexandrian coast: or else (to talk merrily with my merry
friend) thus radiant, as though Phœbus for his ease
would rest him in the castle and not every night so to
travel down to the Antipodes."

An eloquent and observant doorkeeper this.* One
clearly who had missed his vocation. One, too, in
whom the enthusiasm of youth was still on the very

* Or was it the lovely boy Oberon and Titania quarrelled
about ?

surface; though the doorkeeper died in 1580, he notes
already the delicate effect of candle-light.*

"Unto this, his honour's exquisite appointment o
a beautiful garden, an acre or more of quantity, tha
lyeth on the north there. Wherein hard all along th
castle wall is reared a pleasant terrace of ten foot hig
and twelve broad: even under-foot and fresh of fin
grass; as is also the side thereof toward the garder
in which by sundry distances; with obelisks, sphere
and white bears, all of stone upon their curious base
by goodly show were set; to these two fine arbou
redolent by sweet trees and flowers, at each en
one. . . .

"Where further, also by great cost, the sweetne
of savour on all sides, made so respirant from t
redolent plant and fragrant herbs and flours, in for
colour, and quantity so deliciously variant; and fru
trees bedeckt with their apples, pears and ripe cherrie
And unto these the midst against the terrace: a squa
cage sumptuous and beautiful, joined hard to t
north wall. . . . Under the cornice again, every pa
beautiful with great diamonds, emeralds, rubies a
sapphires: pointed, tabled, rok (?) and round; garnish
with their gold by skilful head and hand, and by t
and pencil so lively expressed, as it might be gr
marvel and pleasure to consider how near *excellen
of art* could approach *perfection of nature*."†

When the reader reflects here how repeatedly Bac
in his philosophic works, insists that "it is the du
of art to perfect and exalt nature," it becomes ever m

---

* Bacon refers to this in his "Essay of Truth."

† Note this very Baconian phrase. Also Bacon's love for
scent of flowers was considerable and marked !

KENILWORTH CASTLE ABOUT 1620

Nearly fifty years after the famous festivities.

From a picture at Newnham Paddox.

anifest whose pen is so eloquently describing the joys
Kenilworth, which had so completely delighted and
ptivated his young Shakespearean heart, whilst the
lowing passage is more than ever reminiscent of
phues: " But (shall I tell you) the silver sounded
te without the sweet touch of hand: the glorious
p, without the fragrant wine, or the rich ring with
gem, without the fair featured finger, is nothing
leed in his proper grace and use: even so his Honour
ounted this mansion till he had placed there tenants
ordingly. Had it therefore replenished with lively
ds, English, French, Spanish, Canarian and (I am
eived if I saw not some) African. . . . A garden
n so appointed, as wherein aloft upon sweet
dowed walk of terrace, in heat of summer, to feel
pleasant whisking of the wind above, or delectable
ness of the fountain spring beneath: to taste of
cious strawberries, cherries and other fruits, even
n their stalks, to hear such natural melodious music
tunes of birds." The taste, the smell, the ear, the
the feeling—the effect on every sense is recorded
he young Shakespeare rattles on, telling how the
k stood still at two o'clock, and the significance of
nd how the tent in which Her Majesty was received
ong Itchington vied in size with the bed of Og, King
asan, which was four yards and a half long, and two
s wide: " So this tent had seven cart loads of
pertaining to it—now, for the greatness guess as
an."

t one passage above all in Laneham's letter, as
dy mentioned, betrays at once not only the hand
e poet, but that of Francis Bacon, who dwells so
antly on Pan—*i.e.*, everything—the all in all,

7

the symbol of unity, the value of which Laneham
youthful Orpheus here points out. " Let me tell y
a little of the dignity of one-hood (*i.e.*, unity), wher
always, all high Deity, Sovereignty, Pre-eminer
Principality, and Concord, without possibility of
agreement, is contained. As one God, one Saviour,
Faith, one Prince, one Sun, one *Phœnix*,* and as
of great wisdom says: *one heart and one way*."† 1
motto is the one, above all, peculiar to Bacon, be
a translation of *Unum cor, una via*. Add to this
fact that, five weeks after this letter was printed
was suppressed. Copies were only allowed to L
Burghley and Sir Nicholas Bacon. Proof of its or
seems thus practically complete. At every t
something attests the source from which it came.

In these extracts I have omitted the exaggera
dialect and spellings as being a mere trick designe
complete the concealment. A man with all the cul
of the author of this letter must have known
enough the more polished English, which, at that per
prevailed within fifty miles of London. A country
with the knowledge of four foreign tongues, unabl
write in the better sort of his own, is an absurdity.

We are at 1575. We have established Shakesp
as Francis Bacon, foster-son of the Lord Keeper,
as having been present at Kenilworth, as were all
principal members of the Privy Council. We se
rarely observant eye cultivating already the s
effect of sun and shadow, of candle-light, torchl
fireworks, the glitter of glass and jewelry, the fragr

* " The maiden Phœnix."

(" Henry VIII.," last scen

† " Cor unum, una via." See p. 94.

of flowers and herbs, so peculiarly beloved of Bacon; the effect of such light he compares poetically with the classical Pharos illuminating the Alexandrian coast, or with Phœbus the Sun, Apollo himself, seeking rest in the castle; he even compares Leicester, the Queen's favourite, to Macedonian Alexander and Charles the Great.* His imagination is exuberant. It carries him away. It is essentially a poet, an Orpheus that speaks, and a young one, full of the joy of life—not a doorkeeper, much less an old one. Moreover, he is manifestly practising art and its mission to perfect and exalt nature, on the lines laid down by G. T.—in the " Posies " of George Gascoigne, above alluded to— as to " quickness of invention, proper vocables, and apt epithets,"† and seeks at every turn to experiment with new words, in that manner in which historically Francis Bacon-Shakespeare is known to have studied , and which Puttenham comments upon.‡

His exuberance clearly allowed him to go beyond discretion. He had witnessed scenes not intended to be heard of far and wide. On second thoughts, perhaps, " what these things mean is not for everyone to know." He was held to have gone too far. Young Shakespeare was setting forth truths deemed best untold. It was at Worcester, on August 20, 1575, that, as Robert Laneham or Langham, he published his memorable letter entitled: " A letter wherein part of the entertainment unto the Queen's Majesty at Kenilworth Castle

* The Heroes of Marlowe's " Dr. Faustus " and F. Bacon and Queen Elizabeth.

† See " Gab. Harvey and Thomas Nashe," by E. G. Harman, and Gascoigne's work, 1575.

‡ See " Promus " of Sir F. Bacon.

in Warwick-sheer in this Soomerz Progress 1575 is
signified from a friend officer attendant in the court "
—*i.e.*, the keeper of the council door who supplied
the chamber with fire-irons !

On September 10—that is, just three weeks later—
W. Patten writes to Lord Burghley reporting that
" he has this day received instructions from the Master
of Requests for the suppression of a book complained
of by one Langham. With the exception of 6 copies
to Mr. Wilson and 2 to his Lordship and the Lord
Keeper, has not let 3 copies pass him."* Clearly
" what these things mean was not for everyone to
know." But why were copies sent to these two
Lords ? Only four copies of the original are known
to exist of the eleven which thus escaped.

" The Princely Pleasures of Kenilworth," by George
Gascoigne, are merely the counterpart of Laneham's
letter. The two were evidently written in collusion
The letter gives the scenery and setting; the verses are
the words spoken at the several devices presented to
Her Majesty. They should be studied both as a
whole and in detail, remembering the stress Laneham
lays on one-hood—*i.e.*, unity; and that we are dealing
with the first and earliest dramatic experience of the
youthful Shakespeare at the age of fourteen. He
the great philosopher and poet to be, was fourteen years
old, yet already approaching the end of his university
career. The Earl of Leicester, his probable concealed
father, was making a final great effort of recognition
and acknowledgment. The Queen of England, full of
distinguished majesty and princely grace, was forty
two; Leicester was the same age, some say, to a day

* " Cal. of Hatfield MS.," vol. ii., p. 108.

He was Oberon, the Queen Titania; and who, we wonder, was the lovely boy she had in her attendance?—

> " She never had so sweet a changeling;
> And jealous Oberon* would have the child
> Knight of his train, to trace the forests wild;
> But she, perforce, withholds the loved boy,
> Crowns him with flowers, and makes him all her joy."
>
> (" Midsummer Night's Dream," Act II., sc. i.)

Is this a reminiscence of his youth, of the maternal fondness lavished upon him, not by Titania, but by Queen Elizabeth, in the first flush of his early promise? For what a lovely boy he must have been, this youthful Orpheus, so primed with wit, Hilyard has shown us.

The scene is Kenilworth, 1575. The Earl of Leicester, upon whom all have looked for many years as King to be, is shooting his last bolt. All eyes are upon him. He enlists all the forces of Cupid in his cause. His aim is nothing less than the Queen of England, whose heart, indeed, seems made of flint. He, too, like Oberon, has other loves on hand—his Phillida and his Hippolyta.†
But first he bids the love-god loose his arrow at the highest game to wound:

> " Her whom I loved most
> You cannot choose but call unto your mind
> Zabeta's‡ name, who *twenty years or more*
> Did follow me (Diana), still scorning Cupid's kind
> And vowing so to serve me evermore."

---

* The name Oberon is probably taken from " Huon of Bordeaux " (translated by Lord Berners), one of the books mentioned by Laneham as amongst the many stories of Chivalry and others known to Captain Cox. (See " Kenilworth," H. Knowles.)

† Lady Haworth and Lady Sheffield (see Gilbert Talbot's letter, quoted above).

‡ Zabeta, the last three syllables of *Elizabeta*.

(From 1554 to 1575 is twenty-one years. Queer
Elizabeth met Leicester in the Tower in 1554.)

Long, long afterwards these scenes of his youth a
Kenilworth were vividly brought to mind by the olde
Shakespeare, as he sat writing the play of " Midsumme
Night's Dream." Then he recalled how in one of th
devices at Kenilworth " Proteus appeared, sitting on
dolphin's back. And the dolphin was conveyed upo:
a boat so that the oars seemed to be his finns. Withi:
the which Dolphin, a concert of music was secretl
placed, the which sounded, and Proteus sang this son
of congratulation, as well in the behalf of the Lad
distressed, as also in the behalf of all the nymphs an
gods of the sea." Shakespeare-Bacon writing " Mic
summer Night's Dream," remembered this inciden
and all the glories of that scene in which the gorgeou
Earl assailed and tried to captivate his mothe
England's Queen. He seems almost to hear the mus
—which Laneham describes as " the melody of tl
seven-sorted music of the Dolphin "—and conveys it :
his words, putting the incident—a trifle altered—in·
Oberon's mouth, thus addressing Puck:

> " Thou rememberest
> Since once I sat upon a promontory,
> And heard a mermaid on a dolphin's back
> Uttering such dulcet and harmonious breath
> That the rude sea grew civil at her song
> And certain stars shot madly from their spheres,
> To hear the sea-maid's music.
> That very time I saw,* but thou couldst not,
> Flying between the cold moon and the earth,

---

* " I saw "—that is, Shakespeare-Bacon saw—at Kenilwo:
the Earl courting the Queen.

> Cupid all arm'd: a certain aim he took
> At a fair vestal throned by the west,
> And loos'd his love-shaft smartly from his bow,
> As it should pierce a hundred thousand hearts;
> But I might see young Cupid's fiery shaft
> Quenched in the chaste beams of the watery moon,
> And the imperial votaress passed on,
> In maiden meditation *fancy free*.
> Yet marked I where the bolt of Cupid fell:
> It fell upon a little western flower,
> Before milk-white, now purple with love's wound,
> And maidens call it love-in-idleness."

* * * * *

Well might Castibula, in the device which was suppressed at Kenilworth, exclaim:

> " I dread dame Juno with some gorgeous gift
> Hath laid some snare her *fancy to entrap*,
> And hopeth so her lofty mind to lift
> On Hymen's bed, by height of worldly hap."

Him whom Gascoigne calls Proteus, Laneham calls Arion," the Master of Music of the Gorhambury summerhouse;—and Oberon calls " Mermaid."

" The Princely Festivities of Kenilworth " may indeed be described as drama in real life. What a joy they must have been to the wonderful boy, for whom, as well as his Queen-mother, they were inaugurated. If examined as a whole it will be found they consist of three principal devices. In the first, under the title of the device of the Lady of the Lake, the Queen is welcomed by Sibilla, who assures her of a happy reign. She is then met by the Lady of the Lake, who has been immersed there since the days of King Arthur, and kept the castle " for *Arthur's heirs by right*." Her Majesty is then presented with gifts " as tokens of true love " from him who but of late this building here *did lay*:

" Eccho—Dudley, who gave himself and all, a worth
gift to be received and so I trust it shall."

The next part was to be a device in which Dian
strove to retain Her Majesty in chastity, and " bewar
lest Cupid's Knights invade, by slight, by force, b
mouth or mighty hand." Juno was, however, intende
to triumph and persuade her to accept wedlock:

" Wherefore, good Queen, forget Diana's tysing tale;
Let never needless dread presume to bring your bliss to bale
How necessary were for worthy Queens to wed
That know you well, whose life always in learning hath bee
led.
The country craves consent, your virtues vaunt themself,
And Jove in heaven would smile to see Diana on the shelf.

" Then give consent, O Queen, to Juno's just desire,
Who for your wealth would have you wed, and for you
farther hire
Some empress will you make, she bade me tell you thus.

" I am but messenger, but sure she bade me say,
That where you now in Princely post have passed on
pleasant day,
A world of wealth at will, you henceforth shall enjoy.
In wedded state and therewithal, hold up from great annoy
The staff of your estate; O Queen, O worthy Queen,
Yet never wight felt perfect bliss, but such as wedded been.'

Now young Shakespeare-Bacon at this time kne
nothing of his birth. He was present at Kenilwort
as the brilliant son of his highly revered foster-father—
that is, as Francis Bacon, the son of Sir Nicholas Bacon
If, therefore, as is not improbable, he had any shar
in drafting this device, he did so in the innocenc
of his heart. For, as is generally well known, any tal
of marriage or of the succession was the one thin
that the Fairy Queen sought always to avoid. Thu

this device was not presented, and never came to execution.

What followed is remarkable: this device in which Diana was to favour chastity and Juno to press marriage having been thrown out, "the Earl commanded Master Gascoigne to devise some farewell worth the presenting," and he, in the garb of Silvanus, running by the Queen's side as she departed, held forth to her on the subject of *deep Desire* which he describes as that wretch of worthies, and yet the worthiest that ever was condemned to wretched estate; he was "such an one as neither any delay would daunt him: *no disgrace could abate his passions*, no time could tire him, no water quench his flames; nor death itself could amaze him with terror." This Deep Desire, which had been transformed into a Holly Bush, then addresses the Queen, imploring her to listen to him, and, after explaining his position, beseeches her as follows:

" Vouchsafe, O comely Queen, yet longer to remain,
   Or still to dwell amongst us here; O Queen, command
      again
   This castle and the Knight which keeps the same for you.

' But if your noble mind resolvèd by decree,
   Be not content by me, *Desire*, persuaded for to be,
   Then bend your willing ears unto my willing note:
   And hear what song the gods themselves have taught me
      now by rote."

* * * * *

' If death or dole could daunt a deep desire,
   If privy pangs could counterpoise my plaint,
   If tract of time a true intent could tire,
   Or cramps of care a constant mind could taint,
   Oh, then might I at will here live and serve,
   Although my deeds did more delight deserve.

> But out, alas, no gripes of grief suffice
>   To break in twain this harmless heart of mine,
> For though delight be banished from mine eyes
>   Yet lives *Desire*, whom pain can never pine;
> O strange effects, I live which seem to die,
>   Yet die to see my dear delight go by."
>
> ("Princely Pleasures of Kenilworth.")

And so the Queen passed on "in maiden meditation fancy-free."

"What these things mean is not for everyone to know," yet each can form his own conclusions; and "maidens call it love-in-idleness"; and the great Queen is said to have been married secretly to Leicester the day before Bacon's birth.*

There are two other passages which become worthy of note when we remember, in comparing them, that we are listening to Shakespeare in the boy Francis Bacon describing and extolling his mother, the much admired, quaint, vain, whimsical, capable, and always stately Queen Elizabeth—likewise incomprehensible.

Of the two passages referred to, the first is the welcome of Sibilla, containing the words:

> "As now the dew of heavenly gifts full thick on you doth fall
>   Even so shall virtue more and more augment your years
>   withal.
> The rage of war bound fast in chains shall never stir no
>   more:
> But peace shall govern all your days, increasing subjects' love
> You shall be called the Prince of peace, and peace shall be
>   your shield,
> So that your eyes shall never see the broils of bloody field."†

---

* "Dict. Nat. Biog.," vol. xvi., p. 114; on January 21 1561, the day before the birth of Francis Bacon.

† See "Princely Pleasures at the Court of Kenilworth," G. Gascoigne.

In after years we find Shakespeare elaborating this passage in the last scene of the play of "King Henry VIII." thus:

> "This royal infant—heaven still move about her !—
> Though in her cradle, yet now promises
> Upon this land a thousand thousand blessings,
> Which time shall bring to ripeness: she shall be—
> But few now living can behold that greatness—
> A pattern to all princes living with her,
> And all that shall succeed: Saba was never
> More covetous of wisdom and fair virtue
> Than this pure soul shall be: all princely graces, . . .
> With all the virtues that attend the good,
> Shall still be doubled in her . . .
>
> Her own shall bless her;
> Her foes shake like a field of beaten corn; . . .
> In her days every man shall eat in safety,
> Under his own vine, what he plants; and sing
> The merry songs of peace to all his neighbours."
>
> (Henry VIII.," Act V., sc. v.)

Again, let the reader study the following passage from the "Princely Pleasures," where Queen Elizabeth is again under review:

MERCURY.

Behold where here she sits, whom thou so long hast sought:

*   *   *   *   *

DIANA.
(She wondereth at the Queen's Majesty's Princely Post.)

Is this Zabeta, is it she indeed?
> It is she sure: Zabeta mine, all haile,
And though dame Fortune seemeth you to feed
> With Princely post, which serves for your avail,
Yet give me leave to gaze you *in the face*,
> Since now (long since) myself yourself did seek,
And be content for all your *stately grace*
> Still to remain a maiden always meek.
>
> (" The Suppressed Device," Act II., sc. iv.)

How very beautifully, only a few years later, Shake-speare-Bacon (according to our understanding) elaborated this passage as " Immerito " in the April eclogue of the " Shepherd's Calendar " !   Thus:

> " See where she sits upon the grassy green,
>   O seemly sight !
>   Y-clad in scarlet like a maiden Queen
>   And ermines white.
>   Upon her head a Crimson coronet,
>   With damask roses and daffadillies set,
>   Bay leaves between,
>   And primroses green
>   Embellish the sweet violet.
>
> " Tell me, have ye seen her *angelic face*
>   Like Phœbe fair?
>   Her heavenly haveour, her *princely grace*
>   Can you well compare?
>   The red rose medled with the white yfere*
>   In either cheek depicted lively cheer.
>   Her modest eye,
>   *Her Majesty*,
>   Where have you seen the like, but there ?" etc.

Thus did Shakespeare-Bacon throughout his life, in prose as well as in verse, sing to the glory of Queen Elizabeth, whom we believe to have been his own able Queen-mother.   Moreover, it was Shakespeare's established practice thus at first to express what seemed suitable matter in the briefest and simplest manner, and later to elaborate it to the full bent of his fancy. Many of the famous plays may be shown, and are admitted, to have been by common consent built up in this way, beginning with a brief history, to which,

---

* This Tudor emblem and contrast of colour, roses red and white, was a favourite simile of Shakespeare.

as Bacon says in his "Novum Organum,"* he next makes tables of discovery, a diagnosis of passions, as of anger, fear, shame, and the like, as we see in "Winter's Tale," "King Lear," "Julius Cæsar," and "Hamlet," and then elaborates the same in detail.† These are the types and models, showing "the whole process of the mind in certain subjects" promised in the "Plan of the Great Instauration."

One of the most interesting features of Laneham's letter is the catalogue of old English literature which he gives, known as "Captain Cox's Library" (Furnival). Nashe endorses the views of Ascham on many of these stories of chivalry, which he designates as "the fantastical dreams of those exiled Abbie-lubbers‡ (monks) from whose idle pens proceed those worn-out impressions of the feigned nowhere acts of Arthur of the Round table, Arthur of Little Brittaine, Huon of Burdeaux, the Squire low degree, the four sons of Ammon and infinite others . . . Bevis of Hampton" (Nashe's "Anatomie of Absurdity"). All these are mentioned in Laneham's letter. Similar works receive like scorn in "Don Quixote." It is Shakespeare-Bacon's voice everywhere, imbibed from Ascham's Schoolmaster," as Nashe points out.§

The reader can compare the interpretation of the

* "Novum Organum," i., Aphorism 127.
† See "Winter's Tale," Act. II., sc. ii. and iii.
‡ Ascham says: "These books, as I have heard say, were made the most part in Abbeis and Monasteries," Toxophilus. He calls them "Books of fayned Chivalry," leading only to manslaughter and bawdrie." "Ascham's Works," p. 57, Bennet.
§ See also "The English Novel in the Time of Shakespeare," J. J. Jusserand; and E. G. Harman, "Harvey and Nashe," 104.

events of Kenilworth given above with that of the Rev
N. J. Halpin in 1843.*   He epitomises Oberon's famou
speech as follows:

"A lover (1) seeking vehemently but in vain t
win her (the Queen's) hand, while he was successfull
(2) engaged in winning the affections or corrupting th
virtue of a Lady of inferior rank."

The interpretation given above may be epitomise
as follows:

(1) A lover seeks vehemently but in vain the han
of the Queen in marriage, but—

(2) She prefers love-in-idleness.

(3) Oberon (Leicester) procures that flower, an
pours a love philter into her ear.

(4) She on waking dotes madly on Bottom—*i.e*
d'Alençon.

(5) Until, cured of her hideous fancy, Dian's bu
(*i.e.*, the Queen) returns to her first love for Oberon.

The character assigned to "Deep Desire" as
wretch whom "no disgrace could abate his passions
etc., justifies this view, which the cipher confirm
Moreover, the same expression is used with the san
meaning in the "Complaint of Philomene" of the san
year (1575).

* Rev. N. J. Halpin, "Oberon's Vision," 1843, p. 14.

CHAPTER IX

SHAKESPEARE AND THE QUEEN AT WOODSTOCK

SUCH were the famous " Princely Pleasures of Kenilworth." Princely they were in every way, for Shakespeare, we believe, was there—the Prince of poets—
and, as Laneham, calls himself " The black Prince,"*
and signs himself *El Prencipe Negro*, and there he
received his baptism into the art of the drama: that
drama which to him was in more senses than one the
drama of life. Nevertheless, the events which followed
are even more illuminating as to his true identity inas-
much as recent discoveries show more clearly than ever
his own authorship, behind the pen-name of Gascoigne,
and his close affinity to Queen Elizabeth.

Her Majesty was accompanied by all her Court,
including the Privy Council, and with her went besides
George Gascoigne, John Hunnis, Master of the Children of the Chapel, the Children (actors), and Master
Ferrers and Harry Goldingham, all of whom assisted
in the performances. "Barons, Lords, Ladies, Judges,
Bishops, Lawyers, Doctors . . . what a number of
estates and of nobility had *Jupiter* assembled there,
guess ye by this." She had Queen's weather, too—
" this great gift did his deity cast upon her Highness
to have fair and seasonable weather at her own appointment."† All the gods smiled on Queen Bess and pre-

* Laneham's letter: "Well ye wot ' the black Prince ' was
never stained with disloyalty . . . and will not begin with you."
† *Ibid.*

sented her with thousand, thousand blessings*—sweet
music, fine weather, all the gifts of Ceres, the fruits of
the earth; and of Mars, ladies and gentlewomen of great
beauty and comeliness, and gallant attire, dancing with
comely grace, with sweet voices in a song, " and pleasant
talk with express commandment and charge unto her
sun (Cupid, the son of Venus) that he shoot not a shaft
in the Court all the while her highness remained at
Killingworth."† " I saw, but thou couldst not," says
Oberon, in " Midsummer Night's Dream." " I saw,
but thou couldst not . . . Cupid all armed." In spite
of Venus's commands the little love-god loosed his
fiery shaft at the bidding of the Earl, though unavail-
ingly: " It fell upon a little western flower, and maidens
call it love-in-idleness,"‡ which makes a man or
woman madly dote (with deep desire) upon the next live
creature that it sees. And so the imperial votaress
passed on, to all appearance fancy free, in all her maiden
majesty, though for a while transformed by a love philter
before men's eyes, as was Titania—to dote upon her
lacrymose *grenouille*, her Bottom, the little pock-
marked d'Alençon whom she in turn rejected.

One wonder—I might almost say one fairy tale—after
another opens to our view in this year 1575, when the
Earl of Leicester seemed nearer royalty than ever.
Kenilworth, Chartley, Worcester, Woodstock. At
which place should we prefer to have been during this
great progress? For from Kenilworth Her Majesty
proceeded to Chartley, the seat of Walter Devereux,
Earl of Essex, whose son, the young Robert, later him-

* Laneham's letter, and " Henry VIII.," last scene.
† " Henry VIII.," Act V., sc. v.
‡ Midsummer Night's Dream."

self the favoured courtier Robert, Earl of Essex, was
also there, just eight years old; and there, too, was his
sister, the beautiful Penelope—Sidney's "Stella." It
was a threefold historically interesting occasion. For
in the Queen's train, as all men know, came also Philip
Sidney, and as all may well believe came Shakespeare,
though beclad as Francis Bacon, son of the Lord
Keeper. They were in very truth two cousins, these
famed men. They met again later in Paris, but Sidney
had already spent several years in France, Germany,
and Austria, Hungary and Italy, where he had gained
a great reputation, so that William the Silent of Orange
later proclaimed him " one of the ripest counsellors of
estate that at this day lived in Europe ";* whilst he
had already formed the friendship of Hubert Languet,
a learned political thinker, " humanist and counsellor
of Kings, a friend of Melanchthon, Titian, and Duplessis-
Mornay ";† and he had known Tintoretto, and been
painted by Paul Veronese.‡   Here, indeed, was a friend
after the very heart of the Prince of poets, the royal
Shakespeare—Philip Sidney ! whose biographer, Fulke
Greville, was Bacon-Shakespeare's neighbour at Gray's
Inn, and who " knew him with such staiedness of mind,
lovely and familiar gravity as carried grace and reverence above greater years."§   Such was the renowned
author of " Arcadia." Such as we see it was the
occasion on which our Princely Shakespeare-Bacon
met his cousin, the chivalrous and arcadian Sidney.
They met again in France in 1577, when Sidney had been
an ambassador to Vienna. They met again in 1579

* J. J. Jusserand, " The English Novel in the Time of
Shakespeare."   † *Ibid.*   ‡ *Ibid.*
    § *Ibid.*, and Fulke Greville's " Life," London, 1562.

when Shakespeare-Bacon, as Immerito, was signing letters from Leicester House, the Earl of Leicester being the uncle of Sidney and presumed father of Shakespeare-Bacon. The Queen at that time not infrequently kept her Court at Leicester House,* and there these cousins by blood and in taste, with Sir Edward Dyer, formed as we shall see, that Areopagus† or Crew of Courtly Makers‡ or poets which was to mould the English tongue and build up the English drama. So Sidney and Shakespeare met—the cousins—soldier-poet and Prince-poet. But for Sidney on this occasion there was a yet more portentous meeting. For it was at this time and on this occasion, as said, that he met his " Stella ' —the name he gave to Penelope, the beautiful sister or foster-sister, of the Earl of Essex, by some reputed to be the real brother by blood of Bacon-Shakespeare Poor Sidney ! He was not allowed to marry Penelope He married instead the daughter of Sir Francis Walsing-ham, and consoled himself wisely by idealising Penelope as his " Stella," as Shakespeare, we shall see, idealised a certain Marguerite as his Juliet. For the ideal lies not in the idealised, but in the idealiser, not in the idol but in the idolater. Sidney and Shakespeare ! How sweetly their names sound together ! A pair of heavenly twins indeed. War carried off the brave knight, and it was left to Shakespeare-Bacon to teach the use of knowledge for that end for which God granted it, " the benefit of the state and society of man " by the glorious marriage of science and art, and the initiation of the age of invention.

* Diary of Sir Francis Walsingham.
† Immerito, " Gab. Harvey Correspondence."
‡ Puttenham, " Art and Poesie."

ROBERT DEVEREUX, EARL OF ESSEX

Hilyard.

ROBERT DUDLEY, EARL OF LEICESTER

National Portrait Gallery.

Facing p. 114.

From Chartley—so pregnant of events of importance
r the fame of England—Queen Elizabeth reached
orcester on August 14, and left that place on
ıgust 19. The famous letter of Laneham appeared
ere the day after her departure—*i.e.*, on August 20.
oceeding to Woodstock, she paid it a visit of un-
ınted length, lasting some six weeks, for, though the
te of her departure is unknown, she signed a warrant
Woodstock on September 29 under the signet of the
rd Treasurer.* Moreover, she paid a visit to our
akespeare's home at Gorhambury from Woodstock,
er the play of "The Hermit" had been presented
her on September 23, on which day Sir Nicholas
con, writing from Gorhambury to Lord Burghley
ıcerning the despatch of a certain warrant for the
ıceedings in the north, says: "The Queen is well
ased with it. He trusts that within two hours, the
rk of the Crown will have finished with it."† Clearly
r Majesty must have been with him, on a visit to
concealed son. This, indeed, was the height of
innocent and happy young life, the Queen-mother
ılging her marvellous son, the now fast blossoming
.kespeare, to the full length of her bent; indeed, so
:h so that at last some inkling of the truth must
e entered his head, leading, in 1576, to his being
denly sent, under arrangements made by the Privy
ncil, with Sir Amyas Paulet, to France. For on
·eturn thence he shows in the "Shepherd's Calendar"
knowledge of his royal descent.

·e are, however, now at Woodstock in August and
:ember, 1575. As Laneham's letter and Gascoigne's

* "Calendar of Hatfield MS.," Part II., p. 114.
†*Ibid.* The Privy Council was at Woodstock from Sep-
·er 6 to October 2.

" Princely Pleasures " give a full account of what to
place in this famous year at Kenilworth, so the lit
pamphlet entitled " The Queens Majesties Enterta
ment at Woodstock imprinted for T. Cadman 158
gives us a similar account of the performances the
but there is this marked difference, that, in this ca
the only account extant was not printed until *ten ye*
after the entertainment took place, and was prin
anonymously without any clue whatsoever as to
author,* while Laneham's letter, though published
the time, was suppressed.

Woodstock !   Ancient, beautiful, and roma
Woodstock !   It was much beloved by Queen El
beth, who had once been a prisoner there (1554);
what child does not remember the story of Henry
and the elaborate labyrinth or maze, which tradi
relates he built for his fair Rosamund ?   Investiga
told the author of " The Just Devil of Woodstoc
that this was an invention, and that the house b
for the security of Rosamund, daughter of Wa
Lord Clifford, was a very solid stone building, as se
probable, the foundations being visible.   He goes
to relate how Woodstock was an old Manor H
built by Henry I., and how, before Queen Eliza
enjoyed it and held revels there, her grandfat
Henry VII., had embellished and amplified it.

Alack ! it suffered the same fate as Theobalds.
October 16, 1649—when Charles I. was behea
handing at the time a prayer from Sidney's " Arcac
to Bishop Juxon—Oliver's puritans, in the forn
Commissioners for surveying and valuing H.M. M
Houses, took up their lodging there.   The "

* Laneham's letter had been confiscated.

evil," we are assured, did his best to frighten and
ut them off their job: " But now this late large Manor
House is in a manner almost turned to a heap of
rbbish; some seven or eight rooms left for the accommodation of a tenant." Poor Woodstock! Poor
Rosamund's Bower! Would it still lived!* We may,
however, with advantage try to form visions of what
went on there in those six weeks' revels from August 20
to the end of September, 1575. By what manner of
means did the wonderful Queen train and guide her
ill more wonderful son to the love of that art—which
had been a passion with herself from the day of her
accession—the drama? Having once admitted that
both Laneham's letter and " Euphues," a witty experiment in Elizabethan simile and metaphor,† are from
his pen, we are able to form a very good idea of the
lively and impressionable nature of Francis, the future
Shakespeare, as Laneham, so welcome in the chamber
of Mary,‡ the mother of Sir Philip Sidney, and of the
Countess of Pembroke, always of a gentle spirit, and
by his good-will ever a favourite like Euphues amongst
the Court ladies, in whose company, when pleased, he
became naturally lively. Then effervescing with
excitement this youth, exuberant with as yet half-
conscious delight in nature, foots it with dancing,
plays on his gittern, his cittern, or the virginals (in
which the Queen was skilled), or—nothing coming
amiss to him—carols with a song, till they cry another
and another! He can even amorously ogle the ladies
with his Spanish sighs, his French heighs, his Italian

* It stood where Blenheim is now.
† See p. xviii.
‡ Laneham's letter.

dolces, and his Dutch courtship.* Witty and garrulo
beyond measure, with the classical mythology at h
fingers' ends, accomplished in every art, and with a
the vanity of his youth and race, gay, gallant, an
debonair, intensely high-spirited, yet, in reserv
inspired like his mother with a high purpose nothin
short of divine, and a will stopping short only at ir
possibilities, he is the centre of mirth, interest, an
fun; whilst—though himself unconscious of it—h
likeness to Her Majesty is the cause of many a sile
gesture and whisper amongst the ladies of her Court.

The nature of his wit and genius is nowhere bett
expressed than in the words which he himself puts in
the mouth of one bearing the anagram name of h
love in " Love's Labour's Lost," where, as pointed o
by Mr. R. L. Eagle, *Rosaline* says: †

> " Berowne they call him; but a merrier man,
> Within the limit of becoming mirth,
> I never spent an hour's talk withal:
> His eye begets occasion for his wit;
> For every object that the one doth catch
> The other turns to a mirth-moving jest,
> Which his fair tongue—conceit's expositor,
> Delivers in such apt and gracious words
> That aged ears play truant at his tales
> And younger hearings are quite ravished;
> So sweet and voluble is his discourse."

---

* Laneham's letter. So Euphues exclaims: "Who so co
versant with the ladies as I ? Who so pleasant ? Who mo
prodigal ? Insomuch that I thought the time lost which w
not spent either in their company with delight or for th
company in letters." These sighs, etc., were then the fashio
able indications of love.

† See the *Quest*, October, 1923. R. L. Eagle, "Shakespear
First Play." " Love's Labour's Lost," Act II., sc. i.

What could call to mind more than Jonson's observation in his *discoveries* on Bacon, that " his language was nobly censorious *where he could spare or pass over a jest* " ?

One may sit thus for hours allowing fancy to elaborate the scanty glimpses we get, not of the mature and more worldly philosopher and poet, but of the innocent, unaffected youth of Shakespeare, as yet unspoiled by disappointment and discontent. Vainly do we endeavour to pierce in any detail the veil which shrouds the absolute truth, yet we are vouchsafed just enough matter of fact to form a basis, on which to allow our imaginations to build. Above all, we perceive the same noble aim to actuate both Queen-mother and Prince-son. The drama was to be a means of enlightening—hellenising—the people, in an age when daily newspapers were unknown, weekly magazines were unheard of, books scarce, and the art of reading and writing confined to few. In the minds of both, Alexander the Great stood out as the greatest of heroes. Their aim, like his, was to hellenise all the known world; to make exact knowledge, culture, and good manners and customs the basis of human progress. Strange as it seems to-day, much of this was a new idea then, the means of gathering in the excellent dew of knowledge systematically was the creation of their era. Shakespeare-Bacon grasped its portent through his Queen-mother. She made the bell that Bacon rung and called " Shakespeare." The endowment of human life, with new inventions, discoveries, and powers, by the persistent use of reason helped by the imagination,* was the idea already at the back of the

* See " Steel Glass," Gascoigne.

head of the alert young man, whose first efforts we are
endeavouring to trace—the idea in which, as he told
Fulgentio forty years later, his mind "hath not waxed
older in this design, nor after so many years grown
cold and indifferent." The control of the affections
by reason was, further, a matter in which he differed
materially from Aristotle, and had so differed from his
Cambridge days,* it seems. All, everything, as he grew
to see it, depended, as he saw in youth, upon the co-
operation of that powerful duality in nature, reason and
imagination, so clearly expressed in the " Steel Glass "

> " There is a kind of fame
> The which I seek with science to assault,
> And so to leave remembrance of my name,
> The walls whereof are wondrous hard to climb,
> And much too high for ladders made of rhyme."

Thus wrote the young Shakespeare, as Gascoigne
at the age of fifteen; for that Gascoigne was one o
Shakespeare-Bacon's earliest pseudonyms become
plainer than ever in studying "The Queen's Majesty'
Entertainment at Woodstock."

Of this valuable little pamphlet only one copy seem
to have survived. Even the first few pages of tha
are missing, and, as already stated, it bears date 1585–
that is, ten years after the entertainment took place
and eight years after Gascoigne was dead and buried
The " Play of the Hermit " which it contains is nowher
else to be found. It is a continuation of the " Tal
of the Hermit," usually attributed to Gascoigne, bu
the name of Gascoigne is nowhere upon it, and, indeed
in his letter to the Queen published with the " Ta

* Bacon, " De Aug.," Book VII., chap. iii.; J. M. Robertso
p. 574.

of the Hermit," he specifically repudiates its authorship, his words being as follows:* " I . . . present you
with these rude lines, having turned the eloquent tale
of Hermetes the Herymite (wherewith I saw your
learned judgment greatly pleased at Woodstock) into
Latin, Italian, and French; not that I think any of
the same translations anywise comparable with the
first invention, for if your Highness compare *myne
ignorance with the author's skill*, or have regard to my
rude phrases, compared with *his well-polished style*,
you shall find my sentences as much discorded, as
arrows shot out of a plough." Who was the author,
then, of the first original invention? Gascoigne confesses himself merely the translator. Whose was the
skill and well-polished style with which his rude phrases
could not compare? Indeed, the Queen herself, we
are told, lent her skill to the devisers of the *Play ;* and
who can have been living in 1585 who saw and was so
much interested in this suppressed play (of the Hermit)
as to publish it so long after—anonymously? There
was one person only who answers to the call. The
young Loricus of the Play is the young Shakespeare-
Bacon himself, and he was the author. He was present
as Francis, son of the Lord Keeper. It is he who
speaks to Gaudema, the Queen, and of Contrarenus,
the Earl of Leicester, in terms of such humility and
respect. It is he really who in the frontispiece of
Gascoigne's edition of the " Tale of the Hermit "
kneels before Her Majesty to present his book. Like
Laneham's " Minstrel of Islington," he is but half
disguised. He has Laneham's boyish utterance. He

* See Gascoigne MS., British Museum, Royal MS. 18, A.
xlviii.

holds a sword, lance, and pen, and is crowned with
a laurel wreath on his head, and other figures are said
closely to resemble those in the " Noble Art of Venerie."
The words to the illustration run thus:

> " Behold (good Queen) a *poet with a speare,*
>   Strange sights well marked are understood the better,
> A soldier armed with pensyle in his eare,
>   With pen to fight and sword to write a letter.
> His gown haulf off, his backe not fully bound
>   In doleful dumps which way were best to take,
> With humble haste and knees that kyme the ground,
>   Presents himself to you for dewty's sake,
> And thus he saith: ' No danger, I protest,‡
>   Shall ever let this loyal heart I bear
> To serve you so as may become me beste
>   In fielde, in toune, in court, in anywhere.
> Then peerless Prince employ this willing man
>   In your affairs to do the best he can.' "§

(GASCOIGNE: " Tale of the Hermit.")

The poem on "A Comparison between Two Letters"*
which appeared in the 1572 edition of Gascoigne*
work, but was suppressed in all subsequent editions
clearly itself indicates the <u>alliance</u> between " B "acon
and " G "ascon, as the latter's name was spelt b
Puttenham and others. Also Bascoin was an earlie
form of Bacon;¶ while if B be preferred to A in th
" Christ's cross vow," we get BAC instead of ABC.

It is scarcely possible to conceive a mature poet an

---

* Hazlitt.

† By George Turberville.

‡ Let the reader compare this devotion with Bacon
letters.

§ See " Works of George Gascoigne," Cambridge Universit
Press, T. W. Cunliffe, vol. ii., p. 473.

‖ *Ibid.*, p. 302.

¶ See *Baconiana,* March, 1925, p. 57.

THE "SPEAR SHAKER"
ATHENA PARTHENOS (NATIONAL MUSEUM, ATHENS-GREECE)

PALLAS ATHENA

Athens Museum.

Facing p. 123.

soldier, as Gascoigne was, addressing his Queen thus.
It is the ruse of a young man, the future Shakespeare,
showing already that supreme devotion to the service
of his Queen which, as Bacon, he showed throughout
her life and even after. Mark too, as he bids us, that
he has the symbol of the spear already in view—mindful, perhaps, already, as seems, of the laurel that
sprang from the spear of Quirinus, for he wears a
laurel crown, or of Pallas the Spearshaker,* and remember, always remember too, that, in the " Steel
Glass " the following year, again as Gascoigne, he
declares, as above, page 120:

> " There is a kind of fame
> The which I seek with *science* to assault,
> And so to leave remembrance of my name,"

words which embrace the declared aim of Francis
Bacon. Like as in a kaleidoscope, his character changes
from a poet to a philosopher, from the interlude, the
mask and the play, to the " Novum Organum." He is
the universal, the all-embracing, the growing Pan who
has taken " all knowledge to be his province," as he
wrote later to Lord Burghley, and is destined to
astonish mankind; and he divides all knowledge into
history, poesy, and philosophy.†

The " Tale of the Hermit " (1575) thus translated,
and presented to her ostensibly by George Gascoigne—
to deceive the eyes of men, and so far as possible of her
Court—in fact, emanated really from the inspired
genius of young Shakespeare, the boy of fourteen,
present as Francis Bacon. " The Entertainment of

---

* " In awful hand she shakes her shining speare."
                (Compare Homer's " Odyssey," Book I)
† Bacon, " De Aug.," Book II., chap. i.

the Queen's Majesty at Woodstock," dated 1585,* is divided into two parts, but deals from beginning to end with the same theme as the " Princely Pleasures of Kenilworth "—namely, the love of the Earl of Leicester for Queen Elizabeth.   But the tone here is more earnest, and there is a play as well as " Tale of the Hermit." The end, too, borders in tone on the tragic rather than comic vein, and a third party appears, as said, in the young Knight Loricus, who expresses profound devotion of a platonic kind to the Queen, and receives sage advice from her of a most interesting nature, especially in the play.   The story runs as follows: In the 1585 edition Contarenus (the Earl of Leicester) is enamoured of the fair Princess Gaudema (Queen Elizabeth) and his love is returned.   Occanon, however, Duke of Cambia on the Indus, and father of Gaudema, forbids the marriage, and has Contarenus (Leicester) transported by an enchantress to the extreme bounds of Ocean.   In his wanderings he enters the temple of Venus, at Paphos, and is struck blind for entering uninvited. Mercury then carries him away to the cave of Sibylla, where he lives as a blind hermit.   Meanwhile Gaudema sets out to search for him, and eventually arrives at the cave, outside which she meets the young Knight Loricus, who has also been disappointed in love.   They sit down to tell one another their faithful stories of love which, the blind hermit hearing, is restored—as has been promised—to sight, and at the same time to Gaudema his lost love.   At this point we encounter the Fairy Queen, first mentioned between Tale and

* There is only one fragmentary copy of this little book of 1585.   But it has been recently reprinted with a valuable introduction by A. W. Pollard.

Play. Then Occanon, in search of his daughter, meets her and tells his story; and she asks:

> Q.: Nay, was not that unkindly done of you
> Unknown to her to send her love away ?
>
> *   *   *   *   *
>
> Oc.: But who are you, madam, if I may crave
> To know your name, which seeks them thus to save ?
> Q.: I am the *Fairy Queen*.

Was this the pet name of son for Queen-mother ? It was some years before we hear of Edmund Spenser.

In due course the Fairy Queen then restores Occanon to his daughter, and the sequel is amusing for its *naïveté* and juvenile attempt at pathos. None but a boy could thus have attempted to commit it to paper. The Earl—as Contarenus—is described as a " Knight of estate but mean but of value very great "—and he is now given the choice between " marrying the Queen (*i.e.*, Gaudema) to gratify himself, or resigning her for his country's good." This was indeed exactly the Earl's position. Already, in short, the young Shakespeare was holding the mirror up to nature; and whom but one very near to the Queen would she have permitted to speak so plainly ? Already, too, we read of that war between reason and the affections which figure so much in Bacon's philosophy. It can be none but the young Shakespeare-Bacon who writes; his design, his strength, his colour, his matter; and, moreover, we are told that the Queen lent her own skill to the devisers.

> FAIRY QUEEN: You see, sir Knight, the parent's just request,
> You see the force whereon his *reason* stands,
> *Affection* stays what wisdom thinks for best,
> The matter rests all wholly in your hands.
>
> *   *   *   *   *

CONTARENUS (LEICESTER): Against our love our country's
   good is laid,
For whose avail we ought not death refuse.

*   *   *   *   *

Without, my Lord, your parent's free goodwill,
At home with him what can his child enjoy?

GAUDEMA (Q. ELIZ.): Alas! that such a spirit cannot per-
   suade.
Alas! that State and Virtue sunder so,
But thus from those my love must needes go.
Well sith he yields, which hath most right in me.
Ah! country's good, I yield myself to thee.

*   *   *   *   *

NIPHE: Poor Contarenus, how hath Fortune, fickle dame,
Procured thy grief in offering thee her hand,
Which in thy cause doth now deserve most blame,
When she would seem thy special friend to stand?
Oh, ye that trust the whirling of her wheel,
Beware the wrench at turning of her heel.*

Thus early did young Shakespeare learn and study
to rail at lady fortune in set terms. So favoured was
he by the fair, that he thought the time lost which
was not spent either in their company with delight
or for their company in letters. So devoted was he to
the Queen that he could never cease to use his pen in
her service and cause. The theme, as said, is the same
as at Kenilworth. It is eternally the love of the Earl
of Leicester for the Queen. Allegory, or as Francis
Bacon terms it, parable writing, was a form he
especially favoured, and this love of the Earl of mean
estate but of great value, for the Queen is the theme
alike of the "Shepherd's Calendar," the "Galatea" of
Cervantes, and the "Argenis" of John Barclay—the

* "Play of the Hermit," 1585 edition of "The Queen's
Majesty's Entertainment at Woodstock."

ain difference being that, in these later works, the
tory of the love of Shakespeare himself for Marguerite
f Navarre—acquired as Francis Bacon when in France
with Sir Amyas Paulet—is interwoven.

The veil is not indeed lifted. But we have here
matter that is distinctly biographical and historical,
which enables us to see through the veil. We see before
our eyes within King Henry II.'s old palace of Wood-
ock the great Queen Titania, still dallying with the
arl Oberon. In her train is the young boy Shakespeare, all her joy,* as much the delight of her Court
dies, as he himself loves to delight them by his many
complishments and *letters*. He is known to all as
Francis Bacon, the son of the Lord Keeper, and to give
rce to the delusion the Queen calls him her little Lord
eeper. She makes this explain the interest she
nnot refrain from exhibiting in the already marked
nius, the lively apprehension, and still more remark-
le judgment, of this inspired boy, whom she well
ows to be her son. Above all, and invaluable, this
ry biographical tale and play of " The Hermit "
es us a very distinct idea of the kind of influence
ich the Queen herself at this time was exercising on
 mind, now unfolding, in the embryo of the great
ainary before whose genius all the world in our day
vs—a world far larger than he ever knew—for was
ot foretold of him that:

> " Wherever the bright sun of heaven shall shine,
>   His honour and the greatness of his name
>   Shall be, *and make new nations* " ?
>
> ("Henry VIII.," Act V., sc. v.)

---

* "Midsummer Night's Dream," Act II., sc. i.—the black
ce.

Who more honoured than he by those new nation
which have since sprung into being in America,* wher
he himself as Francis, Viscount St. Alban, and th
two incomparable brothers Pembroke, did so much t
promote our earliest colonies, and so founded the ne
nations we now see.   It is the days of this same man
youth that we are now considering.   He, himself th
great sage that is to be, the new poet just arising, wa
the young Knight Loricus, born with a laurel crow
who thus presented the play of " The Hermit " to H
Majesty.   Unknown to him as yet, he was her so
but natural affinity had already drawn them togethe
As even more touchingly in the later play of " End
mion," so even now he begs leave of the Queen to lo
her " without looking for reward."   He has alreac
learnt to contemn mere bookishness. " Books and beau
make no match,† and it is a whole man or no man th
goddess will have serve her."   Yet " the gods be ju
though women be angry ! Though it is not of t
nature of women to be cruel," yet " touching their va
ableness, who will not apply himself thereto, shall n
long please them, nor much hold them."   Who mc
contrary at times than Queen Bess ?   Lord Burghl
had found it so.   So, too, had young Loricus, w
sagely comforts himself with the reflection that " t
gods be just though women are angry," and " the gc
will receive whom women forsake, and eyes shut fr

* In the United States Francis Bacon is by many regar
as mainly instrumental as promoter in the founding of
English colonies.

† " Why, universal plodding poisons up
   The nimble spirits in the arteries."

(" Love's Labour's Lost," Act IV., sc. iii

delight have minds more open to understanding."
What more Baconian sentiment? Doubtless, he thinks,
" it was the want of his worth that made his service
inacceptable," and, to conclude, he receives that most
wise maternal advice which, as coming from the soul of
his concealed Queen-mother, became the law of his life:

" Knight, prosecute thy purpose, it is noble, learning
by me not to fear and of thyself to take pains, remembering nothing notable is won without difficulty.
Hercules had by his labour his reward, his ruin by
love."

To make the utmost of his talents for the glory of
God and the good of man, to work with ceaseless industry to this end, this, then, was the lesson which
the great Queen impressed upon the mind of her rising
son, the new Solomon; a lesson which he never forgot;
for—

" Poets are made as well as born."

One can imagine how great an inspiration the
majesty and learning of a woman such as Queen
Elizabeth would be to the fiery and apprehensive
mind of a young genius, already the wonder and darling
of the lords and ladies of her Court, counterbalanced
as it was by the philosophic and religious wisdom of
Sir Nicholas and Lady Bacon and the best tutors.
One cannot, in fact, imagine the great plays to have
been written except under some such favourable but
altogether exceptional circumstances of nature and
environment.

9

CHAPTER X

SHAKESPEARE AND MARGUERITE

THE first great crisis in the life of Shakespeare-Bacon
then (like Laneham) the bright, lively, and accom
plished pet and lovely boy of the Court ladies who
surrounded the Queen, and to whom he was already
known as " the black Prince," came in the year 1576
His university career was suddenly cut short. In
August of that year the Queen was on progress, staying
at her pretty little castle at Hertford, still to be seen
and well preserved. The Privy Council, sitting there
on August 26, arranged the details for the conveyance
of the embassy of Sir Amyas Paulet to France " to
be her Majesty's ambassador resident in France, to
take up such carts and cart horses for the carriage of
his staff etc. etc. . . . as he should need for himself
and his train from place to place to the sea coast.
Moreover, George Bristowe of H.M. *Dreadnaught* was
directed to convey him overseas to such part on the
other side as might be deemed most convenient to him
The Court moved to Hatfield on August 27 and to
St. Albans on August 31, on which day the Privy
Council* sat there again, the Earl of Leicester being
present, as also at Hertford. On that same day Sir
Francis Walsingham, always a staunch friend of
Shakespeare-Bacon, reports briefly in his diary: "
went to Gorhambury to dinner and to St. Albans to

* " Acts of Privy Council," 1576, p. 194.

130

:d." Did the Queen-mother go too? We wonder.
ow did she part from the little Orpheus of her
ourt, her lovely boy, her little Lord Keeper—in secret,
we believe, her son? On September 6 Sir Amyas
aulet took his leave of the Queen. With him, as we
now, went he* whom men knew as Francis Bacon,
d, mark this, with the embassy or concurrently went
eorge Gascoigne, concerning whom Sir Amyas Paulet
ports from Paris on October 12, " Mr. Gascoigne
s departed to Flanders."†

We are only able to conjecture what it was that led
the abrupt end of the young sage's university career
d his despatch abroad. The " Complaint of Philo-
ene,"‡ written in 1576, already indicates that he had
come acquainted with the circumstances of his birth,
d the bitterness of the feelings which it at first
gendered. In this sad poem we read:

" I may not say but God is good and just,
    Although He scourge the furdest for the highest,
    The father's fault lights sometimes on the son,
    Yea, four descents it bears the burden still."

Francis Bacon was the fourth in descent from the
st famous Dudley, the extortionist of Henry VII.,
10 was executed. His son, the Duke of Northumber-
1d, was executed and attainted for treason. Leicester
s the third in descent.

Again in " Philomene " we read:

" God's mercy lends you *bridles* for desire;
    Hold back betimes for fear you catch a foyle,
    The flesh may spur to everlasting fire."

---

* Letter of F. Bacon: Rawley's " Resuscitatio"; Madame
1 Künow's "Last of the Tudors," p. 31; and State Papers,
eign series.   † State Papers, foreign
‡ Attributed to G. Gascoigne.

What could more resemble Hamlet's words to hi
Queen-mother:

> " *Refrain to-night*,
> And this shall lend a kind of easiness
> To the next abstinence. . . .
> For *use* almost can change the stamp of nature "?

Hope seeming to revive, he refers to it very unmi
takably in the " Shepherd's Calendar," written on h
return from France, in which he so extols the Quee
and alludes to the Earl of Leicester as her best belove
and to the author, Colin Clout—*i.e.*, himself—as th
Earl's boy. Thus, somehow or another, there is n
reason to doubt the cipher story in this, that it was h
discovery of his true birth as the Queen's son that le
her to arrange for his sudden despatch to France, fo
as the Queen and Privy Council arranged for h
departure, so on his return it was to the Queen that S
Amyas Paulet reported concerning him. We hear
no letter to Lady Bacon, whose husband, Sir Nichola
had just died.

But there is another, and for a poet a most in
portant, experience, which is also noticeable in tl
works published on the return of Shakespeare-Bac
from France, after an absence of two and a half yea
Our gentle, lively, and susceptible young Francis h
in the interval fallen desperately in love. The Ros
linde of the " Shepherd's Calendar " is the *Rosalin*
of Shakespeare, being anagram, as the author poin
out, for *Daiselorn*—*i.e.*, the lost Daisey or Marguer
de Valois, the Juliet whose Italian history and t
feud of the Montagues and Capulets he had studied
enthusiastically from Bandello with George Gascoig
It was a strange passion, the Princess's superlati

beauty striking home to his tender aspiring heart like
a flash of lightning,* the rumble and the thunder of
the busy world around failing to distract his mind for
a while to any other thought, love transfixing him,
though, as in the case of so many young, susceptible,
fiery, and impulsive natures, the fair lady was some
years older than himself, and—so fatally does fortune
harass some—she was not only a Princess by birth,
but already a wedded Queen. Here, reader, is the very
foundation of innumerable fairy tales; the foundation,
also, of many of the stories traceable to Shakespeare-
Bacon himself. This is the substance of it. A concealed Prince, brought up by foster-parents, as it were
a shepherd's boy, espies in the green fields a maiden
fair, a Princess, who sits her down beside him, and they
talk of love. The music that the lady pours into his
ears enraptures him; but he, a simple shepherd, dare
not speak his mind. She passes on. Anon, he,
stricken down and broken-hearted with his passion,
learns that he too is a Prince, born of a parentage as
high as hers. Hope rises high. He goes off in pursuit
of her and finds her, but already a Queen of another.
This is very much the story of the true love and life-
passion of the poet and philosopher whom all the world
adores to-day as Shakespeare, and nothing shows him
to more as a philosopher than the resolution with
which, in spite of its intensity, he renounced love for
her and fell back on his judgment. Thus he tells us—
for example, in " Euphues," which so entirely agrees

---

* " The sweetest rose hath his prickell."
                                        (EUPHUES.)
        " Roses have thorns."
            (SHAKESPEARE: Sonnet XXXV.)

with the view taken in Bacon's essay on love—that in
life it is too like a Syren or a Fury: "You may observe
that amongst all the great and worthy persons, whereof
memory remaineth, either ancient or recent, there is
not one that hath been transported to the mad degree
of love."* So, too, Euphues, our young Shakespeare
in the play is Romeo in spirit, but falls back in life
upon reason, and resolves to bid farewell for ever to the
delight of the affections, as being so far inferior to
those of the sovereignty of mind.

But let us return to history and State Papers,† and
endeavour to trace the actual path taken by the phenomenal man, the full radiance of whose genius is only
to-day becoming apparent to those foreign nations—as
well as his own countrymen—to whose life he laboured
to become a perpetual blessing, by adding to the
knowledge both of men and things, and so endowing
them with new powers and useful commodities.

The Orpheus of our story, known as Francis Bacon,
had just reached the age of fifteen, no more. But he
had the judgment of a man twice his years, and an
apprehensive imagination beyond all parallel. He
seemed gifted, Rawley says, with a beam of knowledge
derived from God, already conscious as no other
that *Deus in nobis* which inspires the young with
an indescribable desire to climb high, even inaccessible
cliffs—in his case cliffs far too high for mere ladder
made of rhyme. Science and reason were the only
instruments with which, as he saw already, he could
hope to scale the heights of his lofty ambition. Even

* See also Mr. A. Barley, article " Euphues and Bacon
Thought," *Baconiana*, September, 1924.

† State Papers, foreign series.

hour of his day was, therefore, spent in gathering in what he so elegantly calls the excellent dew of knowledge—the celestial gift of Ariel (*aërei mellis cælestia dona*),* the heavenly honey that we call science. Such was the idyllic-minded youth, whose fame has to-day risen so high, when, in September, 1576, he arrived in Paris with the embassy of Sir Amyas Paulet to the Court of the French King Henry III., and his eyes were first blinded by love. The massacre of the Huguenots† in 1576 was about four years old. His cousin, Philip Sidney, had been there then. Just before that hideous event the Huguenot Queen, Jeanne D'Albret, had been induced by an embassy, conducted by Marshal Biron (a famous name in the play of " Love's Labour's Lost "), to go with her son, the " matchless Henry of Navarre," to Paris to witness his marriage with the beautiful and accomplished Marguerite of Valois, the Princess of France, of " Love's Labour's Lost." Jeanne D'Albret died before the wedding, of poison, some say by Catherine de Medici,‡ the ill-famed Queen-mother of Marguerite, and instigator of the massacre. Henry of Navarre was saved from murder, but was detained in Paris as practically a prisoner, whilst war raged in the South of France between the Huguenots and the French Army of the Catholic League, commanded by the Duke de Mayenne, or Dumaine, brother of the Duke of Guise, another famous figure in " Love's Labour's Lost." Seeing the Protestant faith of Queen Elizabeth, the

* " De Aug.," Book V., chap. ii.

† See " The Massacre of Paris," by Marlowe.

‡ " The Massacre of Paris," Act I., sc. iii., by Marlowe. But see " Queen Jeanne D'Albret," by W. Ryan, 1911, p. 315 et seq.

principal aim of the embassy of Sir Amyas Paulet became to watch the interests of the Huguenots secretly. When he arrived in Paris, King Henry of Navarre was no longer there under detention. The latter had effected his escape early in 1576,* made his way to Navarre, and left his volatile young wife in Paris. There was already talk of divorce.

Where and how, we wonder, did the young Shakespeare, our Francis Bacon, meet this divine corrupter of so many hearts, herself a poetess and authoress of pronounced ability? She was the third of three successive Marguerites de Valois, all Princesses of France, and all distinguished patronesses of letters of Valois blood. Thus the real Juliet existed in Paris under conditions not so far removed from what became, in the play of "Romeo and Juliet," the feuds and brawls of the Montagues and Capulets, for she herself favoured her very beloved brother, the Duke d'Alençon, him whom we have already seen as the *grenouille* of Queen Elizabeth; and he, true to his character of Consort-in-hopes-to-be of our Queen, was inclined to favour the reformed religion. He therefore also was under detention, and his sister, the beautiful Marguerite helped him to escape. Thus, if for *Montagues* and *Capulets* we substitute *Huguenots* and *Catholics*, there existed, between these two factions in Paris when Shakespeare-Bacon arrived there, just that air of unsettlement and distrust such as we see in "Romeo and Juliet," to which the massacre of the Huguenots gave rise. Here we discover the real Juliet as she appeared to the real and enraptured Romeo. So, too, we discover in Marguerite the Princess of France, of "Love'

* "Mémoires of D'Aubigny," and State Papers, foreign.

Labour's Lost," associated with the matchless Navarre,*
Biron, Dumaine, and Longaville—*i.e.*, the Duc de
Longueville, Prince Henry of Orleans. We find in
the State Papers, foreign series, 1576-1578, that Sir
Amyas Paulet was in touch with all, and his despatches
show how closely he watched events, especially the
endeavours made later with success, to reunite Queen
Marguerite to her husband, the King of Navarre in his
own kingdom. Even Queen Elizabeth herself on
March 9, 1578-1579, wrote to Queen Marguerite, from
whom she had heard, saying, "Your letter seemed to me
an infallible proof of your singular affection toward
me, and of your desire that the affair for which your
brother has sent Mr de Simier here may come to effect."
In short, the two Courts were in such close touch that
there was a quick end to the illicit yet divinely inspiring
love of Francis the real Romeo for his Daiselorn or
Lost Marguerite, the Rosalinde of so many of his
Shakespeare plays, and on his return in "Euphues"
he abandoned love for philosophy, and celebrated
his love in the "Shepherd's Calendar."

Now what can have been the actual position of this
rising Prince-poet in the embassy of Sir Amyas Paulet?
The portrait of the Court painter Hilyard, and what we
glean from "Euphues," Laneham, and the "Shepherd's
Calendar," added to the positive information of Rawley
as to his singular character, the attention which his
judgment and apprehension invited amongst the great
and observant, over and above his thirsty search for
knowledge show that such an individual cannot have
passed unnoticed amongst the great literary lights
which surrounded the throne of the French King,

* See also "The Massacre of Paris," by Marlowe.

including Ronsard and the Pleiades, and such men as de Thou, Du Plessis, Montaigne, and others; and who was the mysterious Du Bartas? It is known that Bacon-Shakespeare studied cipher at this time in Paris. His intellectual activity, his princely appearance, his soundness of judgment, his intimate knowledge of classical mythology, as well as of all the medieval lore recorded by Laneham as contained in the library of Captain Cox,* must have put their mark on him, and there can be no doubt that, whether by reason of his own genius or due to his high credentials, he moved as freely in the French Court as at home he moved in the English Court.

Our young Orpheus, then, be he called Shakespeare or Bacon, amiable, able, learned, and wise, as well as like many youths somewhat conceited, garrulous, and exuberant in his wit,† to the practising of which he, for a time, gave himself up almost entirely, arrived in Paris with Sir Amyas Paulet in September, 1576. I was early in 1577 that the King of Navarre, "regardless of the constant warnings he received of the gallantries of his wife,"‡ escaped from Paris, and placed himself at the head of the Huguenots south of the Loire. His young wife, the beautiful, polished but incorrigible Marguerite, he left behind him in Paris. Let the young, uninitiated Shakespeare tell what happened next in words of John Barclay'

* Laneham's letter: see "The Castle of Kenilworth," E. H Knowles, which has a long and learned treatise on the lette by Mr. Furnival.

† See "Euphues," p. 33. Arber reprint, *Baconian*. September, 1924, p. 277.

‡ "Mémoires of D'Aubigny," p. 36; Cal. of State Paper foreign series, February 6, 1576, p. 241.

" Argenis," which are probably his own. Barclay calls Francis Bacon Archombrotus; Argenis is Marguerite. Poliarchus, as Navarre had left Paris, so he just left Sicily, and stands in the story for him. Translating the names and using the first person, the confession runs thus (the original is in Latin): " While I called to mind the beauty and fortunes of *Marguerite** (after her husband had left), and silently celebrated the good hap of the *matchless Navarre* in such a love, I began myself to like and admire those things which I had before quietly beheld without being moved by them; for what was there to be found more beautiful than *Marguerite?* Who ever to such a grace, and to so great birth, had added so many virtues? Had she no hereditary right, and if out of all the virgins of France, the most deserving were to be elected, there would be none more worthy to be raised to the crown before her. Her wisdom, modesty, and discourse beyond her sex; her beauty almost divine. Thus I ruminated, not esteeming my quality unworthy of such a hope, which also added fuel to the flame. Yet I considered this not as one that was falling in love, but as idle, though not disproportioned or unreasonable desires. Thus by degrees I became infatuated. My imagination dwelt upon these things with curious delight, not yet knowing that if a man desires to be free, and to conquer passion, he has need of much fortitude when love begins to speak. Moreover, in proportion as I loved Marguerite, so much the more the friendship which had before linked me to Navarre was abated and cooled. Envy and the sickness of rivalry grew upon

---

* Marguerite is here inserted where Argenis occurs in the original. See Barclay's " Argenis," Lib. 2, cap. 4.

me. Pensive, and my soul a captive, did I leave that orchard which I had entered free and happy, and to render my malady more vehement, I supped alone. For when silent and in private I heard nothing but love speak, and so little by little gave myself up to those cares which within a few days tortured me a lover, with pains such as before I had never known."* Thus did Shakespeare fall a victim to love.

It is a powerful analysis of the manner in which the inflamed mind of an imaginative young man fired by love (unless controlled by strong will) gradually grows blind, and loses all sense of proportion between right and wrong, good and evil, so that he endows the syren of his adoration in the beautiful flesh, with virtues which exist often only in himself, and not in her; his reason deprived of that judgment which teaches him to discriminate. He thus paradoxically clothes the lady of his fancy with imaginary charms; and so, in the end, builds up a beautiful and almost divine being far more perfect than nature itself. Is it not, indeed, thus that such incomparable creatures as Juliet, Rosalinde, Beatrice, and Portia were evolved in Shakespeare's mind from the fair Marguerite de Valois, who, though she was admittedly extremely beautiful and accomplished, whilst doubtless bewitching in discourse and literary taste, can hardly be regarded as distinguished for constancy, modesty, and wisdom in life ? She is described historically as strikingly impressive in

* John Barclay's " Argenis," p. 90, 1629 translation by Sir Robert Le Grys. On p. 71 we read : " Her *spear* of gold, about which the rays shining through the brightness of the metal made the common people often affirm the goddess did *shake* it." Again on p. 79.

appearance, with a countenance of celestial beauty, as serene as the blue sky, but in complexion marble-white except her cheeks. These like the rosy-fingered dawn were faintly tinged with red, whilst from between them there shone forth, like rising suns, glistening as in the morning dew, two too too* tender eyes, as gentle as the cooing turtle-dove's; which, eloquent as were the eyes of Venus, seemed, like hers, at all times cruelly ready to transfix with Cupid's arrows the helplessly enamoured heart of the beholder. She is said to have become as fond of good living as she was of elegant books and flirting, so that it became as difficult to get her from a book as it was difficult to get her from a meal, when once she had sat down to it.

Thus it is easy to see how true Shakespeare was to the aphorism of Bacon, that it is the duty of art to perfect and exalt nature. Anything beautiful that he saw and touched with the magic of his heavenly art, he strove to make more perfect yet by wisdom and the truth, correcting the idols and affections of the heart by the judgment of the mind and fortitude; and hence behold a Portia, Desdemona, etc. For his imagination lit up all he saw until he made it beautiful as well as true.

One more picture of the woman whose divine beauty inspired in Shakespeare so much that delights man to-day, it may be permitted to me to insert here in the interests of the reader before we proceed to his meeting her. It is of a later date, tinged with a certain cynicism, and comes ostensibly from Richard Braithwaite as the description of "Omphale," but has more than one

* "Too too," an expression common to Shakespeare, Bacon, and Lyly.

very common Shakespeare-Baconism; while also his
own life and experience, as he says, "moved me sometimes to fit my buskined Muse for the Stage." His
satirical picture of "Omphale,"* which so fits the fair
Marguerite, runs as follows:

> "And what more moving pattern could there be
> Than the admired form of Omphale (Marguerite ?),
> *Whose features equall'd Nature and did show*
> *The very spring whence fancy's said to flow?*
> For first her stature's seemly, which I call
> Neither too dwarfish low nor giant tall;
> Her front a rising mount; *her eyes two lamps*
> Which, wheresoe'er she looks, impression stamps;
> Her cheeks *'twixt rosy red and snowy white*
> Attract an admiration with delight;
> Her nose, nor long nor short, nor high nor low,
> Nor flat nor sharp, the token of a shrew;
> Her mouth not ferret-trait, nor callet broad,
> But of an apt proportion, as it should."

The line here given—"The very spring whence
fancy's said to flow"—marks her as a source of inspiration, and omitting the satirical lines the passage
gives an impressive picture. But that which points
most to the hand or suggestion of Shakespeare-Bacon
is the line:

> "Her cheeks 'twixt rosy red and snowy white."

The red and the white rose were, of course, united
in the Tudors, who, from our present point of view,
were Shakespeare's ancestors. Proud of this fact, we
constantly find him using the contrast of red and white
as an epithet in describing female beauty,† and in
Marguerite the marble whiteness of the skin tinged

---

* Braithwaite's work appeared after Bacon's death.
† E. G. Harman, "Gabriel Harvey and T. Nashe," p. 182.

with delicate red is believed to have been very conspicuous. So that we probably have here a very
real and by no means unduly flattering portrait of
Marguerite and her influence on the muse and fancy
of our Tudor-born Prince-poet. The following instances from Shakespeare and Bacon and the " Shepherd's Calendar," etc., are striking examples of the use
of this epithet:

1. " Shepherd's Calendar ":

> " The red rose medled with the white yfere
> In either cheek depicted lively cheer."
>> " Shepherd's Calendar," April eclogue.

2. Shakespeare:

> " In beauty truly blent, whose red and white
> Nature's own sweet and cunning hand laid on."
>> (" Twelfth Night," Act I., sc. v.)

3. Shakespeare:

> " Such war of red and white within her cheeks."
>> (" Taming of the Shrew," Act IV., sc. v.)

4. Bacon:

> " Yea, both roses, white and red, do as well flourish in her
> nobility as in her beauty."
>> (" Discourse in Praise of the Queen.")

5. Sidney (Bacon's cousin):

> " Marble, mixed red and white (cheeks)."

6. R. Braithwaite:

> " Her cheeks 'twixt rosy red and snowy white."

N.B.—Quotations 1 and 4 are both used in respect
of Queen Elizabeth.

There is yet one more play intimately connected
with the history of the embassy of Sir Amyas Paulet

to France, besides "Love's Labour's Lost" and
"Romeo and Juliet"—namely, the first part of
"Henry VI.," which was probably the first of the
Shakespeare plays to appear, except, perhaps
"Henry IV." and the "Two Gentlemen of Verona."
If the scenes in France of this play be taken, they will
be found to form an itinerary of the road taken by the
embassy, to which, according to our faith, Shakespeare
as Francis Bacon was attached; they are: Orleans
Rouen, Paris, Bordeaux, Plains of Gascony, Angiers
Plains in Anjou.—Auvergne, Guienne, Poictiers
Rheims, are other places mentioned, concerning which
no one has yet explained the wonderful scene in which
Talbot is transferred two hundred miles in a breath from
Orleans to Auvergne, and has there a marvellous in
terview with the Countess of Auvergne quite outside
the plot of the play. All we can say is that at the
time when this play appeared the famous Marguerite of
Navarre was a prisoner in the Castle of Ussac, in the
mountains of Auvergne, by order of her brother the
King, and remained there till her divorce in 1598.

We find it impossible, then, to doubt that it was
Shakespeare himself who travelled through these
scenes under the kindly wing of Sir Amyas Paulet—
a Prince-poet, and a Prince of poets, travelling in
cognito under royal auspices as Francis Bacon. Picture
him!—all life and observation!—searching at every
step for new experiences. His senses are, all five, a
alive to all around him. His ears and eyes are no less
alert to hear and see than his pen is ready to set down
and record. He treasures his notes and reflections of
what he sees abroad—at Calais, at Rouen, Paris, Orleans
Tours, Blois, Anjou, Poictiers, Bordeaux, Guienne, and

Gascony. He studies English history in connection
with those places, and he keeps what he sees for future
use in setting forth the history of his race in plays.
His industry is prodigious. His secret aim, which he
never forgets, is the service of his kind; to contribute
by all means that offer, without ostentation, to their
joy, and subdue and in some measure overcome " the
necessities and miseries of humanity for the benefit of the
State and Society of Man." Young as he is, he is *singular*
and attractive, of rare gentleness, and the appreciative
Sir Amyas notes his many *singular* good parts, just
as Whitgift and others before him. Love has at this
time fired his imagination, and he has found that:

> " It adds a precious seeing to the eye."
>
> *　　*　　*　　*　　*
>
> " Love's feeling is more soft and sensible
> Than are the tender horns of cockled snails."

Such are his observations on love as Shakespeare.
He pines for the tender eyes of his Marguerite. Passion
for a time fills him with hope. He is a Prince in concealment.* She is a Princess, too, by birth. They are
equals. True, she is married. But her husband,
weary of her gallantries, has left her. Divorce is not
beyond possibility; and then! What—what a King
and Queen they might make, what a rule of peace,
justice, love, and plenty should be theirs ! What bliss !
Thus he. But Sir Amyas Paulet had his instructions.
He, too, watched this gay Queen and her gallantries,
and reported both her movements and those of her
husband, the King of Navarre, to Queen Elizabeth, the
royal mother. The State Papers are deeply interesting
to read, and the political situation becomes comical

* Compare John Barclay's " Argenis."

beyond measure when we realise the private relations of
the principal actors: d'Alençon, Duke also of Anjou,
aged twenty-seven, had not given up hope of winning
the elusive hand of clever but dissimulating Queen
Bess, aged forty-six.* Was he not her *grenouille?*
Would she not let him swim in the Thames and share
it some day with him ? He accordingly simulated the
reformed religion, and had hopes of becoming Prince
of the Netherlands, and then, he being united with
England's Queen, they would together share honours
as defenders of the faith. He confided all his ambitions
to his beloved sister, the Marguerite of our Prince-poet,
Queen Elizabeth's concealed son, the young and gentle
aspiring and quickly rising Shakespeare. But confidential letters, to be found in the State Papers, passed
between Marguerite and Queen Elizabeth. They kept
the Duke in hopes, while those of our aspiring poet
known to them as Francis Bacon, the concealed Prince
and secret heir to England's throne, were eventually
shattered. Amyas Paulet had to watch the game and
perform a very difficult duty, especially to him, for he
loved our bright and industrious young Shakespeare-
Bacon thus condemned to play a part, and would gladly
have helped him. But he had his Queen's commands
to obey. He was her Ambassador, and she was unre-
lenting. Thus Shakespeare began that painful life of
compulsory dissimulation and suffering that gave him
all the experience of a martyr, and made cruel fortitude
the burden of his whole sad life.†

* State Papers record that those about the French King
laboured to prevent him from having any intelligence with her
but by the King. " Dale to the Queen," October 2, p. 940.

† See Sonnet CXI.

CHAPTER XI

SHAKESPEARE AS ROMEO; AND IN "LOVE'S LABOUR'S LOST"

THE King of Navarre and his wife are further out
1an ever they were." Thus wrote the English
mbassador at Paris (Dale) in January, 1576. Only
few days later he followed this up by reporting, on
ebruary 6, 1576, that "The King of Navarre is
eparted from the Court and fled ";* and he goes on
relate how " he went forth under colour of hunting "
1d had caused horses to be provided for him, by
eans of which he passed over the Loire at Saumur,
ayed three days at Vendôme, and then proceeded to
ençon, where he joined the Duke, and—says our
telligencer—" Biron thinks Monsieur (as the Duke
Alençon was called) will stand to his agreement."
eary of Court and the gallantries of his wife, the
matchless " Navarre tore himself thus away from
atmosphere in which he, at least, could not breathe
ely; and escaped to a region where he was more at
me—the field, still as yet true to the religion which
s brave and able mother, Jeanne D'Albret, had
eathed into him, the Huguenots rallied round him.
e King of France proclaimed the Duke of Maine or

* Cal. of State Papers, foreign series, February 6, 1576:
  " My opportunity may serve me fit
  To steal from France and hie me to my home."
      (MARLOWE: " Massacre of Paris," Act II., sc. iii.)

Dumaine, Lieutenant-General of the whole army of the
Catholic League against him. The Duke was holding
Moulins, " and will not give it up to Monsieur for all
that M. Biron will do."* The Prince of Orange's Horse
had also passed the Loire to Auvergne, now a strong
hold of Protestantism, and the fat was well in the fire.
Huguenot or Catholic, which shall prevail ? The gay
Queen of Navarre left in Paris, meanwhile no sooner
found herself rid of her husband than " she began to
show herself gallant in attire, lofty in words, and full
of jocundity in behaviour."† She was not the one
to mourn for a "matchless" Navarre. She had other
fish to fry.

It was at this time that the embassy of Sir Amyas
Paulet reached Paris, and with it, in 1576, came Francis
Bacon, our disguised Shakespeare in motley. His
Queen, our renowned Elizabeth, was interested in two
events—the cause of the Huguenots and the reunion
of the volatile Marguerite, born Princess of France,
with her husband, the King of Navarre, and Huguenot
leader. She was at the same time dangling her hand
as a bait to d'Alençon, Marguerite's brother. The
account of the arrival of Sir Amyas and his embassy
in Paris at this particular moment is full of deep
interest. Sir Amyas had a secret interview the very
next day with La Noue and young du Plessis, Protestant leaders; but what concerns us more is the
reception at Court of the Ambassador and his train,
amongst whom was to be seen the alert, singular, and
gentle Shakespeare, clad as Francis Bacon. They were,
we are told, well used, " and dinner provided for the

* Cal. of State Papers, foreign series.
† Ibid.

n a special Chamber at Court."* They were in Paris at the very French Court where the jocund behaviour of the fair Marguerite and her gallant attire, no less than her " beauty too rich for use, for earth too dear," the snowy whiteness of her skin and crow-black hair, and her accomplishments, made her the very centre of attraction and observed of all. She was now the recognised leader of Court ways and manners. She shone as no other: but she was a Catholic. Our Shakespeare-Bacon, the young courtier, supping in a neighbouring room, looks in and espies her. He adores. He is more strongly religious, and as brilliant and witty as she, but of the opposite faction—a zealous Protestant, and a reformer at heart to the very core. He is struck all of a heap ! How easy it is under such circumstances to picture the scene. With bashful boyishness he asks: " What lady is that, which doth enrich the hand of yonder knight ?" He follows it up by asking: " Is she a Catholic (Capulet) ?" and feels at once,† for to him Montague and Capulet are Huguenot and Catholic, and he a zealous Calvinist:

> " Oh, dear account ! my life is my foe's debt."

Thus we may legitimately build up, in our fancy, the actual event and scene from whence the immortal words of Romeo on first beholding Juliet sprang. The exact moment when those too too tender eyes of the fair Princess shot forth their fiery darts to strike

---

* Cal. of State Papers, foreign series.

† " Even so my sun one early morn did shine
  With all triumphant splendour on my brow,
  But out ! alack ! he was but one hour mine."
           (SHAKESPEARE: Sonnet XXXIII.)

and move with such extreme force the likewise tender
heart of our contemplative and awe-struck Prince-poet
and philosopher to such deep " mannerly devotion,'
strange as he yet was to foreign Courts and customs,
is not revealed.   Hitherto he had been intent on books
and study and reform.   Was perchance this the very
moment, indeed, which—when their four eyes met—
made him ask himself the question:

> " For where is any author in the world
>   Teaches such beauty as a woman's eye ?
>   Learning is but an adjunct of ourself,
>   And where we are our learning likewise is.
>
>   *   *   *   *   *
>
> " But love, first learned in a lady's eyes,
>   Lives not alone immured in the brain,
>   But with the motion of all element
>   Courses as swift as thought in every power,
>   And gives to every power a double power
>   Above their functions and their offices.
>
>   *   *   *   *   *
>
> " For when would you, my liege, or you, or you,
>   In leaden contemplation have found out
>   Such fiery numbers as the prompting eyes
>   Of beauty's tutors have enriched you with ?"
>
>   (" Love's Labour's Lost," Act IV., sc. iii.)

Especially remarkable in the despatches of this
period is the frequency in them of the mention of the
principal characters of " Love's Labour's Lost "—the
matchless Navarre and his Queen, the Princess (Marguerite) of France; Biron; Du-Maine or du Mayenne;
Longaville or Longueville; Faukenberg, who become
Falconbridge, and so on, including Antonio de Perez,

* Son of Gonzalo de Perez mentioned by R. Ascham, p. 33;
J. Bennet, " Works," 1791.

the Spanish minister who, in 1592, came to England as an exile, and actually lived for a time with Francis Bacon, just before " Love's Labour's Lost " was produced. He walked with familiarity amongst the Court set* of Shakespeare-Bacon; gave copies of his " Peregrinations " to all its members, and is without doubt the Don Adriano de Armado, the fantastical Spaniard of the play, whom Holofernes describes as " too picked, too spruce, too affected, too odd, as it were too *peregrinate*";† with his discourse peremptory, his eye ambitious, his gait majestical, and his general behaviour vain, ridiculous, and thrasonical.

> " Our court, you know, is haunted
> With a refined traveller from Spain."
> (" Love's Labour's Lost," Act I., sc.i., l. 161.)

The embassy remained in Paris till December, when it followed the French King and Court via Orleans to St. Die in March, and to Blois, Tours, and Poictiers, and was in touch at Heidelberg with Philip Sidney, much-beloved of Duke Casimir. He was Shakespeare-Bacon's cousin by blood, and wrote to Sir Amyas to offer his services, and the following year joined him for a time. Only think of it ! These two shining lights of England in amongst Ronsard and French Pleiades. What possibilities ! But for the time being it seems that Shakespeare-Bacon was drifting away from Juliet —Marguerite—and the occasion is notable. For the divine Juliet, the sun so fair that kills the envious moon, had more Romeos than one, and this Romeo,

* See Birch's " Memoirs of Queen Elizabeth." Also M. Mignet's " Life of Antonio de Perez."
† " Love's Labour's Lost," Act V., sc. i.

this Shakespeare, this Francis Bacon—what was his true name?

> "Deny thy father and refuse thy name."

Ah! if he only could! What was his name? If only he could have denied his apparent name of Bacon, so prosaic, so unreal, so hateful to himself, that name of which Juliet said:

> "'Tis but thy name that is my enemy."

How could she ever love a mere squeaking pig,* a Bacon?

Marguerite indeed had other fish to fry, and went off in the opposite direction—to Brabant! and narrowly escaped being kidnapped there by Don John of Austria.

"Did I not dance with you in Brabant?"† says Biron to one of the Princess's ladies, Rosaline, who wears a pearl, which she gives to the Princess, or Marguerite, as a token.‡ And Katherine had seen Dumaine at the Duke d'Alençon's. Did the real Shakespeare, we wonder, follow Sir Amyas to Blois and Poictiers, or did he burst away from him to Brabant himself? How did Shakespeare as Francis Bacon behave under the great illusion common to so many, to all but the fortunate few, of love as a Paradise on earth with lovely Eve—an illusion which falls from the eyes of most men like a dream, and is dismissed as

---

* Masque at Bisham, 1592. "A pipe that squeaketh like a pig, I am he" (Nichols's "Progresses of Queen Elizabeth," vol. iii., p. 124).

† "Love's Labour's Lost," Act II., sc. i.

‡ "Love's Labour's Lost," Act II., sc. i., and Act V., sc. ii., line 459:

> "What, will you have me, or your pearl again?"

dreams are, with a smile? To him, as we have seen,
' Love is the very source whence fancy's said to
flow ";* and it bred in his brain those beautiful, gentle,
pure, guileless, innocent, yet witty and human female
characters which he has depicted in such simple,
delicate, and highly refined language, bringing thereby
infinite joy and admiration to millions of men, generation after generation, of all nations; and, as Don
Quixote observes, to be translated into the language
of all nations, is almost the highest honour that can
be paid to an author.† What would many a man or
woman be without such scenes as those of Romeo and
Juliet? The very thought seems to make all the light
go out of life, when we think of it without the pure
devotion and the tragic words of Juliet:

> " 'Tis but thy name that is my enemy;
> Thou art thyself though not a Montague.
> What's Montague ? " . . .

And Romeo's reply:
> " By a name
> I know not how to tell thee who I am:
> My name, dear saint, *is hateful to myself,*
> Because it is an enemy to thee:
> Had I it written, I would tear the word."‡

How he must have loathed the name of Bacon!
Were these words in the forming at the time of which
I am writing, and have they perhaps a double meaning?
Our Prince-poet, I repeat, was travelling in France
under the name of Francis Bacon, a name which may
well have been very purgatory to him under such circumstances, knowing that he was of Tudor blood.

* Braithwaite (see above).
† " Don Quixote," Part II., chap. xvi.
‡ " Romeo and Juliet," Act II., sc ii.

Queen Marguerite returned to Paris from her visit to Brabant in summer, 1577, and in December of the same year Sir Amyas Paulet reported that "Our only care here is to reconcile the Queen of Navarre to her husband." Poor royal Shakespeare-Bacon, so devoted as his letters to his Queen-mother are, yet always seeming to be at cross-purposes with her. Meanwhile the Peace of Bergerac was concluded on September 14, 1577, between the Protestant and Catholic factions, and the King of Navarre now expressed a wish for reunion with his wife.* It was not, however, till the summer of 1578 that Marguerite set out from Paris where she had remained for a whole year, the embassy being there with the Court; and on August 25, 1578, Sir Amyas was able to report that the Queen of Navarre with the Queen-mother, Catherine de Medici, had arrived at Poictiers on their way south with their Court ladies. At last, on October 4, he reported further that the King of Navarre had met his fair Marguerite at La Reole by Bordeaux, and that nothing was omitted that might serve to make demonstration of sincere amity between those princes: "So the King of Navarre is now in hope to enjoy his government quietly." From La Reole the royal party proceeded to their capital of Nerac, via Agen, a town of the appanage of Marguerite herself; and who can the young M. Baccoуё have been who is reported by Aubigny† to have taken part in certain operations at Agen in this year?

* State Papers, foreign series.
† "Mémoires of D'Aubigny," p. 45. "Le jeune Baccoу estant arrive a Ageins" (1577). His parents apparently lived at Casteljaloux.

The last hope of our Prince-poet had now fled. The royal couple of Navarre took up their abode at their capital, and those scenes of love-making planned by Catherine de Medici commenced of which Marguerite herself has given a description in her own elegant memoirs; they preceded what is known in French history as *La Guerre amoureuse*, and form the foundation round which the play of " Love's Labour's Lost " is built up. This play is unique as the only Shakespearean play on contemporary history, if we except " A Midsummer Night's Dream," and nearly all the characters have been identified.

Let us leave it. Marguerite herself* relates the story of the French love-making that went on in that " King of Navarre's Park," with its avenues and walks and ornamental waters which forms the principal scene in " Love's Labour's Lost," and which our young Shakespeare-Bacon cannot fail to have visited. Sully and Aubigny also refer to those scenes where " all were lovers together," and religion, courtship, and dancing were so fantastically interwoven. Biron was the very ambassador who had been sent by King Charles in 1572 to negotiate her marriage.†

Thus, now at the Court of Paris, now at that of Navarre, and again at Paris, and in many places else-where, did this ever-observant, nameless Prince-poet—known to-day by a hundred names other than his own—such as Shakespeare and Bacon, Spenser and Cervantes—pass to and fro, gathering in, with miraculous avidity, the excellent dew of knowledge from the very lips not

* " Memoirs of Marguerite de Valois."
† Cal. of State Papers, foreign series. See also " Queen Jeanne of Navarre," by W. Ryan, 1911, p. 314.

only of women, but of men of the highest order of his
day. For quite apart from love and woman's eyes,
as the source and inspiration of his muse, his mind was
wonderfully balanced by the soundness and force of his
judgment and reason. What he saw with his eyes he
passed to the judgment of his mind; cast it out if
unworthy, if worthy treasured it in his memory, and
passed it on for all men to see in the most perfect
language known.* Hence later the four rational arts
of the " De Augmentis "—enquiry, judgment, memory,
and elocution or tradition. Picture such a one at the
brilliant French Court, a young and handsome man,
to whom fortune had been bountiful with royal gifts
of presence, position, and tongue; whilst nature's
secret art, in turn, had graved upon his face a certain
charm which, whilst it made him shine with a beauty
almost divine, had the virtue also to attract to it the
love of most who saw it. For he was possessed of an
affability beyond words. He is the Prince of poets,
Shakespeare, amid the élite of Frenchmen of literary
taste and distinction. The whole house of Valois, and
especially three successive Marguerites de Valois, all
Princesses of France, had been famous as patrons
of letters. Charles IX. had recently founded the
Académie de la musique et de la poésie. A chair was
always available for the poet Ronsard by the side of
King Henry III.; and under his influence, and that
of du Bellay and du Baif, a classical French language
was being built up, and rules for French verse framed.
Du Bartas, too, and a myriad lesser stars fluttered

* See the four rational arts, Bacon, " De Augmentis,"
Book V., chap. i.; J. M. Robertson, " Philosophical Works
of F. Bacon," p. 500.

round the famous Pleiades. Into this shining constellation our young Shakespeare entered as a meteor,
but unknown. He was the master of an imagination
more fiery and high-climbing, with a poetic furor more
divine than all; but modesty and youth commended
him to observation, while his impressionable and apprehensive nature took in all he saw and helped him to
form resolutions, which presently on his return he set
down, both in prose as Euphues, and in verse and
letters as Immerito. There we see and learn how
reason taught him to control the affections, and become
blind to any kind of beauty other than the true, as
he depicts it in his matchless men and women: "choosing such subjects as are at once the most noble in
themselves, . . . actual types and models by which
the whole process of the mind in certain subjects, and
these various and remarkable, should be set as it were
before the eyes."* Thus not only women and poetry
possessed him—

> " Thou kenst not Percy how my muse should rage.
>
>   *   *   *   *   *
>
> How I could rear the muse on stately stage
> And teach her tread aloft in buskin fine
> With quaint *Bellona* in her equipage."†

—but philosophers were likewise his friends, and men
of religion, and amongst them he could count such
men as Beza, du Plessis, de Thou, Montaigne, and
many more. Blue blood in his veins, the best tutors

* " Plan of the Great Instauration," p. 253; J. M. Robertson's " Philosophical Works of F. Bacon," p. 299; Aphorism
127 in " Philosophical Works of F. Bacon"; " Novum
Organum."
† " Shepherd's Calendar," October eclogue.

at home that England could provide, with every care and possible attention as to his education, followed by foreign travel, at foreign Courts amongst the élite of men of action, the choicest of women, the sagest of philosophers, the most rare of poets; here, indeed, was an atmosphere capable of producing a Shakespeare— a Shakespeare who was something more than a mere *lusus naturæ*—namely, a man of the highest culture and judgment, in close touch with all the best of his age.

Men say that it is impossible to reconcile such brilliancy of imagination, and such wisdom as a philosopher, in the same man. Shakespeare-Bacon's whole scheme of life is that it is man's first duty to weigh the promptings of fancy and imagination, and to judge of their worth, discarding what is unwholesome and worthless. To imagine that the same man cannot be equally imaginative and philosophic has no basis in fact. The two are not contraries and opposed, but confederates, a duality* working hand in hand together, the one supplying the material, the other passing judgment on it. Poetry, the love of music and rhythm, are born in a man, and inherited. The poet conceives much that no experience can teach. But experience teaches much that no man, by the mere light of his inborn nature, can conceive—those hard facts which counterbalance and correct poetic vision when it is inclined to err.

If, therefore, it be asked whether Shakespeare was more of a poet or a philosopher, the answer is that he was both equally, and that it was in this that the greatness of his genius consisted. He was born a poet,

* See Laneham's letter on One-hood and Duality.

nheriting from a noble and eminent ancestry, noble
mpulses, desire to learn, will to conquer and achieve,
nd the power to judge and discriminate. He was
herefore a poet first, with very marked poetic fire;
ut study, education, and experience—added to his
uick perception and the profound love of humanity
reathed into him by Sir Nicholas Bacon and sweet
ady Bacon, not excluding the example of Alexander
he Great under the influence of Aristotle held up to
im by Queen Elizabeth—made him a resolute philo-
opher, neither to be led away by his imagination nor
isguided by his affections. He thus taught himself
o put philosophy into verse, loving the music of verse
hich charmed his ear; yet, when still quite young,
ason taught him that mere rhyme could never help
m scale the heights he sought to climb, unless in
mpany with science and by force of fact.

> "That so at last my mind may enter in,
>   And *reason rule* where rhymes could never win."

Mere dreamer Shakespeare-Bacon never was. Even
acaulay, and still yet more emphatically Mr. Spedding
his " Life of Bacon "—whom we know as one with
akespeare—insist upon the practically beneficial
ture of his aims and genius; and Mr. Spedding, in one
the most eloquent passages of his generally too dry
Life and Letters," has a sentence which entirely
rees with the view thus taken, saying: "But in him
e gift of seeing in prophetic vision what might be
s united with the practical talent of devising means
d handling. He could at once imagine like a poet and
cute like a clerk of the works." In other words, the
etic power and imagination in Bacon were recognised

by his greatest biographer.   The philosophy of Shake
speare is patent to all, like Bacon's executive power.   N
achievement can in point of duration and value outriva
his.   No greater monument of fame can ever be buil
up in his recognition than the works which he himsel
has left us.   Of no other man of history can it be sai
more truly in his own prophetic words:

> " Wherever the bright sun of heaven shall shine,
> His honour and the greatness of his name
> Shall be, and make new nations: he shall flourish,
> And, like a mountain cedar, reach his branches
> To all the plains about him; our children's children
> Shall see this, and bless heaven."
>
> ("Henry VIII.," last scene.)

To-day all men do, and ever will, so bless the ma
who left his *name* and memory to foreign nations, an
to his own when some time shall have passed.

CHAPTER XII

SHAKESPEARE RETURNS FROM FRANCE

"Euphues" and the "Shepherd's Calendar."

Our Prince of poets, Shakespeare, whom we learn so early to love as our Romeo and Juliet's immortal throstle, returned home under his incognito of Francis Bacon in March, 1579. Sir Nicholas Bacon had just died, and we learn nothing of the whereabouts of Lady Bacon, but the following October he wrote a letter signed " Immerito "* to Gabriel Harvey from Leicester House, the Strand house of the Earl, where, as a Prince and the Earl's son, we should naturally expect to find him, for the Queen was wont to stay there and even hold her Court there,† and " Immerito's " letters are all of the Court and his attendance at it, whilst Gabriel Harvey invariably refers to him as a young courtier. Small wonder. He was already, as his letters show, the centre of that courtly crew of makers who were studying the English language and its adaptability to verse. Moreover, this very year of the return of Shakespeare-Bacon from France saw the publication of his first two really important works: " Euphues, or the Anatomy of Wit "—such a likely title for Shakespeare - Bacon—and the " Shepherd's Calendar." The

* " Immerito," generally supposed to have been Edmund Spenser, another pseudonym of Francis Bacon. See E. K. arman. He was a courtier and close friend of Sidney, Dyer, and Gabriel Harvey, and patron of the theatre.
† Walsingham's Diary.

former was published under the name of John
Lyly, and is said by Edward Blount,* publisher o:
Lyly's six Court plays, to have "made our nev
English." He calls it "my first counterfeit." Th·
"Shepherd's Calendar" appeared anonymously unde
the name of "Immerito," and all the Court must hav·
known well who Immerito was, so clear is its "Gloss.'
In this work the gay and gallant young courtier an·
lover called himself boldly "the new poet." He wa
now fully conscious of his unusual powers, yet no les
modestly conscious of the industry and pains requisit
to train them. Theocritus, Virgil, Mantuan, Petrarch
Boccaccio, Maro, Sanazarus, and other Italian an·
French poets,† he has studied them all. He follow
them all, "yet so as few can trace him out," and :
confident that in time he will "be able to keep win
with the best." Meanwhile, like them and according!
to their example, he chose the simplest form of vers
known as "Eclogues," to start with: "Perhaps doubtir
his own hability . . . following the best poets wh
sought at first to try their habilities, and as young bir·
that be newly crept out of the nest, by little first ·
prove their tender wings, before they make great
flight." So flew Virgil, he says, as not yet well feelir
his wings, so Mantuan,‡ Petrarch, and others. I

* This same Edward Blount published the First Folio
Shakespeare's plays, in 1623, and the six Court plays of Jo·
Lyly in 1630.

† See Epistle of E. K. to the "Shepherd's Calendar."

‡ The "good old Mantuan" of "Love's Labour's Lost
Act IV., sc. ii., l. 100. It is interesting to note that imm·
diately following this mention of Mantuan comes the Itali·

"Venetia, Venetia, chi non te vede, non te pretia."

always places the best before his own high aspiring
eyes. No word written escapes him. His learning is
omnivorous. He had just come back from the very
midst of the most brilliant spirits of France. His
young mind was aflame with lofty enterprise of the
very noblest type. He was no less full of ambition to
brighten and amend the world, than of determination
to do for England what Ronsard and Pleiades were
doing for France. He would excel them. He would
do more than beautify language, which is but an instrument. He would not only frame a new English
language, but a new school of thought, founded not
on what others had done before, and was recorded in
" other books,"* but on the study of nature itself, by
observation and reason, analysing nature as we see her
around, free and noble, knowledge of which we call
science; and as we see her erring and bound, study of
which is art, or nature with man to help.† Thus was

This occurs as an English proverb in the " Book of Riddels,"
referred to as of Captain Cox's library, in *Laneham's* letter,
says Mr. Knowles: " The complete couplet, as given in 'Howel's
Letters,' p. 53, edition 1655, is:

> ' Venetia, Venetia, chi non te vede, non te pregia
> Ma che t'ha troppo veduto te dispregia,'

which has been thus translated:

> ' He who ne'er saw thee, cannot prize thee;
> He who too much has seen thee, must despise thee.' "

Shakespeare gleaned much from Laneham and Captain Cox's
library. See " Castle of Kenilworth," by E. H. Knowles,
p. 182.

* Shakespeare, " Love's Labour's Lost," Act I., sc. i.
† Bacon, " De Aug.," Book II., chap. ii.; J. M. Robertson's
" Philosophical Works of F. Bacon," p. 427. Also Shakespeare,
" Othello," Act III., sc. iii.; "Winter's Tale," Act IV., sc. iii.

man to obtain true knowledge and new powers, new
discoveries, new inventions; and out of this marriage
of art and science man was to be endowed with new
commodities, and his necessities in some degrees met
and his difficulties and troubles alleviated. Such were
the new ideas, the new philosophy, such the resolutions
of Shakespeare-Bacon on his return from the brilliant
and artistic scenes, men and women, whom he had seen
and known in France, and it may be elsewhere. For
there are reasons to believe that he made excursions—
for example, to Germany—where his cousin, Philip
Sidney, was, who also for a time joined the embassy of
Sir Amyas Paulet in France, whilst Francis Bacon-
Shakespeare was still with it. Sidney returned to
England nearly a year before our Orpheus. The
ostensible occasion of the return of the latter was the
death of Sir Nicholas Bacon early in 1579. He returned, however, bearing a despatch from Sir Amyas
Paulet to Queen Elizabeth. There is, as stated above
nowhere any mention of any letter or report to Lady
Bacon, but the personal interest of the Queen in him
could hardly be more accentuated than by the words of
Sir Amyas in a manner unusual, and not used in the
case of any other member of the embassy. The words
of Sir Amyas, who himself returned very soon after, are
" I will not trouble your Majesty with other occur-
rences of which I have written to Sir Francis Walsingham, who I know repeats them to your Highness.
know you will take pleasure to hear of the towardness
of any of your subjects, therefore would not fail to
advertize you that this bearer Mr Francis Bacon is of
great hope endowed with many good and singular parts
and if God give him life, will prove a very able an-

SIR PHILIP SIDNEY

Son of Lady Mary Sidney, the sister of Robert Dudley, Earl of Leicester.

sufficient subject to do your Highness good and acceptable service."*

Thus, as he went out under royal auspices, so he was sent back direct to the royal person. Moreover, Sir Amyas Paulet had the rare privilege of communicating direct with Her Majesty, and very little later, as already shown, Shakespeare-Bacon dated a letter from Leicester House (much frequented by the Queen) under the incognito of "Immerito." Since the publication of Gascoigne's "Steel Glass" in 1576 —in which he had already dedicated himself to science and the force of reason, over and above verse and art, as the true road to knowledge, truth, and power—he had learnt three new experiences: the secret of his birth, love as an inspiration—the very source from which the springs of fancy flow—and the ways of foreign courts and countries. All these new influences become visible at once in "Euphues, or the Anatomy of Wit," which was in circulation early in 1579, wherein he set forth his despised love for the inconstant Lucilla,† forswore love for ever, dedicated himself to the sovereignty of reason, and so rattled on and on, with an excess of Elizabethan metaphor‡ and simile at times ludicrous, if taken seriously, yet delightfully witty and unmistakably boyish, even if overpowering in its exuberance, unless its mixed metaphors be regarded as a study of language and an illustration of the force of epithets in giving vivid colour and strength to word-painting. This was, indeed, its purpose. Like Lane-am, Euphues delights in giving delight to the ladies.

---

* Cal. of State Papers, foreign series, 1578-9.
† Lucilla—*i.e.*, the inconstant Marguerite.
‡ See Introduction, p. xviii, above.

Such was the young Shakespeare, later so masterly a
painter of the most perfect women—and such was
" Euphues " to the ladies of the Court, so that to speak
in euphuisms became the fashion amongst them, and
they must have known well who the real author was
even though to breathe a suspicion of it was beyond
thought a matter of life and death. Nay, the book
itself reveals the author who, whilst "the stumps of
love" still stuck in his friend Philautus, shook it man
fully off as worthless, beside the priceless value of th
understanding and virtue. "It is virtue," he says
" yea virtue, gentlemen, that maketh gentleness: tha
makes the poor rich, the *base-born noble, the subject*
sovereign, the deformed beautiful, the sick whole, th
weak strong, the most miserable the most happy."
Was he, Shakespeare, base-born? Doubtless hi
parents were married,† but why kept secret? The ide
rankled ever painfully in his mind. It must hav
been cruel torture to him at times. It is repeated bot
in Virgil's "Gnats"‡ and the "Shepherd's Calendar.
In the former, dedicated to the Earl of Leicester, h
says:

> " Wronged yet not daring to express my pain
> To you (great Lord) the causer of my care;
> In cloudy tears my case I thus complain,
> Unto yourself that only privie are:

---

* "Euphues and his Ephœbus" is but an adaptation
Plutarch's " περί τῆς παίδων ἀγωγῆς," on which I have show
that young Bacon's mind was fed, and into it he introduc
the proverbs or precepts of Pythagoras, to which may
traced the famous precepts given by Polonius to Laertes. S
"Euphues," Arber reprint, p. 148.

† See p. 106, above.

‡ Under the name of Edmund Spenser.

But if that any *Œdipus* unware
Shall chance through power of some divining spright
To *read the secret of this riddle right,*
And know the purport of *my evil plight,*
Let him rest pleased with his own insight,
Nor further seek to gloss upon the text;
For grief enough it is to grieved wight
To feel his fault and not be further vext."

Likewise Immerito thus introduces the "Shepherd's Calendar," dedicated to Sir Philip Sidney:

" Go, little book, thyself present
As child whose parent is unkent,
To him that is the president
Of noblesse and of chivalry.

* * * * *

" But if that any ask thy name,
Say thou wert *base-begot* with blame."

Were these the forerunners of the thoughts which in the same mind later produced Hamlet ?

As I have shown, in the year when these two works, " Euphues " and the " Calendar," appeared, Immerito-Shakespeare, our young courtier and Prince-poet, was a familiar at Leicester House, where he attended Court.   There he was in close touch with Philip Sidney, Sir Edward Dyer, and other poets about the Court, who had now formed an Areopagus or Senate,* to frame rules to regulate English prosody and verse. The nucleus of this little society had, as said, already published the first so-called edition of the works of Gascoigne and others " gathered from our English Orchards," and the names given by Puttenham of the " crew of Courtly makers, Noblemen, and Gentlemen of her Majesty's own servants who have written ex-

* See " Two Letters " of Gabriel Harvey.

cellently well, as it would appear if their doings could
be made public with the rest," include those of the
Areopagus. The list given by Puttenham of this Court
circle of poets, who were now ranging themselves round
the young Shakespeare, still so young, but already so
pre-eminent, are Edward, Earl of Oxford; Thomas,
Lord Buckhurst; Henry, Lord Paget; Sir Philip Sidney,
Sir Walter Raleigh, Master Edward Dyer, Fulke
Greville, Gascon, Britton, Turberville, "and a great
many other learned gentlemen." He was manifestly
their life and centre—this warbling Orpheus—who had
just returned from Paris, where with Sidney they had
together seen what the French were doing in their
language. All these great spirits of England now
secretly banded themselves together with these two
young leaders, Sidney and Shakespeare-Bacon, to do
for England even better than they, the Pleiades, had
seen done in France. They formed a gallant galaxy,
but nowhere amongst them is any mention of Shakspere
of Stratford, though Puttenham wrote in 1589 when he
had long left Stratford.

How thankful we feel at this stage to Hilyard for
his beautiful picture of the person of our young Shakespeare alias Francis Bacon. The artist was not content
to paint his lively physiognomy. He felt how far the
painter's art here falls short when he exclaimed, almost
in despair: "Oh, would that I could paint a portrait
worthy of his mind," and wrote his words in Latin
round his little picture: "Si tabula daretur digna
animum mallem." Small wonder if there were a little
conceit in our Francis—sweet William. What worthy
lad of that age is without it? This one, too, was very
" singular "—nothing short of a phenomenon. He was

yet a lad, but was already fully aware, both that he
had an imagination, knowledge, and judgment far above
his elders, and a strange history, a secret of birth, as
Gabriel Harvey hints, which ought to, by right even
now, give him a commanding position amongst men,
quite apart from his own private and singular attain-
ments. He had, in short, a unique destiny to work
out. He knew it, and felt fully equal to it, and determined to combat every difficulty and climb to any
height, short only of impossibilities. For hope was
still strong. The clouds had not yet obscured his sun
and made him sad. On the other hand, he had just
become conscious of his powers. The sovereignty of
this young man's intellect, this future Shakespeare,
was, in short, already recognised. His literary leader-
ship was acknowledged, and he had formed a band of
confederates willing and eager to assist him in the
colossal work he had undertaken: the reform of man's
ways of thinking, the new philosophy, by which the
acquisition of knowledge was no longer to be guesswork,
but a sure and certain march forward scientifically, by
logical sequence of facts ranged in order, each part
supporting the other—*i.e.*, by induction and the Great
Instauration of Science, on the one hand; by inspired art
or " learned experience " of human nature on the other,
as illustrated by the great plays. Hitherto inventions
had been fortuitous. The discoveries of gunpowder,
printing, and the needle, as he says repeatedly, were
so. By the force of reason, by a method not entirely
new, but as yet little known, inventions " which may
in some degree subdue and overcome the necessities
and misery of humanity,"* were to be worked out on

* Bacon, " Plan of the Great Instauration."

scientific lines, to meet the requirements of man as
civilisation proceeds.   It was a gigantic undertaking.
He could but make a start.   He could, as said, only
be the bellringer.   The spadework, even, was barely
accomplished within our time.*   To-day, however, we
see science at work in full swing, as the outcome of
the labours of man's best brains, extending over many
generations, and through three whole centuries, during
which the laws of electricity, chemistry, hydraulics,
air, steam, gas, etc., have been painfully worked out.
It is the result of that marriage of Science and Art
which, Bacon-Shakespeare said, was to make the mind
of man a match for the nature of things—the " Great
Instauration " of Francis Bacon and the plays of
William Shakespeare.   What we see around us to-day
is, in the main, the achievement of his gigantic efforts,
of work not lightly undertaken nor of thoughts easily
breathed forth by inspiration; but of industry and
unremitting, colossal—nay, Herculean—labour, pursuing with divine faith an end which its author knew
to be of immeasurable importance to mankind, by
virtue not merely of his prophetic vision, but by mean
of his highly illuminated reasoning power and judgment

From the earliest days, as I have endeavoured to
show, Shakespeare-Bacon realised that he could neve
accomplish his task single-handed.   He had need o
other men's wits.   He sighed for such help as Alex
ander the Great gave to Aristotle.   Failing it, he fel
back upon his own maxims, that a wise man will mak

* " For he must be a trifler and a man of narrow min
who thinks that the perfect art of invention of knowledge ca
be devised and propounded all at once " (Bacon, " De Aug.,
Book V., chap. iii.).

more opportunities than he finds, and set to work to make means. " The Grand Assizes of Apollo at Parnassus" discloses his method.* The Areopagus, the courtly crew of makers working in secret, were the nucleus of the school he formed to propagate his gospel throughout the civilised world, and to translate his works† into the languages of those foreign nations to whom he bequeathed them, the translations often being published as the originals, as in the case of " Don Quixote" and Barclay's " Argenis," and the originals appearing later as translations into English. It was a daring and ingenious system, but unity, and letters such as that of Sir Dudley Carleton,‡ written the day after Bacon's wedding, make the method clear, undeniably, when closely examined.

It was under such circumstances that the " Shepherd's Calendar" appeared, and, as I have already shown, the very curious position in which this great man was

* See " The Great Assizes of Apollo at Parnassus," 1644, where Bacon presides and Shakespeare is tried and Camden is arraigned for detracting " from a great Ladie's glory."

† Also in " Mercury or the Message," 1641, by Wilkins, we learn of Bacon:

"This Dutchman writes a comment, that *translates*,
A third transcribes. Your pen alone creates
New necessary sciences. This art
Lay undiscovered as the world's fifth part;
But *secresy's* now published; you reveal
By demonstration how we may conceal."

‡ Carleton to Chamberlain, Record Office, State Papers, Dom.: " Sir Francis Bacon was married yesterday to his young warde in Maribone chappel. He was clad from top to toe in purple. . . . I send you Don Quixote's challenge which is translated into all languages, and sent into the wide world " (May 11th, 1606).

placed from early youth made secrecy incumbent upon him, and other reasons already given cropped up* for dissimulation and the deferring of that fame which all hunt after in their lives, to the day when, spite of cormorant devouring time, present endeavour would, years after death, bestow upon him that honour which should make him heir of all eternity. Thus, on return-ing to biography, we find him as the young courtier Immerito, now the author of the " Shepherd's Calen-dar " very definitely—in the letter of E. K. attributed to himself—explaining the baseness of the name of his hero " Colin " as chosen " to unfold great matter of argument *covertly.*" Colin, as he says, is himself, whose " unstayed youth had long wandered in the common Labyrinth of love," and his poem discloses the same old story as the " Kenilworth Princely Pleasures " and the tale and play of " The Hermit "— namely, the love of the Queen for the Earl of Leicester, whom he terms " the worthy whom she loveth best." But there is now joined with it the story of his own love for the fair Rosalinde of the *neighbour* town—in the Latin sense, as is carefully explained of *Vicina*— that is, Paris, and the letters making Rosalinde—as this fanciful, new young genuine poet, the coming Shakespeare, tells us—will, if rightly ordered, betray the real name of the divine beauty who so wonderfully inspired him, being Daiselorn—that is, the lost Daisy, or Marguerite.

> " Ah, foolish Hobbinot, thy gifts be vain,
> Colin them gives to Rosalind again;
> I love thilke lasse, alas ! why do I love ?
> I am for*lorne*, alas ! why am I *lorn ?*"

---

* See Chapter VI.

Sometimes she is Rosalinde, then Rosalind, and again Rosalinda, in the order given, but that the anagram of Daiselorn is meant for the fair Marguerite de Valois, with the strong affection for whom he is so sore in travail, he makes quite plain by describing her as the "Widow's daughter of the glen," that is, the daughter of the widowed Katherine de Valois, by birth Medici. She is, he says, a gentlewoman of no mean house, endowed with no vulgar or common gifts, both of nature and manners, such that he needs not to be ashamed to sing of her, or of commending her to immortality for her rare and singular virtues. It is all so exquisitely naïve. The veil of concealment is so thin as to be almost transparent. It is so natural and so truly boyish. A child of born genius, who had also studied deeply and loved study, could alone write thus. All the classical mythology of " Ovid " is called in to help, and prominent above all is the great god Pan, the universal, the all-in-all, who figures no less prominently in the " Advancement of Learning," and yet again more still in the " De Augmentis " and the " Wisdom of the Ancients " of Bacon-Shakespeare. So thin indeed is the veil of concealment in the allegory of this marvellous little poem, that the wonder is that it has not been understood before, as being an un-doubted revelation concerning Shakespeare. As such, and indeed for its own ingenuous ability and delicate beauty, it is of priceless value. What have our pro-fessional literary experts been about in these days when research has been rendered so easy ? Their day of judgment can hardly be far off. The solemn temples which they have erected in honour of that greatest of gulls—Gul: Shakspere of Stratford—must ere long dissolve their insubstantial pageant, and therewith their bubble reputation fade away and leave not a rack behind.

Yet one more revelation of prime importance is referred to in this wonderful Calendar. In autumn, 1578, the Fairy Queen in her progress visited first Kirtling Castle near Cambridge, the seat of Lord North, the brother of the translator of Plutarch's "Lives," so well known to Shakespearians. Thence she proceeded to Saffron Walden, where that Gabriel Harvey was formally presented to her who figures so prominently in the "Shepherd's Calendar" as the author's very singular good friend. To him he gives the feigned country name of Hobbinal, in whom, he says, is hidden the person of "his very special and most familiar friend, whom he entirely and extraordinarily loved." It will be remembered that Francis Bacon-Shakespear was sent to Trinity College, Cambridge, under the auspices of the Queen in 1573, when the Gabriel Harvey correspondence began. On the occasion of his presentation in 1578 the Queen asked the question: "Is this the man that you propose to send for me into Italy?" and Immerito's letter of October 7, 1579, written from Leicester House, is full of the anticipation of immediate travel abroad. The interview was undoubtedly prearranged at the request of Francis Bacon-Shakespear, probably through the agency of Philip Sidney, who was present with the Earl of Leicester, Lord Burghley, and others, to hear Harvey and others dispute on the very Baconian thesis, "whether severity or clemency serves princes best."

The upshot was that Gabriel Harvey now, for a time,

* See Gabriel Harvey's *Gratulationum Valdinensium*.

occupied much the same position in relation to the Earl of Leicester and Bacon-Shakespeare that Gascoigne had, until the latter died in 1577. The early affection of the young Shakespeare for this much older, well-dressed, clever, somewhat affected and cynical Cambridge lecturer on rhetoric and aspirant to courtly honours is one of the most touching incidents in the youth of the famous ever-living Prince-poet. The reason, perhaps, was that Harvey was one of the first (as he afterwards claimed) to recognise sympathetically the real greatness and height of the genius of his magnificent young friend, whom he jestingly addresses as " Il Magnifico Signor " and *Benevolo*—such a very Shakespearean name—and always alludes to as a young courtier, and also a theatre-goer and zealous reformer.

How strong the young poet-philosopher's affection for him was, is shown in the " Calendar " by the way in which the author links his name with that of his lady-love, and this in a manner which shows that he had known Harvey first, putting into his mouth the words:

> " Nor this, nor that, so much doth make me mourn,
> But for the lad whom long I loved so dear.

> *   *   *   *   *

> " Whilom on him was all my care and joy,
> Forcing with gifts to win his wanton heart.
> But now from me his madding mind is start,
> And wooes the *Widdow's daughter* of the glen.
> So now fair Rosalind hath bred his smart,
> So now his friend is changèd for a frenne."

Ostensibly this strong link of affection for some reason seems to have given way after a year or two. The young and very tender heart of the boy Shakespeare, howsoever witty, beat nevertheless very strongly, and even overpoweringly, in the directions of reform. He had been desperately in love. He had vowed a deadly war against the delights of the affections. Reason was to him the sovereign good. Reason was to make man master of all knowledge and give him control and powers yet unknown. It was to kill the delights of the affections—and subject always to its use for that purpose for which God granted it— reason was to be paramount on earth. The cynical Harvey could in this respect do no better than jeer at his youthful enthusiasm, and call his ideas as old as Adam and Eve, and the mere creatures of his imagination. Shakespeare-Bacon, however, stuck to his point without flinching, and answered Harvey later word for word in his philosophical writings.*

Though, however, this difference of temperament conception, and will cooled the tenderness of their feelings, as Shakespeare, known as Francis Bacon rose and mounted above the dear friend of his youth Gabriel Harvey seems never to have been lost to the affection of the greater man. They kept in touch, and not only this, but Gabriel Harvey played a most important part in Shakespeare-Bacon's plan of conceal ment, acting as a screen and shield to prevent the disclosure of his pseudonyms under the characters of Gascoigne, Euphues, Immerito, Greene, Peele, Nashe,†

* "De Aug.," Book VII., chap. iii.: "Culture of the mind affections," etc.

† In his "Strange News of the Intercepting Certain Letters, Nashe says equivocatingly: "This I will proudly boast . . that the vein I have . . . is of *my own* begetting, and *can no man father but myself,* neither Euphues, nor Tarlton, no Greene." In other words, he himself fathered Euphue

Iarlowe, and others. Harvey knew the real Gascoigne, Cuphues, Immerito, Greene, the real Peele, Marlowe, nd Nashe, but he knew also the true author of the vorks issued in their names, and he remained the true nd confidential agent and ally of Shakespeare-Bacon* o his death, helping him in his great work of concealing nd revealing,† of which he speaks so much, declaring is intention to publish part of his works only for a ew select minds.

---

arlton, and Greene. Tarlton acted with the Queen's Com- any, which Shakespeare-Bacon probably trained. See also Gabriel Harvey and Thomas Nashe," by E. G. Harman.

* See " Gabriel Harvey and Thomas Nashe," by the late dward G. Harman, C.B.

† "With regard to the disclosing of a man's self . . . there nothing more politic for a man than to preserve a sound 1d wise mediocrity in declaiming or concealing his meaning particular actions. For although depth of secrecy and oncealment of designs, and that manner of action which fects everything by dark arts and method, be both useful 1d admirable, yet frequently, as is said, dissimulation breeds rors which ensnare the dissembler himself." ("De Aug.," ook VIII., chap. ii.)

And so

" But secresy's now published; you reveal
By demonstration how we may conceal."

ee p. 171 (note).

CHAPTER XIII

SHAKESPEARE'S HAUNTS: GRAY'S INN, BACON HOUSE, THE SHEEPCOTE AT ISLINGTON

WE turn now to consider the haunts of our ever memorable master, both in these young years of his early active life and later. For as the "Immerito" and "Euphues" of literature and a privileged member of the Court, the friend of Sir Edward Dyer and Philip Sidney, he not only walked amongst all the greatest and rising spirits of the day, but he was already a marked man amongst them. On his return from France, as we have seen, Sidney and he had drawn all the young aspirants to the laurel around them in that Areopagus of which he in time became the acknowledged Apollo and Orpheus; and it lived till his death, which event the "Ode of R. P." celebrates with such a deep sigh:

> "Ehew! Ephorus haud lancem* premit
> Sed *Areopagus*. . . .
> Qualis per undas ditis Euridice vagrans
> Palpare gestiit Orpheus. . . .
> Talis placata philologon anigmatis
> Petiit Baconem vindicem, tali manu
> Lactata cristas entulit philosophia;
> Humique soccis repitantem comisis,
> Non proprio ardelionibus molimine
> Sarsit sed instauravit," etc.

---

* *Lancem*—or should this be *lanceam* ?—the spear—i Ephorus no longer shakes the spear. This seems to be suggestion.

No more, alack! the master passes judgment, but the Areopagus without him. As Orpheus sought Eurydice in Hades by touching with his skilful hand the lyre, e'en so philosophy sought Bacon to avenge her, and then he raised her up, and not alone restored, but fresh installed her, as she lowly crept along—at first by means of comedy, then rising higher to the tragic buskin and beyond, he brought even Aristotle by his "Novum Organum" to life again (Manes Verulamiani, R. P.). The unity of Shakespeare and Bacon as one man, combining verse and reason, art and science, could not be more concisely expressed than in this ode, written to his memory the year after his death, and giving the gradual transition of his masterly mind in the very manner and order in which his works appeared, passing from comedy to tragedy,[*] and culminating in the new philosophy and induction. His mind may, indeed, be traced from youth to old age by his difference from Aristotle on the subject of the affections:[†] custom and habit.

Indeed, we feel in suspense—almost as if treading upon sacred ground, after hitting upon this wonderfully illuminating ode, as we pursue his footsteps. Leicester House and the Court and the company of the great men of his time, we have seen that he frequented in early youth; and he has not left us without the means of tracing his footsteps later. He was already entered

---

[*] Charles Sorel, who must have known Bacon, gives this as the natural evolution of a man's mind. Sorel denied to the poet having written the "Francion," and boasted of his English connection. He was but a young man when the "Francion" appeared in 1622.

[†] See Bacon, "De Aug.," Book VII., chap. iii.; J. M. Robertson, p. 574.

at Gray's Inn, though he does not seem to have been
in regular residence there much before 1583. It lay
then clean outside the city in the open country. From
those railings which still bound its garden, to Islington
Highgate, and Hampstead, all was green fields. Walk
ing to the city you passed from Holborn by Ely House
and Holborn Bridge and Snow Hill to Newgate; or
walking by the outside of Ely Garden, later Hatton
Wall—then a country lane, now a dingy street—you
proceeded by the partly demolished buildings, Great
Hall, Chapel, and Gate* of the grand old Knights of
St. John of Jerusalem, across Smithfield, by the gabled
country houses and fruitful gardens of Little Britain
to Aldersgate. Now, inside Aldersgate, and to the east
of it, Sir Nicholas Bacon had a house called Bacon
House, shown very clearly in Stow's map, and he
was residing there in 1578 hard by Recorder Fleetwood
an ally of the Earl of Leicester. He was probably not
infrequently there, York House in the Strand being
his official residence as Chancellor, held from the Arch
bishop of York, for whom it was purchased after York
Place passed to the Crown and became Whitehall
Palace. Thus the space roughly occupied between
Gray's Inn, Newgate, Aldersgate, and Islington is
replete with incidents of Shakespearean interest. In
Little Britain, for example, lived Sir Thomas Bodley
the famous librarian; Sir Ralph Winwood; and there
too, and at Cripplegate beyond, Sir Dudley Carleton

---

* This old gate has been recently restored. The Knights
of St. John hold their meetings here, and the St. John
Ambulance here has its headquarters. The style of the interior
beautifully panelled, is similar to that of Canonbury Tower
at Islington.

and John Chamberlain had relatives. All were friends
deeply interested in Shakespeare-Bacon. For this
region lying round Smithfield rivalled Westminster in
the beauty of Christ Church, its buildings, and aristo-
cratic relations. Next to Gray's Inn stood Brooke
House, where lived Fulke Greville, the staunch advocate
with the Queen of Bacon-Shakespeare when he was in
hopes of becoming Attorney-General, and author of
the life of his dear friend, Sir Philip Sidney. And
mark this! Opposite to Gray's Inn in Holborn stood
the Earl of Southampton's house, where now are
Southampton Buildings. The postern now still leading
into Holborn from Gray's Inn was first made in Shakespeare-Bacon's time, and led straight out to the house
of the Earl of Southampton, to whom Shakespeare
dedicated the first work that bore his name, " Venus
and Adonis." Further down Holborn, next beyond
Brooke House, came what was then one of the most
beautiful houses in London with its chapel—namely,
Ely Palace, the house of the Bishops of Ely, in which
Shakespeare makes old John of Gaunt die in the play
of " Richard II.,"* and to the garden of which the
Earl of Gloucester sent the then Bishop†—to get rid
of him—to fetch him some of his fine strawberries. In
Ely Palace, too, lived later the Spanish Ambassador
Gondemar, another great friend of Shakespeare-Bacon,
who took away with him a copy of the First Folio of
Shakespeare plays to Madrid, where it has since acci-
dentally perished. But before his day Queen Elizabeth

---

* " Richard II.," Act II., sc. i.
† " Richard III.," Act III., sc. iv.:

> " My Lord of Ely, when I was last in Holborn,
> I saw good strawberries in your garden there."

had caused Bishop Cox to make over half of its fine
garden for a house for Sir Christopher Hatton, whose
wife, when widowed, Bacon-Shakespeare courted and
his great legal rival, Coke, married and quarrelled with
So that when Spanish Gondemar sought to borrow her
garden key, and she refused, he declared to King James
that Lady Coke was difficult to understand. She
would neither let him out from, nor her husband into
her house.   Beyond Ely Palace lay Smithfield, famous
for its tournaments, its burnings of heretics, and its
Bartholomew fair, but, above all, noted as the great
horse-market of London for nigh 800 years.   In the
sixteenth century, when Shakespeare-Bacon lived
earls, lords, and barons might have been seen having
horses trotted round, and thither Falstaff sends Bar
dolph to buy him a horse,* and Henry VI. gives sentence
that—

> " The witch in Smithfield shall be burned to ashes."†

Bartholomew fair was dramatised by Ben Jonson
who lived some years in what had once been the close
of the ancient monastery of St. Bartholomew, dissolve
by Henry VIII., the priory of which was now the town
house of Lord Rich, afterwards Earl of Warwick,‡ the
husband of the celebrated Penelope, sister of the Earl
of Essex, and the adored " Stella " of Sir Philip Sidney
so dear to Shakespeare-Bacon.   The Earl of Leiceste
having forbade their marriage, Sidney married the
daughter of Sir Francis Walsingham, another staunch
friend of Shakespeare-Bacon, and their daughter

* " Henry IV.," Part II., Act I., sc. ii.
† " Henry VI.," Part II., Act II., sc. iii.
‡ There was a Warwick House in St. Bartholomew's Close
till recently.

married the Earl of Rutland, and lived later in Rutland House, between Warwick House and Charter House. Both the Countess of Rutland and of Warwick were zealous patronesses of Ben Jonson. Charter House, which still stands next to Rutland Place, passed from Lord North, who received Queen Elizabeth at her accession, to the Duke of Norfolk, who entertained her the last year of her reign, before she passed to Richmond, where she died. This brief survey must suffice to show how closely the whole neighbourhood round Gray's Inn and Smithfield was associated with Shakespeare-Bacon and the friends and Court circle of his acquaintance. All that region radiates with memories of this our Prince-poet, England's greatest glory, and of all the buildings within it. Possibly the great hall of the Knights of St. John and their other buildings then standing around the still remaining St. John's Gateway, restored by King Edward VII., saw him most. For this was the seat of the Offices of the Master of Revels,* and in that ancient hall the boys of the chapel and boys of Paul's rehearsed their plays before acting them before the Queen. It was ten minutes' walk from Gray's Inn. How easy for Shakespeare-Bacon to walk unseen by Hatton Wall to superintend them, and devise scenery under the screen name of John Lyly, the Master of the children of Paul's, and test those delicate effects of candle-light with which, as Bacon, he compares truth in his essay, saying:

" This same Truth is a naked and open daylight, that doth not show the Masques and mummeries and Triumphs of the world half so stately and daintily as candle-light."

* Sir Edward Tilney, Sir George Buck, Sir Philip Herbert.

It was an effect which he had also studied with care at Kenilworth, this effect of candle-light on theatricals. In London, except the Court, the private theatre of Blackfriars, where Lyly's plays were also acted, was in early days the only closed theatre where such effects were practicable.

But we must now return to the earlier days of Shakespeare when, as young Francis Bacon, under the screen name of " Immerito," the friend of Philip Sidney, he was yet making the English language— seeking, as he says, for new and choice, good, and natural English words, that our tongue might be " both full enough for prose and stately enough for verse."* He was but eighteen, but wise enough already to see that an ample choice of vocabulary was the only road to that perfection of expression which he sought as the only means of attaining to the full height of the cliffs he wished to climb. He meant to leave no means unturned. He had thus to forge the instrument with which he must work; but nothing—as he had been taught by his inflexible Queen-mother—nothing difficult and worth doing is attainable without pains. A wise man will make more opportunities than he finds. So he cheerfully began at the very beginning, to mould his crude native tongue to his purpose, putting on a bold face against ridicule, and facing his opponents with a daring wit, the keenness of whose edge made men feel its sharpness, whilst its gentle and pretty humour soothed the wound. He is seen thus unflinching but firm, young but with the rare judgment of a sage, dangerous to attack but eager to heal. His life, his

* " Shepherd's Calendar," Letter of E. K.   This search for new words is already extremely conspicuous in Laneham's letter.

literature, his energy, judgment, and go, never cease
to remind us at this time of his life, of the famous
speech of Polonius to Laertes, written at a later date
in "Hamlet," but already twice in embryo in
"Euphues," and very relevant. This speech is in fact
a close study of the eighth chapter of Ecclesiasticus,*
the last verse of which is introduced in that favourite
translation of the "De Imitatione Christi" of Thomas
à Kempis which is by "F. B.," initials which, no
doubt of it whatever, stand for Francis Bacon. A
modern critic has indeed drawn attention to the
"pointed and antithetical expression" of this work
and the close resemblance of its rhythm to the English
Bible. Thus in the Bible we read (Ecclus. viii. 15,
16, 17, 18, 19): "Travel not by the way with a bold
fellow, lest he become grievous unto thee: . . . Strive
not with an angry man. . . . Do no secret thing
before a stranger; for thou knowest not what he will
bring forth. Open not thine heart to every man, lest
he requite thee with a shrewd turn."

In the F. B. translation of the "De Imitatione "†

* So, too, chap. xxxix. of Ecclesiasticus recalls the last
scene of "Henry VIII." (verses 10-11), and the "Tempest,"
(verse 28): "There be Spirits," Ariel. Here, too, is the fundamental doctrine of Bacon's philosophy that all the gifts of
nature are for use subject to the end for which God granted
them (Ecclesiasticus xxxix. 26, 27). See also Plutarch,
"On the Education of Children," according to whom the
precepts of Polonius seem to have sprung from Pythagoras
(chap. xii.), 1535 translation.

† Roger Ascham, Queen Elizabeth's tutor, mentions in his
"Schoolmaster" a translation of "Kemppes Book de Imi-
tando Christi," by Sebastian Castalio. He refers also to
Quintilian in discussing "paraphrasis" on the same page.
"Roger Ascham's Works," p. 273, by J. Bennet.

this becomes yet more antithetically: " Lay not thy heart open to every one; but treat of thy affairs with him that is wise and feareth God." In " Euphues," written at the time we are now considering, this grows with addition; thus:

" Let thy attire be comely but not costly. Mistrust no man without cause, neither be thou credulous without proof. Be not light to follow every man's opinion, nor obstinate to stand on thine own conceit."*

Now compare the Polonius of " Hamlet," Act I., sc. iii., by Shakespeare:

" Give thy thoughts no tongue,
Nor any unproportioned thought his act.
Be thou familiar, but by no means vulgar.

* * * * *

Take each man's censure, but reserve thy judgment.
Costly thy habit as thy purse can buy,
But not express'd in fancy; rich, not gaudy,
For the apparel oft proclaims the man.

* * * * *

This above all: to thine own self be true,
And it must follow, as the night the day,
Thou canst not then be false to any man."

Strikingly convincing of the unity of Bacon and Shakespeare are the following further antithetical extracts from Bacon's essays:

" Men's behaviour should be like their apparell, not too straight or point device. To apply oneself to others is good. . . . If you will grant his opinion let it be with

* Plutarch gives as precepts of Pythagoras the following and others:

" Taste nothing that hath a black taste.
Leap not over the balance.
Give not to every man thy right hand," etc.

some distinction, if you will follow his motion let it be
with some condition.* And be so true to thyself as
thou be not false to others.† . . . That which maketh
the effect more pernicious is that all proportion is lost."‡

The antithesis throughout is very accentuated, and
at once reminds us of Ascham's account of the great
love of Queen Elizabeth herself for metaphor and antithesis, already alluded to.§ Bacon's essays are, without doubt, his diagnosis of passion, "the tables of
discovery for anger, fear, shame, and the like," referred
to in Aphorism 127 of Book I. of the "Novum Organum." He therein weighs and considers the action
of such passions, and then transfers them to the plays.
Thus in the "Essay of Friendship" we read:

"For there is no such Flatterer, as is a man's self;
And there is no such remedy against flattery of a man's
self, as the liberty of a friend."

* "Essay of Ceremonies and Respects."
† "Essay of Wisdom for a Man's Self."
‡ That both Bacon and Shakespeare borrowed from the
"De Imitatione" is clear thus: Bacon's "Essay of Adversity"
ends: "But Adversity doth best discover virtue."
"De Imitatione," chap. xvi.: "The occasion of Adversity
best discovereth how great virtue each one hath."
Shakespeare, "Love's Labour's Lost":

"Study is like the heaven's glorious sun
        That will not be *deep-searched* by saucy looks,
    Small have continual plodders ever won,
        Save base *authority* from others' books."

Francis Bacon, "De Imitatione," Book V., chap. v.: "We
ought to read devout and simple books as well as high and
learned. Let not the *authority* of the writer offend thee,
whether he be of great or small learning." Chap. iii.: "A
humble knowledge of thyself is a surer way than *deep-search*
after learning."   § See p. xviii.

And in the play of " Julius Cæsar " this is set before our eyes, thus :

CASSIUS: You love me not.
BRUTUS: I do not like your faults.
CASSIUS: A friendly eye could never see such faults.
BRUTUS: A flatterer's would not, though they do appear
           As huge as high Olympus.

(" Julius Cæsar," Act IV., sc. iii.)

Fear, shame, etc., are likewise illustrated.

The learned experience on which this play is founded does not seem far to seek—Cæsar is Essex.   Brutus is Bacon.   They were friends up to the last scene, perhaps brothers.   But it is with the happy youth of Shakespeare-Bacon that I am here dealing before tragedy had overclouded it.

Otherwise in early life versatile, alert, observant, enterprising, painstaking, sound, merry and witty was the young man, aged eighteen, whom we now fancy we see issuing forth from Bacon House, Aldersgate, where then nor trams, buses, nor motors rattled by with busy din.   He is making for the city gate, so called, and finds himself at once confronting just inside Aldersgate an ancient house of the Duke of Northumberland, in which once Percy Hotspur dwelt—a second Talbot, of whose daring " Immerito " speaks in his " Calendar,"* and Shakespeare in the play of " Henry VI."—and strolling on he passes Westmoreland House. Northumberland, Westmoreland, Hotspur, what heroes they became in the play of " Henry IV.," the first probably of the Shakespeare plays to be acted on the stage.   Again, as the young bard, historian, and wit

* " Shepherd's Calendar," gloss for June:
       " The very scourge of France, Lord Talbot."

issued from Aldersgate, he saw on his right the Cooks' Hall. The " Princely Pleasures of Kenilworth " rise now to his memory, for as Laneham he had already immortalised that hall.* From here the north road leads to Islington, and, in the now famous letter, the Minstrel of Islington relates "how the worshipful village of Islington was well known to be one of the most ancient and best touns in England next London at this day; for the faithful friendship showed as well at Cook's feast in Aldersgate Street yearly upon Holy Rood Day, as also at all solemn bridals in the city of London all the year after." Islington was then the Arcadia, the dairy farm of London, in the midst of rolling pastures stretching away to Hoxton and Moorfields. There herds of cattle grazed and " seely sheep " fed, such as we read of in the idyllic "Shepherd's Calendar." Islington, then so favoured by Queen Elizabeth, the Earl of Leicester, Sir Walter Raleigh, nobles and merchant princes, supplied London with milk, and, under the name of Laneham, our young Prince-poet, with his rollicking, euphuistic, distinctly *boyish* wit, goes on to show how intimately he was acquainted with the tricks alike of the dairyman and pastry cook. It is the young Shakespeare studying his trade. For him nothing is too small or lowly for study and fun, nothing human is beneath his notice. He can be as mortal and concrete as he can be divine and inspired. How pretty is his prattle as he makes the Minstrel of Islington go on to tell of the fame of Islington in well serving of these bridal feasts " of furmenty for porage not over-sodden, till it be too weak: of milk for the flawnies (cheese cakes) not pild

* See Laneham's letter, under " Ministrel of Islington."

(watered) nor chalked: of cream for their custards, not frothed nor thickened with flour," and so on *ad lib.* His tongue wags ceaselessly, the coming of Falstaff can almost be seen, the merriment is so natural, so unrestrained and endless. His great delight in Islington is manifestly genuine and not to be denied; and all students of Bacon know his great love for Islington; how he brought it into his masque of the " Prince of Purpool," played at Gray's Inn with the " Comedy of Errors " in 1594, and held a long lease of Canonbury Tower as it still stands at Islington, with its Latin list of English Kings in the top room in which the letters " Fr—— " are entered between Queen Elizabeth and King James.

Now Queen Elizabeth had a house at Islington called the " Sheep," or " Shipcote " (the i and double ee being interchangeable, as in seely or silly).* This is established by State Papers, which record that: " On Aug. 9th—24 Elizabeth (*i.e.* 1582), the Queen presented the Earl of Leicester with a house at Islington called the Shipcote."

Furthermore, the Calvinistic Bishop Hall, in his satires, which are admitted by all parties to be an attack on Shakespeare under the names of Labeo and Gallio (*i.e.*, Prince of Wales) for writing " Venus and Adonis " and " Love's Labour's Lost," after inviting attention by the line " Should Bandell's† throstle die without a song?" gives this remarkable

* SPEED: Twenty to one, then, he is *shipp'd* already,
And I have played the *sheep* in losing him.

(" The Two Gentlemen of Verona," Act I., sc. i.)

† Bandello (Bandel in French), author of " Romeo and Giulietta." See Hall's " Satires."

information concerning Labeo—*i.e.*, Shakespeare—namely, that, e'er his muse her weapon learnt to wield,

> " The SHEEPCOTE first hath been her *nursery*,
> Where she hath born her idle infancy,
> And in high start-up walked the pasture plains
> To fend her tusked herd that there remains,
> And winded still a pipe of oat or beer*
> As did whilere the homely Carmelite
> Following Virgil and the Theocrite;†
> Or else hath been in Venus chamber trained
> To play with Cupid,‡ till she had attained
> To comment well upon a lady's face,
> Then was she fit for an heroic place."§

The most hostile critic, with these words placed thus before his eyes, could not deny that every line of them is biographical, or that they refer to the author of the "Shepherd's Calendar," who refers so pointedly and repeatedly to Mantuan,‖ Lydgate, Virgil, and Theocritus as his models, and who—Hall here distinctly tells us—wrote his pastural eclogues, his "Shepherd's Calendar," living on the green plains and amongst the lowing herds of the then rural Islington. There it was, he tells us, that the young Francis, the inspired Orpheus, fresh from the vain pursuit of his Eurydice, the beautiful Marguerite in France, was

---

* *Cf.* Laneham.

† The very models quoted by " Immerito " in the ' Shepherd's Calendar," Letter of E. K.

‡ Laneham and Euphues were both specially devoted to the ladies, and Bacon and Laneham frequented the Court, as well as Immerito.

§ After the "Shepherd's Calendar" came the heroic "Faerie Queen."

‖ The " good old Mantuan " of " Love's Labour's Lost." What a ring it has of to-day! ("Love's Labour's Lost," Act IV., sc ii.)

wont to wander out from Bacon or Leicester House, to pine away in manful mood the pangs of despised love, and set down his brave words in his Calendar, feeling inspired beyond all durance, in words quoted above:

> " Oh, if my temples were distained with wine
> And girt in garlands of wild ivy twine,
> How I could rear the muse on stately stage,
> And teach her tread aloft in buskin fine,
> With quaint Bellona in her equipage."

" I found him so besotted," says the father in " Don Quixote "* of Laurence, " with *poesy and that science,* if so it may be called, that it is not possible to make him look upon the law which I would have him study;"† and nothing could probably better express the feeling of young Bacon-Shakespeare at this time when he wrote to Lord Burghley of " things of greater delight and no less preferment than the law," to the study of which he most unwillingly resigned himself. Again, the above passage from Hall cannot fail to remind the reader of the young Euphues and Laneham, both so addicted to the ladies and to delighting them; and was it not to the chamber of Mary Sidney above all that it was Laneham's special joy to resort ?‡ She was his aunt and the mother of his

* Part II., chap. xxi., Shelton translation.
† This was Shakespeare-Bacon's very case. See " Don Quixote," Part II., chap. xxi. Also, " I am as it were more than duncified twixt divinity and poetry " (T. Nashe, " The Unfortunate Traveller," p. 38. H. F. B. Brett-Smith, Perc Reprints, No. 1).
‡ The " Shepherd's Calendar " is the title of one of the books mentioned by Laneham as contained in Captain Cox' library.

dear friend and colleague in the Areopagus—Philip
Sidney; and to conclude, the April gloss of his Calendar
confirms the words of Hall, in which he refers to himself as " a shepherd's boy brought up in the sheep-
fold," and towards the end of the December eclogue
says that as time advanced—

> " Also my age now passed youthly prime
>   To things of riper reason selfe applied,
>   And learned of lighter timber *cotes* to frame,
>   Such as might save my sheep and me fro' shame."

The gloss explains that shepherds' cots are referred to.
  It would be difficult to find any passages showing
more clearly how this sweet Tudor rose spread its
fragrance around under so many names.   Immerito
and Shakespeare, Francis Bacon, Laneham, and John
Lyly or Euphues, Don Quixote and Nashe, these are
only a few of the many names from all of which the
same sweet scent pours forth, and of these authors
the "Shepherd's Calendar," and its curious gloss, are
especially illuminating.

CHAPTER XIV

SHAKESPEARE'S FURTHER TRAVEL — RESIDENCE AT GRAY'S INN—MEMBER OF PARLIAMENT

It is, as I have shown, in his motley of "Immerito" that we are able to identify that author most unmistakably with both Shakespeare and Bacon. He returned from France lovesick and forlorn:

> "Delight is laid abed, and pleasure past.
> No sun shines now, clouds have all overcast.
>
> *   *   *   *   *
>
> Here will I hang my pype upon this tree,
> Was never pipe of reed did better sound.
>
> *   *   *   *   *
>
> Winter is come that blows the baleful breath,
> And after winter come thy timely death.
> Adieu delights, that lulled me to sleep,*
> Adieu, my deare, whose love I bought so dear.
>
> *   *   *   *   *
>
> Adieu, good Hobbinal,† that was so true;
> Tell Rosalind her Colin bids her adieu."

Thus did the stricken muse of England's newly budding and lovely rose sing his farewell to his Princess of France, his lovely Marguerite, his Daiselorn. He pulled out whatever stumps of despised love still stuck painfully in his gums, and turned once more soberly to the achievements of the dreams of his youth, the

---

* The delight of the affections and their control by habit was the cause of his difference from Aristotle ("De Aug., Book VII., chap. iii.; J. M. Robertson, p. 574).

† Hobbinal, he says, is Gabriel Harvey. "Shepherd Calendar," December eclogue.

triumph of reason and the perfection of the means of
expression. These things, to him, were those of greatest
delight, and he believed of no less preferment even than
the law. Study of the law was not inviting to him.
He was conscious of having to bear a yoke in his youth,
*tolerare jugum in juventate mea,** as this mere boy—and
ostensibly mere subject—did not hesitate to write to
the Queen, knowing her to be his mother, concluding
that "nothing under mere impossibilities could have
detained him from earning so gracious a veil as it
pleased your Majesty to give me."† In words so like
those of Endymion to Cynthia in John Lyly's play of
"Endymion"‡ did he express himself, who says: "I
am that Endymion, . . . who divorcing himself from
the amiableness of all ladies,§ the bravery of all courts,
the company of all men, hath chosen in a *solitary* cell
to live only by feeding on thy favour, accounting in the
world, but thyself, nothing excellent, nothing immortal." What could be more dutiful, more sub-
missive, or more touching ? And it was always thus
that Bacon-Shakespeare addressed the Queen, in terms
not ever customary for a young man and subject, to
address Her Majesty, but far more as a son to a mother,
who knew all about him *and cared*. Even after he had
become most highly distinguished as a lawyer he wrote

* Compare Gascoigne, "Philomene":
> "Some think that *jugum* is
> The jug she jingleth so,
> But jugulator is the word
> That doubleth all his woe."

† Letter to the Queen, July 20, 1584 (Spedding, "**Life
and Letters**").

‡ Act V., sc. iii.

§ As do the heroes in Act I., sc. i., of "Love's Labour's Lost."

to the Earl of Essex in 1595 when he had failed for the
Attorney-Generalship: " I am purposed not to follow
the *practise* of the law, (if her Majesty command me
in any particular I shall be ready to do her willing
service:)* and my reason is only, because it drinketh
too much time, which I have dedicated to other purposes." Thus already, at nineteen, the sudden revelation that he (by birth a Prince) was to study the law
as a means of living, as though he were a subject, came
to him—so full, moreover, of his own projects—as a
stunning blow, as may well be believed. Sir Nicholas
Bacon was no more. He had made no provision for
this Francis. Though it is easy to conceive the painstaking care and conscientiousness with which such an
earnest and pious couple as the Bacons would rear and
bring up one whom they knew by birth to be a Prince
the last Tudor and England's heir, they would naturally
think it quite outside their sphere to provide for the
future of such an one. On the other hand, the real
mother, the inflexible Queen Elizabeth, was adamant
The dissimulation must be maintained. Francis, as the
son of a lawyer, must follow his (foster-)father.

The letters of Immerito to Gabriel Harvey in this
dilemma work in exactly as might be expected with
those written by the Prince-poet Shakespeare in his
character of Francis Bacon. He has begged some
favour of the Queen by Burghley. He is expecting
every hour to be sent abroad—his very heart's desire—
to continue his travels and gain experience of the
world—ever more experience—so he writes to Harvey
After October, 1580, he disappears. Nothing more is
heard of him till April, 1582, and Rawley tells us that

* Strange words for a mere subject.

having delivered to the Queen a message sent by Sir Amyas Paulet, with great approbation, he returned back to France.

The political situation here comes to our aid. It was the year 1580, the year of the anticipated Jesuitical attack. Anxiety was at its height. That very June Fathers Parsons and Campion had stolen into the country. They had left Rome in April, where Pope Gregory had spoken to them of Queen Elizabeth as " that impious Jezebel, whose life God hath permitted thus long for our scourge."* Many more young Jesuits who had gone out from Oxford to be trained in foreign colleges at Douay and Rheims† were expected to follow their leaders. The Pope had further stimulated their fanaticism by declaring, in his opinion— though their crusade was to be a purely religious and not a murderous one—" the doer if he suffer death simply for that (*i.e.*, for assassination) to be worthy of canonisation."

Here clearly was a situation which required investigation. Our great poet, philosopher, and historian, though young, was already an accomplished linguist. The Queen was wont to call him her " Watch candle."‡ He was the essence of judgment and precaution. Who more fit for such a service ? And he was begging some suit of the Queen. It was granted, and he wrote to Burghley: " And now, seeing it hath pleased her

---

* Froude's " History of England," vol. xi., chap. lxiii., p. 45.
† " The Massacre of Paris," Act III., sc. ii.:

> " Did he not draw a sort of English Priest
> From Douay to the seminary at Rheims ?"
>
> (MARLOWE.)

‡ Letter to King James I.

Majesty to take knowledge of this my mind, and to vouchsafe to appropriate me unto her service, preventing any desert of mine with her princely liberality; first, I am moved humbly to beseech your Lordship to present to her Majesty my more than humble thanks therefore," etc. With that he is off,—as we believe, to Paris! Vienna! Padua! Verona! Rome! Florence! He disappeared for two years as Bacon, and we hear no more of Immerito. Our great versatile and immortal Shakespeare, or if you prefer it Bacon, had thus his first practical political mission, and on return, it seems, issued his "Notes on the State of Christendom" anonymously, as, being on secret service, he was bound to do, if for no other reason. This is what literature closely studied seems to reveal. The diaries both of Montaigne and Anthony Munday tell the same tale. Both were secretly on the tracks of the Jesuits, and Nicholas Faunt and Anthony Bacon—both devoted to our Francis Bacon-Shakespeare—were travelling about at their service, and on the alert to help them.

The "Notes on the State of Christendom" date, it is said, from the return of Bacon-Shakespeare from this journey in 1582. It is impossible to believe that they were written by one who had never visited the places and people he alluded to, or been in their neighbourhood, and it will be found that, so far as it goes, it covers much the same ground travelled over by Montaigne and his young friend and companion, M. d'Estignac, except Spain. For d'Estignac parted from Montaigne in Italy in 1581, just at the time when Shakespeare-Bacon was probably in Spain.* The

* At the very time when Cervantes returned to Madrid after imprisonment in Algiers.

enquiries concerning Catholics made by Montaigne are noteworthy. The journal mentions, for example, the picture of the royal French family, including Marguerite de Valois, to be seen in the Farnese Palace, which place is also mentioned in the "Notes on the State of Christendom." Anthony Munday visited Rheims and Rome. In his journal no attempt is made to conceal the cause of his mission; he assumed disguise, even penetrated into the Jesuitical colleges, and assisted to say Mass.

The situation is not clear. We should like to know more. We long to know for certain how, and when, and under what circumstances Shakespeare travelled in those places in Austria and Italy which he has made so familiar to British ears—Vienna, Padua, Venice, Verona. They seem almost ours. Certain it is that Montaigne and M. d'Estignac travelled and were received as persons of great notability, almost princes, and we are fain to believe that it is just under such circumstances as these that our Prince-poet visited, and observed, those famous places to which his plays have added so great a lustre, over and above their native interest. The journey fills an otherwise curious blank in Bacon's life and Shakespeare's.

This mission and the detection after his return of several popish plots to assassinate the Queen in 1585 are also curiously connected with the entry of our gifted Prince in concealment—our Shakespeare—into Parliament, of which he continued to be a leader and ornament for nearly a quarter of a century, under the name always of Francis Bacon, and into which he entered very soon after his supposed return from the Continent, when he settled down at last submissively at Gray's Inn to study the law, much as it went against the grain.

What career, indeed, is more lightning in its cinematic changes, what great man was more hydra-headed in talent than this whom—mortal as he was and erring—we believe to have had the most far-seeing and immortal mind of all known mortal beings? Since 1579 he had been condemned against his own inclinations to study the law. His flinty-hearted but admiring Queen-mother could not be moved either to acknowledge him or release him from the feigned and dissimulating life to which he seems to have been ordained. Only so far would she relax as to allow him to travel as her "watch candle," for the security of her life and realm, as her confidential and secret agent. She thus in her own words "appropriated him to her service," and he, overjoyed, at once gratefully snatched at this respite from the law. But the mission performed, we find him at last settling down to that residence in Gray's Inn with which he is so closely associated, not indeed as Shakespeare, not as a Tudor, but as Bacon, to become the untiring Lord Chancellor whom his countrymen so strangely and paradoxically accused of bribery, though it is said that no sentence he ever passed was ever reversed or even appealed against.

Gray's Inn, however, was not then as it is now. Up to the beginning of the sixteenth century it had been a private house. In the day of the poet-philosopher it still stood in open country, on its own grounds, in which the famous man later caused a mound to be erected, amid a group of trees, on which stood a chair. There he loved to sit and ponder, gazing northwards, reclining

as we see him in his monument, and thence could be
seen for many years after his death a lovely view of
undulating pastureland, such as poets, shepherds and
their flocks delight in, stretching right away to Highgate
and Hampstead, and to nearer Islington, wherein
Canonbury Tower is distant about two miles from
Gray's Inn. The open railings are there still. The
green fields and the view beyond them are gone.
Houses, houses, houses everywhere!

Such was the Gray's Inn in which the future Prince
of poets, the most illustrious of philosophers, and the
most just of eminent judges, was caused to ensconce
himself, an unwilling student of the law, with occupa-
tions " of more delight and no less preferment " on his
mind, to which he had from early youth dedicated
himself. He and his (foster-)brother Anthony had
been admitted to Gray's Inn—then only open to the
select few—as boys. There is, however, no sign of his
having resided there steadily till 1582, and, as Spedding
points out, there is no clear record of him at all from
September, 1580, to April, 1582. Then, as I have
suggested, on his return from the travels which led to
the paper styled " Notes on the State of Christendom,"
he was admitted as Utter Barrister on June 27, 1582,
and is said by Faunt* to have been frequently seen
about town in his gown. Was it, we wonder, at this
period that he from time to time joined with the young
bloods at St. Paul's in the cry " Eastward ho!"†
which it appears was the signal for a rag with the
clerical element returning home? There was much
work for the lawyer then in wondrous old St. Paul's,

* Spedding, " Life and Letters of Francis Bacon."
† Leigh Hunt, " The Town."

a thoroughfare where men of all classes high and low
congregated.* Both Bacon and Shakespeare were well
acquainted with it. There many a *si quis* was posted
and many a debtor caught. Each part, it seems, had
a separate name and function, and it was a common
practice to use some bookseller there as a post office
There, in fact, Dudley Carleton found the letter† to
Chamberlain, in forwarding which he tells him, in 1606
that "Don Quixote" is translated into all languages
and sent out into the wide world;‡ which letter also
gives an account of Bacon-Shakespeare's wedding the
previous day. Let the student read also Dekker's
"Gull's Hornbook" of 1609, in the *proœmium* of which
he tells us: "I sing like the cuckoo in June to be
laughed at. . . . The *motley* is bought and a coat with
four elbows . . . *a fig* therefore for the new-found
college of critics. . . . Consider what an excellen
thing sleep is . . . look upon Endymion the moon's
minion, who slept three score and fifteen years and
was not a hair the worse for it. . . . All the diseased
horses in a tedious siege cannot show so many fashion
as are to be seen for nothing in Duke Humphry's Walk
The top of St. Paul's contains more names than Stowe'
Chronicle." What student of human nature would
avoid such a haunt, or again the Boar's Head Tavern
in Eastcheap, which all the rank and fashion of London
passed daily in crossing old London Bridge to ride
hawk, and hunt beyond Southwark. Such, withou
any sort of doubt, were the occasional resorts of ou
Shakespeare, in relief of his study of the law as Franci
Bacon. On the other hand, he was about to put hi

* See Dekker's "Gull's Hornbook."
† In the Record Office.   ‡ See p. 171.

variegated powers now to a new test as orator and Member of Parliament—the art of elocution. In respect of this period of Shakespeare-Bacon's life (1583-1593), nothing could be more instructive than to follow M. Jusserand* as, quite innocent and unconscious of the supreme comedy being played under his eyes, he proceeds to compare, for example, Nashe and Dekker, and quite rightly associates them as one in mind with the rest of the Shakespeare-Baconian school, saying of Dekker: " He had many traits in common with Nashe, the same excellent faculty of observation, the same gaiety and *entrain.*" Thus Dekker in his ' Knight's Conjuring " relates how " Grave Spenser was no sooner entered into this Chappel of Apollo, but these elders (Chaucer, etc.) of the divine furie, gave him a lawrer and sung his welcome," to which M. Jusserand adds in a note: " In the same happy retreat Dekker gives a place to Watson, Kyd, Greene, Peele, Nashe, Chettle." To him the unity in the works written under all these names is visible, but he does not grasp that this arises from the fact that they are practically all pupils, and some merely pseudonyms for the same great name " Shakespeare "—*i.e.*, what the great man himself so specifically calls his " motleys," the *scribimus indocti,*† under which he sought liberty to speak his mind, his *medicine*—each one a volume of the propaganda by which he sought " to cleanse the foul body of the infected world." Never was so measured and

* J. J. Jusserand, " English Novel in the Time of Shakespeare," pp. 332-336. 1890.

† Unlearned scribes.—" Scribimus indocti, doctique poemata passim." This line is referred to by Samuel Daniel; also by Gabriel Harvey and the " Return from Parnassus."

deliberate, so serious and profound, so earnest yet so
sparkling, so truly practical a joke carried out with
such wonderful method and inspiration, and, to borrow
Sir Tobie Matthew's expression, with such " *prodigious
wit.*" As M. Jusserand says with true insight (so far
as he goes): " Nashe's ghost was most certainly hovering
over Dekker," and " Intimate literary ties existed
between Nashe and Dekker; many passages in the one
remind us of similar things in the other," which in his
innocence M. Jusserand regards as " the result sometimes of actual imitation, sometimes of involuntary
reminiscences." No, my dear friend, they came from
the very same ingenious, fluent, and facetious pen,
the same great mind from whose abundant pen " honey
flowed to his friends and mortal aconite to his enemies,"
to paraphrase Dekker. Each of them—both Dekker
and Nashe—had his fat hostler, his Falstaff, like their
master. " Dekker's man is not thinner, cleaner, nor
braver than Nash's victualler. He is a country inn-
keeper, ' a good fat burger he was, with a belly arching
out like a beere-barrell, which made his legges, that
were thick and short like two piles driven under
London Bridge.' "*   (Dekker's " Wonderful Year,"

* Another author says: " For mere consistency of detail
Nashe cared no more than Shakespeare "; and " to Shakespeare
Nashe has not infrequently been likened by historians of the
English novel," and quotes Sir Walter Raleigh: " It is the
likest of all others to Shakespeare. . . ." We get one sentence
from his " Sidership " that is the very burthen of Sir John
" Oh (quoth he), I am bought and sold for doing my country
such good service as I have done. They are afraid of me
because my good deedes have brought me into such estimation
with the Comminaltie. I see, I see, it is not for the lamb to
live with the wolf " (" The Unfortunate Traveller of Nashe,"
p. xiii, ed. by H. F. B. Brett-Smith).

1603.) What a true touch of real Elizabethan wit,
such as the great Queen might herself have uttered,
much more her brilliant son. Yes, indeed, there is a
strange resemblance between Nashe and Dekker. Not
strange, however, so far as they were one and the
same—namely, variously coloured *motleys* of the same
man who claimed " as large a charter as the wind,"
to blow on whom he pleased. " The motley is bought,"
he tells us. Here we have him in the very act, blowing
with all his might, " And they that are most galled
with my folly, they most must laugh." He who laughs
last laughs most. Did M. Jusserand ever dream of
looking at the likeness between Nashe and Dekker
from this point of view? Would he might kindly do so
now, and help our countrymen and the world to rightly
understand and do justice to Shakespeare, who, as
Bacon, thus wittily set about his great work of reform.

The ten years from 1583 to 1593 may, in short, be
described as the period devoted by Shakespeare-Bacon
to the fundamental study of the English language—
witty as well as wise—as a means of elocution and
tradition and power, till he had brought it to that state
of perfection in which we find it after 1593 under the
proud name of Shakespeare. Add this to ten years'
study as a boy, and we arrive at the conclusion that
it took this great master of art and his assistants twenty
years to fashion the instrument which he found so crude
and poor—as E. K. tells us in the " Shepherd's
Calendar "—till he had amassed a vocabulary, it is
said, of 15,000 words—nearly double that of the later
Milton—and had brought his native tongue to the
refined state of perfection which could alone give that
sweetness, that precision, that fullness and melody

which the greatest of masters alone could touch
Poetry and prose and recitation he had practised from
youth. He was now resolved to test and perfect his
powers of persuasion with the tongue, as an orator—
his eloquence and address in public.

The public circumstances under which he first took
his seat, on November 23, 1584, as Member for Melcombe
in Dorsetshire, have a special interest in respect of the
probable object of his earlier travels. Rumours and
discoveries of plots against the Crown were everywhere
current, so that, as Mr. Spedding observes, " the first
breath of Bacon's public life was drawn in a very
contagious atmosphere of loyalty and anti-popery."*
An association had been formed to " prosecute any
person by whom or for whom violence should be offered
to her life."

It was in a Parliament thus inflamed with passionate
loyalty to the Queen's Majesty herself that the Prince
poet Shakespeare, himself of Tudor blood, concealed
under the name of Francis Bacon, and knowing himself
—from the point of view we are now considering—to be
her son, took his seat. He was her " watch candle."
As such he had just been traversing the Continent
from end to end in her service. He would now cham
pion her cause in Parliament. He could not be allowed
to say—he dared not say—he *loved* her. Like Endy
mion, he would be content to call it *honour*, and vow
the last degree of fidelity to her in his efforts for her
cause, falling short only of impossibilities. To him
so far as concerned her, it must be " duty and all duty.
Young as he was, he was already a master of the new
growing, classical English. Of his maiden speech w

* Spedding, " Life and Letters of Bacon."

know nothing. We can but imagine it. What a scene
to reconstruct! Shakespeare as Member of Parliament
at the age of twenty-three! Think of Portia! Think
of the fixed star-like height to which he has since risen
in the eyes of all the world! His brilliancy was already
known as he rose to address the great mother of Parliaments with that sweet persuasive eloquence for which
he became famous, having also a presence which was
impressive, and a countenance on which nature's
pencil had graved highly earnest and attractive features.
It is said that when J. S. Mill, whose early youthful
genius was also marked for its precocity, first addressed
the House in later life, the silence was so intense that
a pin could have been heard drop. But what a contrast! He was no orator, and powerful reasoner as
he was, his intellect had been cultivated at the expense
of his imagination. Yet his character and genius
commanded a very unusual respect. What was it,
then, when the concealed Shakespeare, great master
alike of reason and imagination in his motley of Bacon,
addressed the same House three hundred years ago
and more? What were his own feelings supposing
him to have been not only a concealed poet, but a
concealed Prince—a Tudor, a born ruler? Probably
there were present men who silently knew or sus-
pected it, for, judging from portraits even, there is
enough to arouse suspicion. Remembering how his
own mind was bent, above all, on the coming of that
age of the art of scientific invention which he saw
must come in time, and which we have present before
us, the power of distant penetration of this young
man, his marvellous apprehensiveness, seem to us to
have had in it of a truth, as Rawley said, something

divine or "of God." In addition to all this, remember
that it is Romeo himself before us, he who calls his
muse his rose, which by any name would smell as
sweet, and who painted Juliet, Rosalinde, Portia,
Desdemona, Lady Macbeth, Old John of Gaunt,
Henry V., Hamlet, Macbeth, Falstaff, and a hundred
other characters, whose names are household words in
every cultured home, in every country throughout the
whole wide world! This being the man, what would
we not give to have—by means of those inventions
now at our service—a photograph, a cinematic repre-
sentation, of this young sage, this Shakespeare, now
the world's hero, this inventor of plays, then addressing
the mother of all the world's Parliaments!

All we know is that he introduced a style of eloquence
such as that House had never known before. For is
not eloquence a branch of his fourth rational art*—
i.e., Elocution and Tradition? Thus he assumed very
rapidly an influential attitude, taking an active part
on committees, especially regarding subsidies to the
Crown. He was always on the side of reason rather
than force, and of moderation in the demand and
granting of subsidies. Perhaps the best idea of the
impression which he probably made in the House of
Commons may be gathered from that similar occasion
when, ten years later, at the urgent request of friends,
he consented to plead as a barrister in the King's
Court. The occasion was to remove the obstacle raised
to his being granted the Attorney-Generalship, because
it was urged by his opponents that his power as
barrister had never been tested. The only account

* Bacon, "De Aug.," Book V., chap. i.; J. M. Robertson,
p. 500.

we have of this incident is that given by Harry Gosnold.
The Court, he tells us, was crowded with judges and
others to hear him, and the strange words with which
he "spangled his speech,"* and used to enforce his
arguments, called forth much comment and applause.
This was in 1594. His fame as a master of language
was then established. His preliminary studies as
linguist, lawyer, philosopher, and parliamentary orator
had been completed, and the plays of Shakespeare had
begun to appear. He had, as he told Lord Burghley,
at the age of thirty-one taken all knowledge to be his
province, and become a sorry bookmaker.†

Scenes such as this are memorable and graphic in
the history of so very great a man as Shakespeare.
Common sense says that the author of his famous
plays must have had, and have gone through, dramatic
experiences such as this to be able to conceive and
represent them. Without them the empty life of the
rustic actor, Shakspere of Stratford, dwindles and
shrinks sensitively into an absurdity. The one por-
trays at once the genius, perseverance, and experience
of a great master, the other testifies to no experience
beyond that of a clown. Such an expert at language,
with observation and powers of expression so exquisite,
must also have possessed an inexpressible charm in
conversation such as could not fail to attract the
attention of the learned and wise, and we know from
Rawley and Jonson that Bacon had just that gentle,
considerate, and unassertive, affable manner in con-
versing which we should expect to find in one so refined
and accomplished, even though his inability to over-

* Spedding, "Life and Letters."
† *Ibid.*

look a jest may at times have made an opponent wince.
This, in fact, was Bacon-Shakespeare's sharpest weapon
in debate, and it was in the calm and self-possessed,
self-confident manner which he used it that he outdid
his intemperate rival Coke. It was this same gentle
persuasive humour which also made him a power in
the Commons, where he took, for the times, a really
independent line, maintaining there the attitude of
wise concession on behalf of the Crown, which he
deemed most calculated to the dignity and honour
of the Queen, because fair and just to the people; and
certainly on one occasion he commended concession
to an extent which, for some time, banished him from
Court. He was, however, taken back into favour
without withdrawing anything he had said.

Bacon-Shakespeare was returned for Taunton early
in 1587, and sat on a Committee to provide a single
subsidy, after which another hitherto unaccountable
hiatus occurs in his career. This, too, at that period
when the Spanish Armada was threatening the realm
Then, of all times, one feels that the filial loyalty of
the Prince-lawyer-statesman-poet would demonstrate
itself; and so—there is reason to believe it did—not in
the capacity of a soldier, or sailor, but once more as
his Queen-mother's "watch candle," in that secret
diplomacy which Queen Elizabeth permitted herself
with the Duke of Parma in the Low Countries, till it
was discovered by the Privy Council, and her disowned
agents, Bodenham* and Sir James Croft, were hauled
up before Lord Burghley and Walsingham and severely
reprimanded. Bacon's dear friend, Sir John Norris

* Who was this Bodenham ? See Froude's " History of
England," vol. xii., p. 71.

was at this time in the Low Countries with the Earl of Leicester, and it is to him that, under the name of Peele, the "Farewell" is addressed. The paper entitled "A brief discourse touching the Low Countries, the King of Spain, the King of Scots, the French King and Queen Elizabeth, with some other remarkable passages of State,"* is also of interest in this connection.

We hear of Bacon-Shakespeare next in connection with a masque at Gray's Inn in February, 1588, and he sat as Member for Liverpool in the Parliament which met in November, 1588. In February, 1593, he was returned as Knight of the shire for Middlesex, and it was in connection with the triple subsidy voted by this Parliament that he offended the Queen by venturing to express publicly the opinion that, what was above a double subsidy, should be regarded as extraordinary and exceptional, "for precedent's sake, and for discontent's sake ought not to have been levied on the poorer sort." Let us give due honour to our Shakespeare for this stand for the people, and his refusal to retract. Why did the Queen dally thus with this ostensibly private member and subject? It was not her wont. Who was he thus to offend Her Majesty and yet go scot free? Here we see him not as philosopher, not as poet, but as fearless man of action, having in his mind that "The least part of knowledge . . must be subject to that use for which God hath granted it, which is the benefit and relief of the state and society of man"; or, as the "brothers of common life" would say, whose faith is expressed in the "De Imitatione," "Work not for fame, praise, or self-glory, but for the common good of all." Don Quixote's

* Spedding.

error lay in thus not rightly fixing his ends. Glorious as the errant Knight's aims and ideas were in themselves, his actions were directed toward self-glory. He did not say, as Shakespeare says:

> " Let fame, that all hunt after in their lives,
> Live registered upon our brazen tombs."

Note to p. 199.—Montaigne's journal was found in 1774. Up to February 16, 1581, it was kept by an amanuensis, on which date he gave leave to one of his followers who, up to this time, he says, had written it in admirable fashion. " All interest in the places he now passed vanished, and the humour of the road appeals to him no more." (See " Montaigne's Journal," translated by W. G. Waters, 1903.)

The following entry is noteworthy:

" *September* 1.—Took the Road to Bagnaia. . . . The cardinal was not there, but being *francesco* at heart, as he was Francesco by name, the people in charge of the palace showed *me* the greatest courtesy and friendship."

CHAPTER XV

SHAKESPEARE: GRAY'S INN AND THE DRAMA,
1583–1593

THE simplest thing, often repeated, gains a strong hold on the mind, and in youth does much to mould character. An experience, constantly present for any length of time, makes a lasting impression. It is thus not difficult to discern what was passing through Shakespeare's mind when he wrote the exquisite passage in " Romeo and Juliet " containing the famous apostrophe:

" What's in a name ?"

He discovered early that he was committed to a life of dissimulation under a name other than his own by right of birth. To ask this question must have become a habit. Call him Shakespeare or call him Bacon, neither name was his own. He, a concealed Prince by birth, lived under pseudonyms of which as the Prince of poets we love best that of " sweet William Shakespeare"; but he had many others. Thus, regarding his muse—*i.e.*, himself—as his rose,* how pathetically true of him is the line " a rose by any other name would smell as sweet," and yet more the line, " My name, dear saint, is hateful to myself." He was for ever making fun of his name " Bacon," calling himself, as shown, a little squeaking pig, in one of the most beautiful of the Court masques attributed

* Sonnet CIX.: " Save thou, my rose, in it thou art my all."

to John Lyly—one produced when the Queen was on
progress at his own supposed aunt's house. He and
Anthony Bacon were invited to witness it, but excused
themselves. Further, this mood culminated in his
will, where, with such a sly smile, such inexpressible
pathos and superb humour, he leaves his name to the
next ages and to *foreign nations*.* What was his
name ? Dudley by birth, he was Tudor by blood, but
never baptised or known by the name which by right
was his.

Now it is very easy to see how this sensitiveness as
to his name, knowing himself to be by birth a Prince,
would be on his mind when, in the infatuation of his
youth—at a time when he still hoped for recognition—
he was madly in love with his sweet Juliet, the Princess
of France, and Queen of Navarre, the beautiful Marguerite. He was her equal and knew it, if only he
dared openly divulge it. " Deny thy father and refuse
thy name." How he must have longed to do so, to
proclaim himself, as in a fairy tale, a Prince in disguise,
and he clearly signifies his consciousness of his right
to the title in the October eclogue of the "Shepherd's
Calendar," where he exclaims, in pondering his love:

> " O peerless Poesie, where is then thy place
> If not in Prince's pallace thou do sit
> (And yet in Prince's pallace the most fitt)?
> No breast of baser birth doth thee embrace,
> Then make thee winges of thine aspiring wit
> And, whence thou camest, fly back to heaven apace."
>
> (" Shepherd's Calendar.")

---

* This is in the first will. Another copy has: " And to min
own countrymen after some time be past."

The beautiful Rosalinde, his Daiselorn, his Marguerite, as Puttenham says, had written volumes too. Braithwaite also tells of a Prince-poet, and the writer of the above lines, as we know, frequented Leicester House and the Court.

In all the earlier works attributable to Shakespeare-Bacon his connection with royalty is thus evident, and it never quite disappeared. Not only did the Queen still recognise him as her "watch candle," but she made him—at an unwontedly early age—her learned counsel extraordinary, and whilst she, without any apparent or justifiable cause, refused him remunerative employment in the State, she never allowed him from her side, and in his public life he invariably advised her in the highest interests of the Crown.   From Laneham to Hamlet we see in him the Black Prince.*

When, however, he finally settled down at last to study the law at Gray's Inn, he realised that his flinty Queen-mother intended him to make his own way, and, obedient to the policy which he followed throughout towards her, and which he vainly recommended to the Earl of Essex, he in the end submitted cheerfully to her will,† whilst at the same time he determined, as we have seen, with indomitable Tudor energy and perseverance, to pursue also in secret those great and noble aims " of more delight and no less preferment," which had captivated him in youth, and which were

* See Laneham's letter and Gabriel Harvey's four letters. The Black Prince signifies Prince of Wales.

† " Lady and Queen and Virgin deified
    Be she all sooty black or berry brown,
    She's white as morrow's milk or flakes new blown,
    Sure will he saint her *in his kalendar*."
                                    (HALL: Sat. vii., Bk. I.)

to him the very soul of existence. Despite every obstacle, he strove to perfect every side of his nature, and has shown how he set about it in his delightful essay " Of Nature in Men," in which there is much food to be chewed with advantage concerning fortitude, resolution, and habit. For, as in the " Shepherd's Calendar," he likens both Henry VIII. and Queen Elizabeth to the great god Pan, the all-in-all, the universal, and as he writes of Pan in the " De Augmentis," so he aimed to be himself; and never has the world known a more universal genius than he. Thus, though study of the law came as an uncongenial task to him, he bent himself to it, setting apart, we are to believe, so many hours a day to this duty as a habit, since, as he says, " in studies whatsoever a man commandeth upon himself let him set hours for it; but whatsoever is agreeable to his nature, let him take no care for any set times: for his thoughts will fly to it of themselves."* Thus wisely proportioning his day, allotting a fixed time to the law, remembering always the sage advice of his Queen-mother, the pleasure and zest which difficulty confers upon industry and labour Bacon, the great lawyer and judge, found time for those studies to which his mind naturally flew, and became also Shakespeare, the great poet and philosopher. He thus found time to gratify his innate taste for those higher delights on which his mind remained fixed throughout his life.

We have seen the very decided and unalterable direction in which his taste thus ran to be due recognition and use of the relative functions of the mind and the imagination, reason and verse. His nature, his

* Bacon, Essay " Of Nature in Men."

musical ear, and his inborn and inspired soul, in its pious Baconian nursery, flew to Ovid, to poetry, to rhyme. But he saw that this alone could never help him to climb the giddy heights to which he aspired. Like his Queen-mother, he felt that not musical sounds alone, but sound matter must underlie all useful writing, whether in poetry or prose. Knowledge and experience of nature, rather than of books, can alone ensure beneficial and philanthropic progress. *Science* based on the force of reason must therefore be his instrument. With *this* he must force an entrance into the citadels which hold human nature imprisoned in misery, unable to rise to greater heights through poverty of invention. Thus he advanced to the marriage of Science with Art, which together were to subdue and overcome in some degree the necessities and miseries of humanity, and so climbing steadily and surely up the logical ladder which he built, he arrived at those splendid pronouncements:

(*a*) Science is the interpretation of nature, free as we find it—*i.e.*, by induction, or the "Novum Organum," etc.*

(*b*) Art is nature bound, or nature with man to help† and mould it, by the aid of science and invention and learned experience.

(*c*) "The true and lawful goal of the sciences is none other than this, that human life be endowed with new discoveries and powers" (Robertson, "Novum Organum," p. 280).

* "This science (being of so excellent a use both for the disclosing of nature and abridgement of Art is) therefore placed first, as a common parent" (Robertson, "Philosophical Works of F. Bacon," p. 91).

† "De Augmentis Scientiarum," p. 427.

(*d*) " It is the duty of Art to perfect and exalt nature "
(Robertson, " Advancement of Learning," p. 114).

The mind, in other words, analyses nature, and
discovers and teaches the structural components and
action of things, by reasoned and logical induction,
each part supporting the other. The imagination
seizing hold of the particulars thus disclosed arranges
them in a new order, by deduction gives them a new
direction appropriate to the ends and purposes man
has in view, and so we have a new invention. It may
be a new play based upon a new and deeper analysis
of human nature, or a new gramophone, motor, or
flying machine. His method, as he expressly says,
was to apply to all sciences. (" Nov. Org.," Aph. 127.)

Such, generally, were the philosophical lines upon
which we gather that Bacon's mind was working in
these ten years, from 1583 to the wonderful year
1593,* when he first appeared in his most perfect
motley, as Shakespeare, in his thirty-third year. This
may be gathered from Bacon's philosophical works.
Both with the drama and with philosophy he advanced
slowly and deliberately. He was, as we see in Shakespeare, a great student of perfection. He quotes
Colossians on charity as " the bond of Perfection,"† and mentions the word repeatedly in his essays.

* Gabriel Harvey, Sonnet, " Gorgon, or the Wonderful
Year, 1593."

† Coloss. iii. 14; Bacon, " De Aug.," Book VII., chap. iii.
Robertson, p. 577. He also links Perfection with Time, as
Shakespeare:

　　" Although myself have been an idle truant,
　　　Omitting the sweet benefit of time
　　　To clothe mine age with angel-like perfection."
　　　　　(" Two Gentlemen of Verona," Act II., sc. iv.)

He was, in short, probably as well acquainted with that striking work, the " Scala Perfectionis,"* of Walter Hilton as he was with the " De Imitatione Christi" of Thomas à Kempis. Both deal with the contemplative as apart from the active life. There are known to have been copies in manuscript of both in the lost library of Sion House, still standing, which adjoined his estate at Twickenham†—especially of the three first books of the " De Imitatione," known as the " Musica Ecclesiastica," being rhythmical writing, and by many attributed also to Walter Hilton till recently. One can conceive our Shakespeare in his beloved retirement, as Francis Bacon, poring over such books. They appeal strongly to the ear, and under certain conditions give inexpressible fullness to the mind by the variety of senses which they touch and play upon, and to Bacon-Shakespeare no detail, no particular, was too small, no experience too slight, to be lost or undervalued. All added to the source whence he produced his delightful harmonies. " It is not enough," said he, " for a man only to know himself; for he should consider also of the best way to set himself off to advantage;

" Experience is by industry achieved
And perfected in the swift course of time."
(" Two Gentlemen of Verona," Act. I., sc. iii.)

* The " Scala Perfectionis " of Walter Hilton was " Englished and printed by desire of Margaret (Beaufort) Countess of Richmond and Derby, in W. Caxton's house by Wynkyn de Worde, anno Salutis, 1484." The venerable Margaret herself translated the fourth book of " De Imitatione Christi," from the French into English. (She was in my belief Shakespeare-Bacon's great-great-grandmother.) " Life of Margaret Beaufort," by Caroline Halsted, pp. 99 and 170.

† Hard by Brentford, mentioned in " The Merry Wives of Windsor."

to *disclose and reveal* himself."* He proceeded in all things with measured and dignified footsteps, never hurrying lest he should trip, but, as he said, in all things giving time his due, testing little by little his tender wings, like young birds which be newly crept out of the nest. For no man recognised, as he did that experience needs ripening, and, as the fruit of trees must pass through certain natural processes before it becomes grateful to the taste, so philosophical thought must pass through certain mental processes, such as comparison, elimination, and final judgment, before it is fit to be served up as ripe for public entertainment and use.

Thus gradually also did this divine Orpheus, or settling down at Gray's Inn, commence to develop the English drama. It had received its first impetus from his Queen-mother. Not until after many attempts advancing with infinite patience stage by stage under various names, did he bring his song to that wonderful degree of perfection which he thought worthy to dignify with the name of Shakespeare. It is generally assumed that this name was evolved from that of Shakspere of Stratford, the actor. But nothing is more certain than that he had some such title in his mind long before Shakspere was known, telling in the "Shepherd's Calendar" in 1579 how Pallas, on issuing from the head of Jupiter, "Shaked her spear" at Vulcan, and on the frontispiece to the "Hermit Tale" we read:

> "Behold (good Queen) *a poet with a speare*,
>   Strange sights well mark't are understood the better.
> A soldier with pencil in his ear,
>   With pen to fight and sword to write a letter."

---

* "De Aug.," Book VIII., chap. ii.; Robertson, p. 599.

PALLAS ATHENE
The Vatican (see p. 299).

Facing p. 22

And in the "Faerie Queene" of "Spenser" (so-called):

> "Yet is not all of gold that golden seems,
> Nor all good Knights that *shake the spear* and shield."

Again, in the "Argenis" of John Barclay, describing the adored Pallas: "Her *speare* of Gold, about which he rayes shining through the brightness of the mettle, made the common people often affirm that the Goddesse did *shake* it" (p. 71, translation of Sir Robert Le Grys). And again, on p. 76:

> "Her armes, her armes she threat'ning *shakes;* her *speare*
> Sounds on her golden Shield."

Probably the poetic idea of the spear of Quirinus and of Pallas, the goddess of invention, early impressed his young mind, and contact with Shakspere the actor, who was a member of Burbage's company, crystallised it for appropriate use.*

This, however, came later. The genius of this nameless man for the drama went through many stages ere that was reached, and went hand in hand with improvements in, and study of, the English language and verse, as gleaned from the pages of Gascoigne's "Instructions," Webbe's "Discourse," and Puttenham's "Arte" of English Poesie. I have already referred to his juvenile efforts at dramatic writing before he went to France. His travels in no way diminished his enthusiasm, for we find Gabriel Harvey writing to him as "Immerito": "I suppose thou wilt

---

* Similarly in "The Tempest":
> "The strong based promontory
> Have I made shake; and by the spurs plucked out."
>
> (Act V., sc. i.)

go nigh hand shortly to send my Lord of Leicester
or my Lord of Warwick, Vawsis (Vaux) or my Lord
Rich's players, or some other fresh upstart comediantes
unto me for some new devised interlude or some malt-
conceived comedy fit for the Theater, or some other
painted stage whereat thou and thy lively copesmates
in London may laugh their mouths and bellies full for
pence or two pence apiece." He addresses him, as
said, half humorously as " Il Magnifico Segnior,'
" Immerito-Benevolo," for he was a young courtier,
dating a letter from Leicester House, and the
Earl of Leicester's players were then acting at the
only " Theater " (except perhaps the Curtain), which
London then possessed—other, that is, than those
courtyards of certain inns where plays were staged.
Leicester, his brother Ambrose Dudley, Earl of Warwick, Lord Vaux, and Lord Rich, the husband of
Penelope, Philip Sidney's " Stella," all were members of
that Court circle in which Shakespeare-Bacon moved,
and to Lady Elizabeth Vaux is dedicated the F. B.
translation of the " De Imitatione," with its unmistakably Baconian and euphuistic preface, which is so
deeply interesting that an extract can hardly be
omitted; " perfection " is again his theme:

" Of all the books which are written that treat of
the spirit and Christian perfection, the holy Scripture
excepted, it is inferior to none, if it excelleth not all.
No book hath been more approved by general consent,
none more often printed and translated into diverse
languages, none more esteemed, commended, yea
commanded also by the chief Maisters of Spirit of some
religious orders to be often read by everyone in private
and once a week publicly to all. *So full of sweet sense
is this genuine flower that the most spiritual bees*

*nay daily draw from thence great plenty of celestial honey."**

So distinctly does this last characteristic passage, underlined by me, bear what Bishop Tenison, writing in 1670 his " Baconiana," calls the strength, design, and colour of Bacon, that I give below for comparison an extract from Bacon's own " De Augmentis ":

" For he that shall attentively observe how the mind gathers this excellent dew of knowledge like to that the poet speaketh of—' Aërei mellis cælestia dona ' (Celestial gifts of heavenly honey)—for the sciences themselves are extracted out of particular instances, partly natural, partly artificial as the *flowers of the field* and the garden—shall find that the mind doth of herself by nature manage and act an induction much better than logicians describe it."†

Compare, again, the following " Author's Preface " to the earliest translation into English of Bandello's " Historie of Hamlet," 1608 (Shakespeare Library Edition):

" I have ventured to visit the History of Denmark that it may serve for an example of virtue and contentment to our nation (whom I especially seek to please), and for whose satisfaction *I have not left any power whatsoever* untasted, from whence I have not drawn *the most perfect and delicate honey*, not caring for

* Compare " Novum Organum," Book I., Aphorism 95; " Philosophical Works of F. Bacon," J. M. Robertson, p. 258: The reasoners resemble spiders, who make cobwebs out of their own substance. But the bee takes a middle course: it gathers its materials of the garden and the field, but digests it by a power of its own. Not unlike this is the true business of philosophy."

† " De Aug.," Book V., chap. i.; J. M. Robertson's " Philosophical Works of F. Bacon," p. 503.

the ingratitude of the present time that leaveth (and as it were rejecteth) without recompense such as serve the commonwealth and by their travel and diligence honour their country."

The dedicatory letter to Lady Vaux ends thus:

" The practice of that which this book doth teach covereth the soul with the rich garment of grace, and adorneth it with the splendent pearls of Evangelica perfection, which maketh us more pleasing in the sigh of God than the decking of all earthly jewels make the fairest lady in the Kingdom where you are, appea beautiful in the eyes of men."*

The likeness of this to the metaphorical style of Euphues and Queen Elizabeth can hardly escape notice, and the letter, which does not appear in the earlier editions, is signed:

> " The first of January 1620
>> " Yours ever assured
>>> " F. B."

Thus do Immerito, Bacon, and Euphues all betra the same mind, the mind also of the author of " Rome and Juliet," as well as of " Love's Labour's Lost " an of " Venus and Adonis "—that is, of Shakespeare. I is under the names of John Lyly the pseudo-author of " Euphues " that Shakespeare, on his return from h second tour of travel abroad in 1582, also continue his study of the drama. It is as the young bird newl crept out from his nest again that he proceeded, ad vancing ever gradually from the interlude and masqu to the classic form of drama; and for informatio

* Compare this again so euphuistic metaphor with the specimen of Queen Elizabeth's youthful style given on p. xv of the Introduction.

concerning him and his counterfeits, we turn naturally to his very special and singular friend, Gabriel Harvey, he "so entirely and extraordinary loved," and to whom he confided his innermost secrets and woes. The famous correspondence between Shakespeare-Immerito and Gabriel, carefully examined, reveals uniformly the same phenomenon. In alike the cases of Gascoigne, Lyly, Greene, and Nashe, whilst he reveals the true characters and lives of the real men, he extols in like manner the writings of the real author, saying, for example: " I once bemoaned the decayed and blasted state of M. Gascoigne; who wanted not some commendable parts of conceit: but unhappy M. Gascoigne, how Lordly happy in comparison of most unhappy M. Greene."* Again, " Signor Immerito " (mark the Signor)—" for that name will be remembered—was then, and is still, my affectionate friend, one that could very well abide Gascoigne's 'Steel Glass.' "† Gascoigne, Immerito, Greene, and Nashe, whom he styles he "butler of Pembroke," beside others, he thus inks in his own mind as mere false names for the same author, whom he admires and ever again addresses and exhorts impersonally—e.g., "Good sweet Orator, be a divine poet indeed: and use heavenly eloquence indeed: and employ thy golden talent amounting dance indeed, and with heroical Cantoes honor right virtue, . . . not according to the fantastical mould of Aretine or Rabelais,‡ but according to the fine model of Orpheus, Homer, Pindarus, etc. . . . Such lively

* Second letter of Gabriel Harvey; four letters.
† Third letter of Gabriel Harvey; four letters.
‡ This is the same advice as Hall gives in his " Satires " concerning Venus and Adonis.

15

springs of streaming eloquence: and such right Olym-
pical hills of amounting wit: I cordially recommend to
the dear lover of the Muses: and namely to the pro-
fessional sons of the same; *Edmond Spencer, Richard
Stanihurst, Abraham Fraunce, Thomas Watson, Samuel
Daniell, Thomas Nashe,* and the rest:* whom I affec-
tionately thank for their studious endeavours com-
mendably employed in enriching and polishing their
native tongue, never so furnished or embellished as of
late. For *I dare not name the honourabler sons and
nobler daughters of the sweetest and divinest Muse
that ever sang in English or other language:* for fear
of that suspicion I abhor: and their own most delectable
and delicious exercises (the fine handywork of excellent
nature and excellenter *art combined*) speak incom-
parably more than I am able to insinuate."† He
alludes thus clearly to the courtly crew of makers, who,
as Puttenham says, concealed themselves. He, too,
dare not give their true names. The names he does
give are Shakespeare-Bacon's pseudonyms.

John Lyly he mentions contemptuously elsewhere
as " a dapper and deft companion, a pert, conceited
youth that had gathered together a few pretty sentences
and could handsomely *help* Euphues . . . sometime
the fiddle stick of Oxford now the babble of London."
The real Euphues whom Lyly helped as master of the

* All apparently pseudonyms of Shakespeare-Bacon or
school.

† Third letter of Gabriel Harvey's " four letters." It is
noteworthy that he here admits having matter to *insinuate*,
and easy to see that the insinuation refers to the buyer of
motleys, Shakespeare—that is, Francis Bacon—who made a
study of nature and art his own, saying " the Art itself is
Nature."

children actors of Paul's, and by lending his name to the plays they acted, was, as we see it, Shakespeare-Bacon. The six Court plays first published anonymously* are mostly written in praise of Elizabeth, of Leicester's love, and of Shakespeare-Bacon's own devoted duty to the Queen. Alexander, in Campaspe, is her favourite hero. The " Galatea " appeared first about the same time as the " Galatea of Cervantes "—which again deals in eclogues, and prose, with the lovers of Queen Elizabeth—and in this play the device of women disguised in boys' clothes, so beloved by Shakespeare, first finds place.† " Sappho and Phao " is again a Queen's love story, and, as John Lyly, Shakespeare touches his highest note in the pathetic platonic and filial love of Endymion (who represents himself) for Cynthia the Queen, and is of its kind, when thus understood, one of the most beautiful idylls in any language. Philologically, moreover, it is easily identified with Bacon's own letters, as also are Lyly's fragmentary letters and petitions.

True to his resolve to try his wings little by little, these Court plays are as simple in language as in plot. They are the earliest serious dramatic attempts of the still studious Shakespeare. As he himself grows, and his own knowledge of mankind grows, so proportionately his knowledge and mastery of language grows, as, bit by bit, assisted by conference with his secret areopagus, he builds it up, and publishes it as Webbe's Discourse on Poetry," and the anonymous " Art of

* Published later together by Edward Blount, who also published the First Folio of Shakespeare plays.
† This device is conspicuous in the " Two Gentlemen of Verona," which is put at about the same time, 1582.

Poesie," attributed, admittedly without sufficient
reason, to an almost unknown " Puttenham."

As Lyly the dramatist, Shakespeare the Prince-poet
the young courtier of Gabriel Harvey, the son of
England's Queen, living at Gray's Inn, condemned to
study the law, devoted those hours not set apart for
the law to those greater delights, which he knew were
peculiar not only to himself, but to his Queen-mother
who, he says in one of Lyly's petitions, had instructed
him to aim all his courses at the stage.   Of their rare
beauty and the impression they made, some idea can
be formed from the words of Edward Blount, who, in
publishing the collected edition of the six Court plays
says: " It can be no dishonour to listen to this poet's
music whose tunes alighted in the ears of a great and
ever famous Queen.   His invention was so curiously
strung that Eliza's Court held his notes in admiration.
As Lyly, Shakespeare confined himself scrupulously to
Ovid and the classical mythology of the "Meta
morphoses": Pan, Syrinx, Echo, Apollo, Diana
Cynthia.   He even goes so far as to make one of his
characters quote a satirical paraphrase of the line
used by Dr. Rawley in his biography, who says of him
" as if it had been natural to him to use good forms
as Ovid spoke of this faculty of versifying:

> ' Et quod tentabam scribere, versus erat.' "

So in "Endymion" we read, as given on p. 53:

> (Sir Tophas): " Quidquid conabar dicere versus erat."
> (Epi): " I feel all Ovid de arte amandi."

Shakespeare, in short, thus disguised his style
following Ovid as Lyly, and adopting the heroic style
as Spenser with Homeric similes.   He thus rose to

legrees from unassuming comedy to tragedy, and
ouched his highest note (outside Shakespeare) in his
notley of Marlowe. Then he started afresh. He had
now reached perfection in expression, sufficient to
attempt those heights which he had dreamed of
assaulting in his young days, and he assumed the
famous name of " Shakespeare "—*i.e.*, Shaker of the
spear of Pallas Athene, the Goddess of Invention,
Wisdom and Power—under which he later issued the
complete collection of his best conceptions in the great
First Folio of 1623—the most perfect works of art
moulded by the hand of man.

CHAPTER XVI

SHAKESPEARE AND THE GREAT YEAR 1593

THE time had now arrived when England's throstle—the sweetly singing throstle of " Romeo and Juliet "—felt that he had tuned his beautiful voice to that high degree of clearness and perfection which must give it precedence over everything that man had heard heretofore. The spirited but modest little bird which fifteen years before, had newly crept out of its nest as " Immerito," resolved " by little at first to try it tender wings," had now become an accomplished singer soon to win the applause of all mankind. In the year 1593 Shakespeare-Bacon reached his thirty-third year known amongst his contemporaries as " the great year 1593."* It was the year in which, casting away all other pseudonyms, the great philosopher, called whilst living Francis Bacon, appeared secretly before the world as " Shakespeare," the author of " Venus and Adonis," the sweetest songster ever heard in any clime, the most human, the most divine. His voice, the voice of nature free and noble, erring and bound, sweet and glorious, sad, desperate, uncontrollable and tragic, can already be recognised in the plays of Marlowe, which are partly written according to his method, as afterwards described in the " Plan of the Great Instauration." " Nature "—" natural

* See Gabriel Harvey's sonnet, referred to above, " Gorgon or the Wonderful Year, 1593."

and "unnatural"—is clearly visible before us, for example, in Marlowe's "Edward II.";* whilst "The Massacre of Paris" deals with contemporaneous French history immediately preceding the period of "Love's Labour's Lost," when Bacon was in France, and many of the characters are the same, including the King of Navarre, Marguerite de Valois, and Dumaine; also Bacon's friend du Plessis (Pleshé) is prominent. But the following passage in this play is eloquent above all, when we bear in mind what has been said above, concerning the probable travels in France of Shakespeare-Bacon in connection with the Jesuitical plots against Queen Elizabeth. It is the King of France who speaks, saying of the Duke of Guise, who had just been murdered:

> " This is the traitor that hath spent my gold,†
> In making foreign wars, and cruel broils.
> Did he not draw *a sort of English priest*,
> *From Douay to the seminary at Rheims*,
> *To hatch forth treason 'gainst their natural queen ?*"

This is true history. It was during the treasonable plots that followed the removal of the English Jesuitical college from Douay to Rheims that Shakespeare-Bacon took his seat as M.P. This English Jesuitical College at Douay—to which Oxford Catholics were sent—was moved from Douay to Rheims‡ as a preliminary to the attempt of their leaders, Fathers Parsons and Campion, which was—as I have shown reason to believe—the

---

* See p. 285.

† Bacon's Apothegm 149 says: " They would say of the Duke of Guise, Henry, that *had sold* and oppignerated all his patrimony . . . that he was the greatest usurer of France, because all his state was in obligations."

‡ Froude, vol. xi., p. 51.

cause of young Francis Bacon-Shakespeare's being sent secretly abroad on some service to the Queen, in his motley of " Watch candle," in 1582, before the fragmentary play "The Massacre of Paris"* appeared, and immediately before his entry into Parliament.

To what extent, however, Shakespeare was indebted to others for assistance in attaining his sweet pre-eminence—to what extent he may have designed or coloured or strengthened works, which appeared in their name—is a matter which can, of course, never be accurately gauged, any more than we can draw an exact line as to how much Raphael or Rubens owed to the handiwork of their pupils. As these great artists, thus assisted, painted whole galleries of pictures, so Shakespeare-Bacon has been said to have written a whole library of books.† It is probable, indeed, that all worked together at times under the master's direction, according to his method and dictation,‡ and certain it is that, as Bishop Tenison wrote in 1679, the hand of Bacon can always be traced by the design, colour, and strength of any book, by anyone skilled in his work, just as that of a great artist can; while in matter his difference with Aristotle concerning the affections is always a guide. Research indicates of a

* The date of this play is uncertain, but the whole period of the Marlowe plays lies between 1583 at the earliest and 1593. It is probable that " The Massacre of Paris " (a fragment) was one of the earliest attempts under that name. The fact that it is a fragment is ominous. So much left by Bacon was " unfinished."

† J. M. Robertson, " Philosophical Works of F. Bacon," p. xvi.

‡ Bacon had a great admiration for Cæsar's said capacity of dictating to five persons at once.

certainty that Shakespeare-Bacon was the centre and
dominus of a secret school of at first mainly courtly
poets and authors, whose names Gabriel Harvey dare
not mention and who, Puttenham says, concealed their
names and doings. He was the Apollo, the Orpheus,
the Ephorus, of this little coterie, which at first called
itself the Areopagus.* He presided at it, and as we
know, from both Ben Jonson and Rawley, his judgment not only was perfect, but he was as good a listener
in conversation as he was lively in repartee. " Neither
was he one that would appropriate the speech wholly
to himself, or delight to outvie others, but leave a
liberty to the co-assessors to take their turns." What
a President of such a debating society! Our Shakespeare shone in this as in all else. As Bacon, moreover,
he dwells insistently on *conference* as an aid to study
and knowledge surpassing almost everything, and he
never omitted to make use of anything that might
help to perfect, or add to, his knowledge and power,
or help reveal his best self.

Now Puttenham, although like Gabriel Harvey he
conceals the names of some of this courtly crew,
nevertheless names a goodly few, at the head of
them giving the Earl of Oxford, all the rest being
also well established historic friends of Francis Bacon.
Oxford and Lyly—whom we identify as Shakespeare-
Bacon—were, in short, very closely linked together and
confederates during this " Endymion " phase of our
Prince-poet. Oxford had rooms in the Savoy, nearly
opposite to his father-in-law, Lord Burghley, in 1578,
and in the dedication of " Euphues " the author, Lyly,

* There is some reason to believe this was merged in the
Rosicrucian order.

says he was " sent to a nobleman of great worth who with great love brought him up for a year." This no doubt was the Earl, whose actors he trained. Oxford was a prime favourite with Her Majesty the Queen, a bold and fearless swordsman, apt to duel, and a good dancer. Such a courtier would not fail to do his utmost to shine as a patron of the drama, and to such a man of all others Her Majesty would be likely, under the very peculiar circumstances, to commend her son. Thus Shakespeare-Bacon as John Lyly dedicated " Euphues " to the Earl of Oxford. Both were wards of Lord Burghley as Master of the Court of Wards; Oxford was also his son-in-law, and Francis Bacon was ostensibly his nephew. In fact, by marriage Francis Bacon-Shakespeare and the Earl of Oxford were ostensibly cousins, and it came about quite naturally, so far as men could see, that the Earl took Shakespeare-Bacon, as Francis Bacon, under his wing. At that same time it appears that he took also the original John Lyly, as his secretary, and under that name Shakespeare thus wrote the Court plays. These were presented, both at the Court and Blackfriars, which was a private theatre. Another link in this connection was Arthur Golding, already mentioned, who was uncle to the Earl of Oxford, and who dedicated his Ovid's " Metamorphoses " to the Earl of Leicester from Cecil House. He also wrote a little thin book of a few pages on that earthquake* which Shakespeare-Bacon-Immerito discusses with Gabriel Harvey. Thus the Earl of Oxford was in the forefront of the courtier who helped promote the drama. Like him, however

* See also " Papp with a Hatchet," about " the natural causes of an Earthquake."

the Earls of Southampton, Derby, Essex, and Rutland, Lords Buckhurst and Vaux, Cecil, Sir Philip Sidney, Sir Walter Raleigh, and Fulke Greville, all exhibited, as did the whole Court, a deep interest in poetry and the drama. But only think what a hotch-potch and patchwork the English drama would have presented as the result of combined but unguided authorship of such.

It is the unity, the one-hood, of the works written under the pseudonyms of men who helped and of others who sold, or allowed their names to be used by Shakespeare-Bacon—the sameness of design, strength, and colour—that identifies them as the original work of one and the same man. Add to this his adoption of the heathen god Pan himself as especially representing unity, the all-in-all, the universal, and little else is wanted to fix upon him the guiding mind, the master, who alone could breathe into his work, that divine spirit which God had alone breathed into him.

A prolonged discussion as to the merits of the evidence which has been adduced to show Shakespeare-Bacon's mind as revealed in his many pseudonyms is not, however, within the province of this work. The notes in my possession agree with the researches of others, but cover a much wider and more general field. Abandoning a mere comparison of mind, design, and colour in various works, Mr. Bhutshenshu, it will be seen, has dived into independent channels, searching to see how far the authorship of those works can be connected with the *life* and ancestry of Bacon-Shakespeare. He found it to agree wholly and altogether at every step. He traced Shakespeare-Bacon from the time when he began to think—when he was so intimately connected with the great translators—to the doubtful identity of Laneham and Immerito and so on in succession, and found that the growth and evolution of his mind fitted in exactly with the gradual growth of the drama, as it advanced stage by stage, from "The Hermit" at Woodstock to the plays of John Lyly, under which the mighty Prince-poet essayed his tender wings, then to Greene, Peele, and Marlowe, till at last, after ten years of original experiment, feeling fully fledged, he rose aloft as with the sweet voice of the throstle borne on the strong wings of an eagle, under the name of William Shakespeare. Whatever else may be thought of "Venus and Adonis," this cannot be denied, that it is the highest art put forth in a garb of the highest culture, and although it may seem too much "Nature unadorned," it is nature—nature painted with a master's hand—and Shakespeare knew it, or would not have put his name to it. As to its being "the first heir of my invention"* of a young man, this expression might pass the observation of the minds of the uninitiated. "Unpolished lines," as he modestly calls them, they certainly are not. It requires but little thought to see that such perfection of language and touch, in a tongue just emerging from barbarity, could never have been reached by any but a man, who had bestowed a painstaking study on words with a view to giving the greatest beauty of expression to all that is most human, ravishing, and sacred in nature.

In a word, as I have said, Shakespeare-Bacon felt that he had now reached command of language as perfect as even he dared hope for, and now he felt

* Dedicatory letter to the Earl of Southampton.

sure of the strength of his wings. He had no more
need for models. He had moulded a style and language
of his own, more superlatively beautiful than anything
before known, unless it be Homer, and henceforth he
shines forth in English verse and drama under one
only name as Shakespeare, "the greatest genius of all
times and nations."*

I propose, therefore, to conclude for the present,
limiting myself only to one passage at this period, in
the known life of Francis Bacon, which to some is alone
conclusive proof of his identity with Shakespeare.
The previous decade from 1582 to 1592 had been
dedicated to two principal objects: to perfect his
own genius for expression, by the study of language fit
to give meet form to his experience, whether as a man,
an orator, a philosopher or poet, and further to win
the Queen by his assiduity and devotion to her service.
This may be deemed the period of "Endymion," whose
expressions are the same as those used by Bacon in
his letters, so expressive of his sadness and despair at
not receiving princely recognition. "Endymion" appeared early in 1592 when Bacon, our Shakespeare,
was writing to Lord Burghley: "The contemplative
planet carrieth me away wholly," and to the Earl of
Essex on March 30, 1593 (when he appeared as Shakespeare), he writes: "I will . . . retire myself with a
couple of men to Cambridge and there spend my life
in my studies and contemplations, without looking
back." Such was the bitter mood which produced
"Venus and Adonis," and is re-echoed in "Endymion,"
who says: "What company have I used but con-

* Alfred Weber, Austrian Bacon-Shakespeare Society. See
Baconiana, March, 1924.

templation ? Whom have I wondered at but thee ? (the Queen, Cynthia). . . . *Have I not spent my golden years in hopes*, waxing old with wishing nothing but thy love ? With Tellus, fair Tellus (the world) have I dissembled . . . from this contemplation if I be not driven, I shall live of all men the most content . . . *such a difference hath the gods set between our estates that all must be duty*, loyalty, and reverence. . . . My un-spotted thoughts, my languishing body, my discon-tented life, let them obtain by princely favour, that which to challenge they must not presume on by wishing impossibilities."*

With precisely similar despondency and with identical language we find Bacon-Shakespeare, full also of dis-content, writing at the very same time to Lord Burghley: " I wax somewhat ancient: 31 years is somewhat of sand in the hour glass,"† and to the Lord Keeper Puckering: " It might please her sacred Majesty to think what my end should be, if it were not *duty and all duty*."‡

Our Shakespeare, our Bacon, our Prince-poet, and Prince of poets, had at this time failed in the two chief objects of his earthly desires: first, to obtain princely recognition, which he had so long, so eagerly hoped for, and failing that, to obtain at least some office of State which might secure him a competence, and help him in his great projects for the reform of thought and the generation of a new philosophy founded on the logical study of nature.

* John Lyly, " Endymion."
† Spedding, " Life and Letters of Bacon," attributed to 1592.
‡ *Ibid.*

It was then, early in the year 1592, that Anthony, the dearly-loved foster-brother of Bacon-Shakespeare, returned from a twelve years' sojourn in the South of France. There he had acted as agent to Francis, keeping him in touch with both the men of foreign nations and their politics. Living now at Marseilles, now at Bordeaux, but principally at Montauban, whence he paid visits to the King of Navarre at Pau in Bearne, on the very borders of Aragon in Spain, he contracted very close relations with that country in particular. On his return he joined Francis and the Earl of Essex; and together, as Mr. Spedding points out, they formed a little foreign office, designed to advise the Queen on foreign affairs, especially Spanish affairs. No stranger triumvirate ever existed, if the facts as they are now gradually dawning should be established—the Queen's two sons and Anthony Bacon: Shakespeare, the myriad-minded and universal, but ostensibly a private subject; the young Earl of Essex, quite inexperienced; and Anthony Bacon, another private subject. Or was this a triumvirate of three brothers thus formed to undermine the influence of Lord Burghley and transfer it to the Earl ? Sir Thomas Bodley, whom Essex approached, would have nothing to do with it. Feeling himself between two stools, he retired from the Queen's service, and set to work on his famous library. There were clearly too many wheels within wheels, and he did not know whither they might lead him. Meanwhile Anthony and the Earl of Essex saw clearly that, everything else apart, Francis, the rising star, was not receiving the encouragement which all London recognised to be his due. His wisdom and executive power had been tested

on Committees in Parliament. His high reputation as
a master of law was admitted on all hands, even before
he ever appeared in court to plead as a barrister.
Deeply as he resented having to study the law—
grudging time taken away from things more congenial
and important—he had nevertheless overcome all
dislike to it, and triumphed over his objections. Yet
preferment, any office under the Crown, was denied
him from first to last by the Queen who had shown
such deep interest in his genius from youth. Poor
Endymion ! Cynthia was obdurate. She would not
grudge him a kiss to save his life, but there her grace
ended.* Shakespeare must fend for himself, and he
was fully equal to it. He had weighed his services.
They had been despised. He had been told to " aim
all my courses at the revels, for which these ten years
I have attended with unwearied patience," walking,
we guess, all those years backwards and forwards to
and from Gray's Inn by Hatton Wall to St. John's
to witness rehearsals at the office of Revels, devise
scenery, and study the effects of candle-light.† Ten

* See " Endymion," by John Lyly.
  † The quarto edition, 1622, of " Othello " was handed to
the publisher by Sir George Buck, Master of Revels, whose
office at St. John's was ten minutes' walk from Gray's Inn.
We have thus a very good indication as to how the plays
found their way into print. Buck himself was a poet of
mystery, and also wrote the Appendix to Howes's " Annales.'
It is remarkable how many Shakespearean incidents are to be
found in Howes's " Annales," written under a promise to
Whitgift, and in which the name of Sir Francis Bacon stands
eighth in the list of poets. The suspicion that Bacon and
Buck as well as Sackford collaborated in writing these annals
has thus substantial foundation. See Madame von Künow's
" Last of the Tudors."

ears added to 1582 would be 1592, just the period we
re at, and he repeated this later, saying: " Thirteen
ears your Highness' servant but yet nothing . . . a
housand hopes but all nothing, a hundred promises
ut yet nothing* . . . thus casting the inventory of
iy friends, hopes, promises and times, the *summa
talis* amounteth to just nothing." Thus might a
rivileged son write to his royal Queen-mother, but
ot a mere theatre manager—a witty son to a witty
nother, whose humour he well knew.

But Her Majesty was adamant. Even when he
emoved Burghley's last objection, that he had never
ractised at the Bar, she refused to grant him place,
1 spite of the sensation he created in court, as alone
Shakespeare could, spangling his speech with unusual
ords which " were rather gracious for their propriety
han strange for their novelty." How this scene
eminds us of Portia! Shakespeare pleading, a con-
ealed Prince of the Realm, in the Court of King's
Bench, which then sat in Westminster Hall; judges and
nen of fame crowding to see him, and the respect
hown to him by the judge attracting the attention
f the beholders—respect which, " although it was
xtraordinary, was well noted but not envied."

Probably our Prince-poet knew well enough before
.e attempted it that it would be vain, for the Queen
emained unmoved, and he had already taken the bull
y the horns some time early in 1592. He reached the
ge of thirty-one that year, and shortly after addressed
o Lord Burghley what, from the point of view we are
ow considering, must appear one of the most mar-

* John Lyly's second petition, a good specimen both of
Bacon's wit and the freedom he took with the Queen.

16

vellous letters ever written by a great man. He ha
spent ten years of valuable time, given, we believe
every hour of it, with *unwearied patience*, to the per
fecting of his talents in every possible direction. Openl
he had shone in Parliament and Law Court. Secretl
he had spent hours on those studies of greater delight
the perfection of language and other purposes, to whic
he had dedicated himself; and still, so far as concerne
his own duty, he could say: " I am as far from bein
altered in devotion towards her as I am from distrus
that she will be altered in opinion towards me whe
she knoweth me better." Her behaviour towards hir
had, however, now convinced him that he must loo
out for himself, though, " if her Majesty command m
in any particular I shall be ready to do her willin
service." As office of the State was denied him, h
would turn the fullness of his mind toward those othe
purposes which so possessed him. He was thirty-on
He had wasted no time. He had trained himself in th
highest degree. He knew that he had abundance c
matter with *aliquid salis* to put before mankind " fc
the benefit of the state and society of man," and h
knew, above all, that he could dress it up in languag
such as no man before him had used, or attempted
saving always Homer. He felt that he was no long
a young bird newly crept out of its nest. He kne
his powers. He cared no longer for Burghley or anyor
else, saving only the Queen, and he let himself g
with the *naïveté* of genius in tomes as solemn, as we no
see, that such an occasion deserved. After expressir
his devotion and commending himself to his Lordshi
he proceeds (as before quoted): " I wax now somewh;
ancient; one and thirty years is a great deal of sar

ı the hour glass." Then, pointing out that " I account
ıy ordinary course of study and meditation to be
ıore painful than most parts of action are," he declares
is mind " to serve her Majesty, *not as a man born
nder Sol*, that loveth honour; . . . but as a man born
nder an excellent sovereign, that deserveth the dedica-
ıon of all men's abilities." Finally, after expressing
is desire to deserve well of his Lordship, " to whom he
ı tied by all duties both of a good patriot and of an
nworthy kinsman," he comes to the point. It is
hakespeare's voice he uses now, who wrote:

> " Our court shall be a little academe
> Still and contemplative in living art."

He is thinking philosophy, and has in his mind the
ew school he means to form; as he pens the lines:
Lastly, I confess that I have as vast contemplative
ıds as I have moderate civil ends: for I HAVE TAKEN
ıLL KNOWLEDGE TO BE MY PROVINCE."* He is pro-
aiming himself PAN, and cares not what may be
ıought. " This, whether it be curiosity or vainglory
ı nature, or (if one may take it favourably) *philan-
ropia*, is so fixed in my mind that it cannot be re-
oved. And I do easily see that place of any reason-
ıle countenance doth bring commandment of more
ts than of a man's own; which is a thing I greatly
ıect." With that he flung down his ultimatum.
cretly he had longed for many helpers, as Alexander
d helped Aristotle. He sought no place to which
yone nearer† to his Lordship might aspire. He
ıyed for " *means‡* and occasions to be added to my

* *I.e.*, History, *Poesie*, and Philosophy.
† *E.g.*, Robert Cecil.   ‡ Compare Sonnet CXI., p. 253.

faithful desire to do you service." But "if you Lordship will not carry me on, I will not do as Anaxagoras did, who reduced himself with contemplatio into voluntary poverty, but this I will do—I will se the inheritance I have and purchase some lease quick revenue, or some office of gain that shall b executed by deputy, and so give over all care for servic *and become* SOME SORRY BOOKMAKER, or a true pionee in that mine of truth, which (he said) lay so deep."

"He would become some sorry bookmaker." Autho ship was not the thing at Court. He would cut himse adrift. He would henceforth go his own way as a tru pioneer of truth—and from that time forward th famous plays pour forth,* at first anonymously, whic were afterwards collected in the great First Folio, the masterpieces of **William Shakespeare,** and pul lished contemporaneously† with the "Great Instaur tion" of Francis Bacon.

Marlowe died on June 1, 1593, and "Venus ar Adonis" appeared the same year with the new nan of William Shakespeare, as in turn "the first heir my invention," just as "Euphues" and the "She herd's Calendar" had been produced ten years earli Each was, in fact, only a new departure by the sar man. Thus of Marlowe one biographer writes: "Duri the six years which elapsed between his quitti Cambridge and his death we know literally nothi of him except that he *must have composed* the wor above enumerated; that he had the evil reputation being a free-liver and free-thinker; that he tried

---

* One or two had appeared before.

† "Novum Organum," 1620; "De Augmentis," 16 "First Folio of Plays," 1623.

To the Reader.

This Figure, that thou here feeſt put,
    It was for gentle Shakeſpeare cut;
Wherein the Grauer had a ſtrife
    with Nature, to out-doo the life:
O, could he but haue drawne his wit
    As well in braſſe, as he hath hit
Hisface; the Print would then ſurpaſſe
    All, that was euer writ in braſſe.
But, ſince he cannot, Reader, looke
    Not on his Picture, but his Booke.

                                    B. I.

THE DROESHOUT PORTRAIT, 1623

Note the coat is part back, part front.   Back-Front is anagram for Fr. Bacon, Kt.

MO NITI MELIO RA

Honble Francisc.⁹ Bacon.⁹ Baro de Veru:
lam Vice-Comes S.^{ett} Albani, mortuus 9° Aprilis,
Anno Dñi. 1626. Annoq, Ætat 66.

fortune upon the stage. The curtain is for a moment lifted, but it is only to show him in the agonies of a violent death."* What if, instead of composing them, he merely lent his name to them? Little more is known, whether of Lyly, Greene, Peele, Marlowe, Spenser, Cervantes, or Shakspere of Stratford. They were all men who were born in obscurity, lived in obscurity, and died in obscurity, whilst the little that is known of them shows, that they mostly lived in very doubtful company, or filled very insignificant offices. On the other hand, the works that appeared in their name show the steady evolution of one mind, gradually moulding the tongue and material with which it has to work, advancing stage by stage, to that perfection and pre-eminence which all men of all nations associate, without envy, with the name of Shakespeare, the great inventor of the great plays, the great prophet of the wonderful inventions by which modern man is surrounded, who left, lest we forget, his name and memory to the next ages and to foreign nations, not even mentioning his own.

* Lieutenant-Colonel Francis Cunningham, introductory notice to the works of Christopher Marlowe.

CHAPTER XVII

SHAKESPEARE'S LIFE—CONCLUSION

My endeavour to trace and depict the early life and character of the youthful Shakespeare, as it is now gradually unfolding itself, under the research of earnest men and women of all nations deeply interested in doing justice to him, from England to the Antipodes— here comes to an end.* Howsoever I may have erred innocently in detail, whether in imagination or judgment, I hope that I have at least drawn the portrait of the rise of a great man—call him, if you will, Shakespeare, as he might have been—something more than a yokel out of whose mind our littérateurs would have us believe that the great plays leapt forth, like Pallas from the brain of Jupiter, "*ready made.*" Perhaps it would be more correct to claim having unfolded the nurture, education, and environment of a man of great genius, whose own unrivalled perseverance and suffering made him all that Shakespeare-Bacon grew to be†— *i.e.*, Bacon as the *natural* counterpart of great Shakespeare. I draw the line at his approach to maturity. I make no attempt here to portray the active life of

* I refer the reader to Madame von Künow's " Last of the Tudors."

† " Some allege, they travel to learn wit . . . that wit, which is thereby to be perfected or made staid, is nothing but *experientia longa malorum*, the experience of many evils " (" The Unfortunate Traveller," T. Nashe, p. 94, ed. by H. F. B. Brett-Smith).

his divinely inspired yet human and erring being. He was moulded by the world against his will into a great lawyer, judge, statesman, and Member of Parliament. He was a man who in his life played many parts, but I have limited my attention to the growth and promise of the bud, instead of attempting to describe the beautiful rose, as Shakespeare calls his muse—the rose which also so often suffers from the storms it has to face, but is nevertheless a rose.

The point is that so beautiful a rose could not grow without culture, so brilliant a light cannot have burst forth spontaneously, from parents wholly undistinguished, and without any visible education or favourable environment or contact in youth with great spirits.* A rare combination of advantages and opportunities alone could produce results so sublime, and cultivate faculties so varied, as are displayed in the great plays—knowledge of history, the law, horticulture, and men and women of every degree of life; breathing of success not only in a contemplative, but in an active career, in a life providing "*public* means, which *public* manners breeds";† the life to which Shakespeare's sonnets tell us he was condemned, and which we know Bacon entered upon with dislike.

Lest, however, I be thought to have exaggerated the love and literature and learning of those now believed to have been Shakespeare's ancestors, as well as the love of sports and pastimes of such as Henry VIII. and his curious and capricious daughter, Queen Elizabeth, the supposed grandfather and mother of Shakespeare,

* See also Lord Sydenham's recent article on "The Shakespeare Myth," *English Review*, August, 1924.
† Sonnet CXI.

I give below that which another citizen of another foreign country—France—says concerning them. As my assumed Japanese friend might describe them, they are amongst nature's prodigies, almost freaks, these highly cultured, but strangely contradictory descendants of Margaret Beaufort. Compare this with what the distinguished and elegant French author, M. J. J. Jusserand, has to say. French art stands high. In the sixteenth century the French, too, had their "master of the enchanters of the ear," Ronsard, and their Rabelais, from both of whom our Shakespeare learnt much. M. Jusserand's verdict on Queen Elizabeth in particular, and on Henry VIII. and his children generally, is startling in the direct influence they exercised on the literature of their time. M. Jusserand is no Baconian, yet nothing stronger than his words could be wished to support the view which I have ventured to propound. He says:

"But besides these elegant languages (Italian and French), Greek and Latin were becoming *courtly*. They were taught in the schools and out of the schools; the nobles, following the example of King Henry VIII and his children, made a parade of their knowledge. Ignorance was no longer the fashion, any more than old towers without windows."

Sir T. More, according to Erasmus, "is the sweetest softest, happiest genius nature has ever shaped." In a word, "Literature is triumphant among the English. The King himself, the two cardinals, almost all the bishops, favour with all their soul and adorn letters. To learn Greek and Latin was to move with the time and to follow the fashion. . . . Dazzled by what he saw and heard, Erasmus was announcing to the worl in enthusiastic letters that ' the golden age ' was to be born again in this fortunate island."* Well might he be dazzled. Never was a truer prophet. Never did wise man see more clearly whither that which he saw immediately around him led. It was no exaggeration—the golden age of Shakespeare was at hand, and such a man could not fail to feel it, moving as he did at Court in the very forcing house, the hotbed, the actual nursery, that gave birth to Shakespeare. Turning next to the English ladies of the sixteenth century, M. Jusserand continues: " They too began to read Greek, Latin, Italian, and French; knowledge was so much the fashion that it extended to women. Here Ascham bears testimony in their favour; the Queen herself gives the example: ' She readeth now at Windsor more Greek, every day than some prebendary of this church doth read Latin in a whole week.' "

Not that this " in any way imperilled the grace and ease of their manners." You need not fear being welcomed " with a quotation from Plato, or dismissed with a verse from Virgil." On the contrary, " It was the custom at that time with English Ladies to greet their friends and relations, and even strangers with kisses."

We remember how later the gay Pepys enjoyed this custom. Even the Queen when she invested Dudley as Earl of Leicester " could not refrain from putting her hand in his neck smilingly tickling him, the French Ambassador & I [Sir James Melville] standing by. Then she turned, asking at me ' how I liked him ?' "

M. Jusserand continues: " Queen Elizabeth, who was

* J. J. Jusserand, " The English Novel in the Time of Shakespeare."

wholly representative of her age, and shared even its follies, liked and encouraged finery in everything.

" . . . The learned queen who read Plutarch in Greek, a thing Shakespeare could never do [*sic*],* and translated Boethius into English, found, in spite of her philosophy, an immense delight in having herself painted in fantastic costumes. . . . Sometimes she recreated herself in playing upon the lute and virginals "† (as did Laneham-Shakespeare). She liked to be overheard or caught playing and seen dancing, and yet " This woman, nevertheless, with so many frailties and ultra-feminine vanities was a sovereign *with a will and a purpose.* Even in the midst of this talk about buskins, lovebooks, and virginals it shone out. . . . The same singular combination may be observed in the literary works of her time: flower of speech and vanities abound, but they are not without an aim. Rarely was any sovereign so completely emblematic of his or her period. She may almost be said to be the key to it; and it may be very well asserted that whatever the branch of art or literature of this epoch you wish to understand, *you must first study Elizabeth.*"‡

Such is the view of the great Queen Elizabeth held by a foreigner. " She was emblematic of her times, which cannot be understood without her." What more could we expect to hear said of the woman who, not only herself inaugurated the study of the classical drama in this country, but who herself actually inspired,

* On the contrary, in our opinion the learned son Shakespeare-Bacon followed his mother, delighting in Plutarch, having indeed been fed and nurtured on him.

† J. J. Jusserand, " The English Novel in the Time of Shakespeare."

‡ *Ibid.,* pp. 87-95. Translated by Elizabeth Lee.

if not gave birth, as we cannot but believe, to the great Prince-poet, who was to bring it to such unrivalled perfection, and to glitter before the eyes of all the world, outshining as a human star the most brilliant competitors, to an extent that makes all admire and none envy—his superiority is so assured. Elizabeth, as we know, at heart was far from being without an aim. Her hero was Alexander the Great,* as it was that of her son, Bacon-Shakespeare, and nobly she expressed her desire to outrival him at Cambridge in 1564 in Latin, praying that before paying her last debt to nature she too might erect some passing good work, which, "if I must die before I can complete this thing . . . yet will I leave some famous monument behind me, whereby my memory shall be renowned, and I by my example may invite others to like worthy actions; and also make you all more ready to pursue your studies."† What more noble monument to her wish than Shakespeare's plays?

Thus Shakespeare-Immerito seems fully justified when, in his "Shepherd's Calendar," he describes both Henry VIII. and Queen Elizabeth as partaking of the nature of the great god Pan, so universal was their genius, their love of nature in everything, small as well as great. The allusion is indeed strikingly apt

* See "Advancement of Learning," where his name occurs copiously as well as in other works. "My admiration for whom, when I consider him not as Alexander the Great, but as Aristotle's scholar, hath carried me too far" ("Advancement of Learning," p. 69; J. M. Robertson's "Philosophical Works of F. Bacon").

† Queen Elizabeth, Oration at Cambridge, 1564, Nichols's "Progresses." "A sovereign with a will and a purpose," as I. Jusserand says (p. 250).

both in respect of them—*i.e.*, his ancestors, and of himself. No sovereigns, that one can call to mind, at once retained so lofty a dignity yet never refrained from mixing freely with their subjects. None took such a keen interest in the things of this world, and yet had equally distinctly—however much at times absent from their minds—a noble ideal. This dual frame of mind no one has more beautifully expressed than Shakespeare in his sonnets, asserting there so pathetically that though he may have ranged, like him that travels, far away, he had ever returned and been constant to it, just as Bacon late in life told Fulgentio that his mind " had never waxed older in this design, nor after so many years grown cold and indifferent."

In short, to myself the quotations on the title-page of this my book tell the whole secret of the life of Shakespeare-Bacon. He himself was Jacques in his innumerable motleys, and Hamlet in his inky coat— the black Prince. Juliet, inspired by Margaret de Valois, was his ideal, his muse, which in Sonnet CIX. he addresses as his Rose, and, as he sits there, like his statue as shown in the frontispiece, looking back in leaden contemplation on the past, with all its hopes, its aims, its troubles, its temptations, and its strange dissimulation, spreading such a veil of mystery and gossip all round him, methinks it not difficult to follow the train of his thoughts as they wander in remembrance over the old ground—" My name, dear saint, is hateful to myself, and is, indeed, not any part of me; gladly would I deny my father and refuse my name, and, since it is an enemy to thee, had I it written I would tear the word. But yet, that which we call a rose by any other name would smell as sweet. So would my

muse, by whatsoever name, retain that dear perfection
which is hers:

> " As easy might I from myself depart
> As from my soul, which in thy breast doth lie:
> That is my home of love: if I have ranged,
> Like him that travels I return again,
> Just to the time, not with the time exchanged,
> So that myself bring water for my stain.
> Never believe, *though in my nature reigned*
> *All frailties that besiege all kinds of blood*,
> That it could so preposterously be stained,
> To leave for nothing all thy sum of good;
>   For nothing this wide universe I call,
>   Save thou, *my rose ;* in it thou art my all."
>   (Sonnet CIX.)

To him his muse was everything.   His name, what
was it ?   He has been called myriad-minded.   So also
is he myriad-named.   He confesses it candidly.   He has
worn a many-coloured coat (Sonnets CX., CXI., CXII.):

> " Alas ! 'tis true I have gone here and there
> *And made myself a motley to the view*,
> Gored mine own thoughts, *sold cheap what is most dear*,
> Made old offences of affections new;
> Most true it is that I have looked on truth
> Askance and strangely: but, by all above,
> These blenches gave my heart another youth,
> And worse essays prov'd thee my best of love.
> Now all is done, save what shall have no end."
>
>   *   *   *   *   *
>
> " O, for my sake do you with Fortune chide
> The guilty goddess of my harmful deeds,
> That did not better for my life provide
> *Than public means which public manners breeds*.
> Thence comes it that my name *receives a brand*,
> And almost thence my nature is subdued
> To what it works in, like the dyer's hand:
> Pity me then and wish I were renewed."
>
>   *   *   *   *   *

" Your love and pity doth the impression fill
 Which *vulgar scandal* stamped upon my brow;
 For what care I, who calls me well or ill,
 So you o'ergreen my bad, my good allow ?
 You are my all-the-world, and I must strive
 To know my shames and praises from your tongue;
 None else to me, nor I to none alive."

Is not this the very life and sufferings of Shakespeare-Bacon epitomised ?

If the premises herein assumed are right and true, it is easy to imagine the vulgar scandal which must have been current from time to time concerning Shakespeare. He tells us here plainly that he shook it all off. His muse was all-in-all to him. From her tongue alone he could feel shame or praise, his sense was dead to others' voices, whether raised to criticise or praise. So long as he could fulfil her behests and so attain his own purpose, to him the outside world was as good as dead; he was unconscious of it, so profound was the abyss in which he drowned all care for all else. He was a mystic above all:—a mystery.

The only interpretation possible to put upon these words is that they come from a man of lofty spirit communing with himself, thus: He is conscious of his many frailties. He has been compelled by fate to lead a public life uncongenial to himself, and for which he felt unfitted, regarding it, moreover, as a brand on his true name (his birthright as a Prince). The position he was thus forced by circumstances to fill was to him one of torture; a man of the highest birth and noblest aims condemned to live, as a subject, a life of drudgery. His frailties, his want of strength pressed upon him. His muse, his child-born ideals—nurtured in him before he knew his royal origin—alone cheered him on.   He admits that he wandered from the path, looked askance at truth, as hope for a time died, yet like the traveller he ever returned home to his muse, his rose, his divine mission, his ideal.   Nothing could deprive him of that.   It was his solace throughout that outward public life in which at last he rose so suddenly, when once the chance came to be Lord Chancellor.   Then envy of his great name and high place in public life reared up a great host of enemies.   To follow him stage by stage as he thus shot with lightning swiftness into the highest eminence in the State is not within the scope of my present effort, or to show how he mingled verse and philosophy with the law and his duties as judge.   It should be borne in mind, however, that he received no chance of public life so long as Queen Elizabeth lived.   For the first forty-four years of his life he was entirely master of his own time, except for slight parliamentary duties, and such services as he from time to time rendered to Her Majesty.   Once opportunity given, when James I. ascended the throne, he rose like a meteor, and plays came scarcely, but enemies in numbers.   It was not indeed his muse, not his scientific fame men envied, but his pride of place and power.   By nature a poet, he had always felt himself better fitted for a contemplative than an active life, but *necessity* is the mother of *invention*. Need tempted him into the arena, and nature made him unconsciously a partaker of the frailties of his times.   He felt his weakness.   His errors were not calculated or concealed.   He erred openly, in ignorance and blindness.   There had been no bribery when he fell, much less the least miscarriage of justice.* No sentence which he passed as a judge was ever appealed against even by his accusers, but he had by the King's command issued patents of monopoly to his favourite, the Duke of Buckingham, and he had himself allowed his servants to take presents in a few cases—for expedition, not affecting his judgment—in a manner then customary.

He had erred, though in a minor degree. He would not mince matters. He would not defend himself. Perhaps he had been far more guilty in other instances. He would disappear.

And so this great judge, leader in Parliament, orator, philosopher, and poet, this great student of science, this bold and delicate, refined, cultured, and gentle delineator of human nature, erring, yet at times almost divine, the force of whose intellect had impelled him, from the days of Gascoigne and Euphues, to climb heights so lofty by the sheer weight of reason—

> " The walls whereof are wondrous hard to climb,
> And much too high for ladders made of rhyme,"†

—this great man who essayed so much and who achieved so much towards the endowment of human life with new discoveries and powers, for the alleviation of human misery, and the benefit of the state and society of man, who had mounted like a meteor to the very pinnacle of power, and had himself so eloquently

* " But his fault was laxity, never iniquity, and he could truly claim . . . that he had been the justest judge of his day. Not one of his thirty-six thousand (36,000) decrees as Lord Chancellor appears to have been overturned on the score of corruption " (J. M. Robertson, " Philosophical Works of Francis Bacon," p. viii).

† Gascoigne, " Steel Glass."

warned the Duke of Buckingham against the perils of
it, fell with a crash, in an instant. He barely left
himself time to indite and publish his "Great Instauration" and the great First Folio of his plays;
then he was gone and did disappear from ken, lost
not only to the eyes of men but to their thoughts,
leaving indeed his name and memory to foreign nations.

High as his ideals were, he too was none the less
frail. His enemies even still have more than one case
to bring against him, and, above all, the fate of the
Earl of Essex, possibly his brother. Here also Mr.
Robertson—not, however, acknowledging consanguinity—is eloquent in his defence, and argues as
follows:

"When it is remembered that Essex, on his part,
had received from the Queen a hundred times the
benefits she had bestowed on Bacon . . . the attack
seems to break down. Bacon, who held the normal
view of his duty to the State, acted on principles of
public fealty, which then, as now, were as clearly of
plenary force as his obligation to Essex was limited.
And his action in the prosecution was that of a man
concerned *to save* the offender, who, unwise to the
verge of madness, would *not let himself be saved*"
(. M. Robertson, "Philosophical Works of Francis
Bacon," p. vii.   Compare Spedding).

Bacon-Shakespeare himself, in fact, owed immeasurably more to the Queen than to Essex; and, if she was
their mother, the case knows no like tragic parallel,
unless it be Œdipus, of which we hear so much at this
period. These things are in truth beyond our judgment, amongst those things which it is not for us to
know. Like his great ancestors he was a contradiction.
In no man are the two spirits—the divine and the

17

sublime—the human, passionate and erring, so conspicuously contrasted as in him, as we now see him
He had untold trials. His life is involved in situation
and mysteries beyond all parallel. Let us pass on
reflecting in the terms of Philip Sidney:

"So uncertain are human judgments, the sam
person most infamous and most famous, and neithe
justly" ("Arcadia").

Nor should it be forgotten that "Francis Meres"
calls the "Countess of Pembroke's Arcadia,"* Phili
Sidney's immortal *poem*. It was published by Sidney'
sister, Countess of Pembroke, the daughter of tha
Mary (Dudley) Sidney to whose chamber young Shak
speare-Laneham as Bacon so loved to resort at Keni
worth. And Sidney held that poetry, a poem, can b
written in suitable prose as well as verse, which is th
very position taken up by Bacon in his "De Aug
mentis," where, in defining poesie, he says: "Verse
only a kind of style, and a certain form of elocutio
and has nothing to do with the matter; for both tr
history may be written in verse, and feigned histor
in prose, . . . and under the name of Poesy, I tre
only of feigned history."†

So completely at one were these twin spirits ar
cousins—Sidney, the son of Mary Dudley, and Shak
speare, as I believe, the son of Robert Dudley, but
"These things are not for all men to know."

* The "Arcadia" was originally written by Sir Phi
Sidney to entertain his sister, in 1580, when he had offend
Queen Elizabeth by pressing against the French marriage wi
d'Alençon. His Queen Gynicia may have been suggested
what he had seen of Queen Elizabeth at Kenilworth and Cou
 † "De Aug.," Book II., chap. xiii.

N.B.—It is a strange fact that two translations of Sidney's "Arcadia" were published consecutively in Paris in 1624 and 1625, when Bacon was publishing his great works; and one of them was by M. Baudoin, who translated also some of Bacon's works. Both were in three volumes, both were adorned with engravings. (See "The English Novel in the Time of Shakespeare," Jusserand.)

CHAPTER XVIII

SHAKESPEARE'S ART AND INVENTION—
A SUMMARY

THE magnitude of the influence on human powers and possibilities of the mind of this nameless man, this modern Solomon and Prince of poets, whose genius itself was already so very great, and who added to it himself so much, by industry so strenuous, and devotion so nearly superhuman, cannot be measured. Our admiration for him is such that, as we read his inspired word we feel that, however frail and erring he may at times have been, in the course of an inconceivably troublous life, he is so great of soul and so exquisitely sublime in diction, howsoever human and humorous the action, as to seem in spirit almost divine. Dr Rawley says of him that " if there were a beam of knowledge derived from God upon any man in these modern times, it was from him."* The *Est Deus in nobis*† was never so powerfully, so vividly, so mystically mingled in any man, with the liability to err common to all. It is probable that the intellect and imagination of no other single individual man, since the world was the world, has contributed so much to

* " Life of Sir Francis Bacon."

† " The poet is naturally born a poet from his mother womb, and with that inclination that heaven hath given him without further study or art he composeth things that verify his saying that said *Est Deus in nobis*," etc. (Shelton's " Don Quixote," Part II., chap. xvi.).

increase the happiness of mankind, promote their welfare, and teach men how to add to it themselves *ad infinitum* " till the world's dissolution."* He is careful always to show that under " invention "† he includes artistic and literary, as well as scientific and mechanical, invention. Thus M. Jusserand‡ traces the origin of the English novel to Shakespeare and his period—for example, in Greene's " Pandosto." In " Euphues," moreover, which comes from the same concealed hand, we have the first introspective novel,§ and to-day the world teems with works of imagination or fiction. Still more, new mechanical inventions, founded on the laws of science now in active operation, surprise us daily. Ariel is at work everywhere, " the airy spirit " —*aërei mellis cœlestia dona.*‖ Puck's girdle round the world is an accomplished fact. We can talk with the Antipodes either by aerial or wire, " before you can say ' come ' and ' go ' or cry ' so so ';"¶ " in a twink " or " e'er your pulse twice beat."** Ariel is in fact magic—*i.e.*, scientific art—or is nature bound, and set free by the skill of Prospero, who stands for Bacon himself. By it we can to-day hear music

* " Shepherd's Calendar," epilogue.
† " Invention is of two kinds, the one of arts and sciences, and the other of speech and arguments " (" Advancement of Learning," " Philosophical Works of Francis Bacon," p. 112, ed. by J. M. Robertson).
‡ " The English Novel in the Time of Shakespeare."
§ John Barclay's " Argenis " is a yet more striking example almost Homeric in some scenes.
‖ " The heavenly gift of ethereal honey."
¶ " The Tempest," Act IV., sc. i.
** *Ibid.*, Act V., sc. i.

leagues away.* It seems, too, as it were, to come from heaven. Science is so like magic. We can even by gramophone hear once again the voices of the dead. We fly. Wonder succeeds to wonder till we cease to wonder. It appals. Yet we are only at the beginning of realising the value of the discovery of the laws of electricity, hydraulics, chemistry, gases, flying, X rays, antiseptic treatment, psychology, and so on. We are but just beginning to appreciate the wondrous foresight and apprehension of Shakespeare-Bacon. We are only at the foot of the great mountain or ladder of achievement which this mysterious and nameless man, whilst yet a boy called Francis Bacon, in the name of Gascoigne,† wrote that science, with the force of reason, might assault and climb. Moreover, of recent years, we seem to be more than ever in need of direction, which indeed is inevitable as life becomes more complicated; and this is the very thing which, as Bacon-Shakespeare tells us, he was working at with all his might.‡ It is on this, too, that we now see men beginning to concentrate, striving to eliminate passion bringing all available mechanical inventions to the aid of the reasoned conferences of experts, collecting

* " Man has come into his heritage and seems now to possess some particle of the universal creative force in virtue of which he can wrest from nature the *secrets* so jealously guarded by her, and bend them to his own desire. But let there be no mistake; much has been done, but much more remains to be done. . . . It is the duty of science to go steadily forward illuminating the dark places *in hope of happier times*" (Sir David Bruce, Toronto, British Association for Advancement of Science, *Times*, August 7, 1924).

† Gascoigne, Preface of the " Steel Glass."

‡ Bacon, " De Aug.," Book V., chap. ii.

and collating learned experience and particulars, seeking to make sure that our efforts may be made in the right direction and not fail. This is the real teaching of Don Quixote. He is a picture of wasted effort madly expended in search of deeds to his own glory, tilting at windmills like the German Emperor. So, too, if the "Dr. Faustus" of Marlowe be compared with "The Tempest," one will be found the counterpart of the other. Thus Bacon and Shakespeare give the name of "Magic" to science—*i.e.*, scientific art in "the production of wonderful operations."* It is used in the same sense both in "Dr. Faustus" and "The Tempest." Learned Faustus is—

> "The wonder of the world for *magic art*."†

And Prospero says to Miranda:

> "Lend thy hand
> And pluck my *magic* garment from me;
> Lie there, my *art*."‡

The difference between the two is made very plain. Dr. Faustus, like Don Quixote, uses his powers for his own glory, pleasure, and pride:

> "Whose fiendful Fortune may exhort the wise
> Only to wonder at *unlawful* things."§

But in "The Tempest" Prospero uses his art lawfully; he had fixed his ends in the right direction—that is, as Bacon says, "for the benefit of the state and society

* Bacon, "De Aug.," Book III., chap. v.; J. M. Robertson, "Philosophical Works of Francis Bacon," p. 474.

† Marlowe, "Dr. Faustus," Act III., sc. iii. Hamlet, like Faustus, goes to school at Wittenberg.

‡ Shakespeare, "The Tempest," Act I., sc. ii.

§ Marlowe, "Dr. Faustus," Act V., chorus.

of man."* He effects his restoration and vengeance without revenge, to the good of all. Thus, when he says: "I'll drown my book," he is accompanied by "solemn music,"† and he pardons the rankest fault: "I do forgive, unnatural though thou art."

When, on the other hand, Dr. Faustus says similarly: "I'll burn my books," he is accompanied by "Thunder, lightening and rain and exeunt Devils with Faustus" (*1604 edition*).‡ So also with Cæsar. His end, too, was self, not man and the use of power for his relief, as God granted it.

Great and noble as he was, nothing could be more conclusive in respect of this point of direction than Bacon's acknowledged verdict on Julius Cæsar—*i.e.*, "He worked only for his own present and private ends, . . . he endeavoured after fame and reputation, as he judged they might be of service to his designs . . . he courted reputation and honour only as they were instruments of power and grandeur . . . the same thing at last was the means of his fall which at first was a step to his rise—viz., his affectation of popularity. . . . His error was the *not rightly fixing his ends.*"§ This was the very error of Don Quixote, a wanderer up and down in search of his own glory, on the right way to the wrong place.‖ And now mark this: it is the very *motif* of Shakespeare's play of "Julius Cæsar," in which the famous speech of Anthony shows in detail

---

* Bacon, "De Aug.," "Valerius Terminus," chap. i.

† Shakespeare, "The Tempest," Act V., sc. i.

‡ Marlowe, "Dr. Faustus," last line.

§ G. W. Steeves, "Francis Bacon," p. 110; Bacon's "Imagines Civiles Julii Cæsaris et Augusti Cæsaris."

‖ "Valerius Terminus," chap. ix.; a fragment.

how all Cæsar's acts were directed towards his own
ambition, by courting popularity, rather than the real
benefit of Rome, and Brutus, who loved him, yet
justifies himself, deeming the ends of Cæsar wrong:
" As he was valiant I honour him, but as he was ambitious I slew him."* And yet—

> " His life was gentle, and the elements
> So mixed in him that Nature might stand up
> And say to all the world, ' This was a man.' "
>
> (" Julius Cæsar," Act V., sc. v.)

Thus ever Shakespeare is the bell. Bacon is the
ringer. Two or one ? I believe *one*, whose bell still
continues to ring and to call, beseeching and imploring
men to listen to his merry peal, and to all that it
invites them to pursue for their own good: Science and
art, reason and wit, learning and nature, imagination, philosophy, religion and induction. Such is his
chime. What practical and substantial ends may not
man yet achieve by aid of these powerful instruments,
bestowed on him, be it ever remembered, " for the
benefit of the state and society of man " ?

Such was this great master's teaching, in spirit. He
strained every faculty unsparingly; he called upon
everything that wit, wisdom, reason, learning, philosophical earnestness of purpose, poetical love, and joy
of life could bring to bear in order to advance effec-
tively the interests of his fellow-men. From earliest
youth to his last day, wander though he might off the
path,† he kept his aim ever in view—returning always
to it, when tempted to depart from his overpowering

---

* Shakespeare, " Julius Cæsar," Act III. Also Bacon in
" De Augmentis " quotes Plutarch as saying of Cæsar, " He
had rather be first in a village than second in Rome " (J. M.
Robertson, p. 601).   † Sonnet CIX.

desire—in some degree to help subdue and overcome the necessities and miseries of humanity, his practical method being invention rightly directed, the co-operation or marriage of science and art, intellect, and vision. The great plays and the " Novum Organum " under one name coming from one pen; what a revelation! Together they express unity indeed! that " One-hood " to the full, of which young Laneham in his wonderful letter makes so much—Pan. For the discourse and working of the mind, together with the analysis of things, forms the complete " Interpretation of Nature " as a whole, comprising everything, mind and things, by precept and example—*i.e.*, the " Great Instauration " and the plays, reason and imagination. Thus Bacon expressly says that his method applies to all sciences, and embraces everything;* and this method may in its fullness be well called one of scientific and artistic induction, for the two meet and differ only in degree, the induction of things being exact, that of the mind tentative, and dependent upon correct and learned experience and anticipation.

The plays, which are intended to be select examples of the discourse and working of the mind in subjects the most remarkable and noble—set upon the stage as in a mirror before our very eyes to show what " idols " we worship†—are thus now being acted and read all

* " Novum Organum," Aphorism 127; " De Aug.," Book II., chap. i.: " All human learning is embraced under History, Poesy, and Philosophy, and so his method applies to all."

† Bacon, " Plan of the Great Instauration"; J. M. Robertson's " Philosophical Works of Francis Bacon," p. 253. Bacon, " Novum Organum," Aphorism 127; J. M. Robertson's " Philosophical Works of Francis Bacon," p. 299. I am indebted to Colonel B. R. Ward, R.E., for drawing attention to this important Aphorism.

over the world, even across the Atlantic and Pacific, in America, Asia, and Africa, by those very nations, then unknown, which he did so much to make, and of which he foretold that: "His honour and the greatness of his name shall be, and make new nations."

Similarly, the great nameless spirit who lived under a hundred motleys, of which "Shakespeare" and "Bacon" are only the most famous, also, as I have said, anticipated as in a dream, which he strove to put vividly before us in his "New Atlantis," the coming of the wonders of scientific invention now at hand and before our eyes, with their beneficent effect on health and life, over and above the new commodities and increased powers they afford, and their immeasurable further possibilities. He maintained especially the importance of recognising, I venture to repeat, the inter-relation, the relative value, of reason and the imagination, and of getting the most out of both together, as well as out of each separately. For the true beauty of the picture conceived as a whole depends upon its unity, and that in execution depends upon the accuracy, truth, and proportion of its relative parts, each supporting the other; so that science and art, reason and imagination, going hand in hand, the mind of man becomes a match for the nature of things. Most men constantly assert as fact things which their minds have in fact anticipated by imagination; it is often not until they are contradicted that they set to work to prove themselves right, by observation, conference, and induction; and so come to a peaceful agreement, for our senses often deceive.

It is thanks also to this marriage of art with science that the arts of discovery and invention to-day hold

the field with such *éclat* undisputedly, and are now
perpetually at work endeavouring to subdue and overcome both the necessities of civilised life and the
miseries attached to it; but to which unfortunately
they still sometimes add, through want of direction,
and this raises Shakespeare-Bacon's new point. The
"Novum Organum" and the "De Augmentis," the
"Great Instauration" and the great plays, the forces
of reason and of the imagination together, interpret
nature. Both deal with natural history, and induction
is the key to both. Thus the same mind naturally
conceived both, and saw not only the new powers that
they might confer upon man, but, as I have shown,
their dangers—the supreme need of direction, and of
the guidance of man in the use of those powers, on the
right way to the right place.* This indeed is a problem
which no induction can scientifically and accurately
solve, for, although God "hath placed the world in
man's heart, yet cannot man find out the work which
God worketh from the beginning to the end,"† and
"A man may wander in the way, by rounding up and
down,"‡ as Satan wandered to and fro in the earth
and up and down in it,§ or lost as one on the right way
to the wrong place.‖ This—as we have so severely

* Bacon, "Valerius Terminus," chap. ix.; J. M. Robertson's
"Philosophical Works of Francis Bacon," p. 194.

† "Advancement of Learning," Book I., chap. i.; J. M.
Robertson's "Philosophical Works of Francis Bacon," p. 44.

‡ "Valerius Terminus," chap. ix., and "Don Quixote";
" J. M. Robertson's "Philosophical Works of Francis Bacon,"
p. 194.

§ Job i. 7; "Don Quixote."

‖ "Valerius Terminus," chap. ix.; "Don Quixote"; J. M.
Robertson's "Philosophical Works of Francis Bacon," p. 194.

learnt in our day*—remains always the greatest difficulty; to penetrate without passion the problems and
citadels of the human mind; to array the facts on
which their solution seems to depend in our imaginations; then to arrange those particulars with care;
finally, to confer with patience and solve them, steering
clear of cruelty and war, and of the use of civilised
inventions for the infliction, instead of the alleviation,
of human misery.† Thus whereas the "Great Instauration" was to furnish the natural instruments to
power, and general precepts concerning the working
of the human mind, and the conflict of nature and
custom, use, and habit, the plays were to be the actual
mirror of nature, setting before our very eyes upon
the stage‡ the effects both of the good and evil use
of man's powers under the influence of human passions
and weaknesses,§ as in Shakespeare's "Hamlet,"
"Macbeth," "Othello," and "The Tempest," and
Marlowe's "Edward II." and "Dr. Faustus." Nothing more remained. There exists no more sublime and
perfect artistic unity of design and purpose in any
work of any age than in the "Great Instauration"
and Great Plays viewed as a whole—the interpretation
and direction or the right use of power. As Bacon

* The European War.
† The success of the Experts Commission and Reparation
Conference is a happy omen, and the League of Nations.
‡ "Plan of Part IV. of Great Instauration"; J. M. Robertson's
"Philosophical Works of Francis Bacon," p. 253.
§ "The poets and writers of history are the best doctors of
this knowledge." It was in the influence and power of custom
over those actions that are natural that Bacon differed from
Aristotle, and that Shakespeare illustrates. Bacon, "De
Aug.," Book VII., chap. iii.; J. M. Robertson, p. 574.

shows, God alone really creates; man interprets and directs the working of nature to his own ends by discovering its powers.

Our progress since has recently been immense. Order has at last been introduced into the several sciences. The working of the forces of nature has become known by rule and precept. In Shakespeare-Bacon's day newspapers were unknown, and the horse was the swiftest means of locomotion, whether for the traveller or for transmitting news. To-day news from the remotest parts of the earth is broadcasted every evening by wireless for all men to know throughout the wide world; we travel by steam and rail, or by road and motor, at fifty miles an hour, and by air at double that rate; whilst the sound of music in London can be heard in Calcutta, and even records of the voices of the men of to-day can be handed down for future generations to hear, by reproduction on the gramophone. These are but a few of the new powers that have been conferred on man for daily use by science, and by that method of induction of which Shakespeare-Bacon was the bellringer. What would we not give to-day to be able to hear the voice of Homer, Cæsar, Cicero, and Shakespeare himself, or, if it may be said without sacrilege, the voice of Pontius Pilate and even Christ. So wonderful are the achievements of science to-day, and with due precaution, D.V., our descendants a thousand years hence may be able to hear the voices of to-day. The new Atlantis is no longer a dream.

Who, again, has done more to illustrate the value, not only of beauty but of purity of speech and action, than the same great nameless master in motley, the supremacy of whose universal power is to-day undisputed in all countries? And he tells us in his works that secrecy and concealment of design "by dark arts and methods is *useful* and *admirable*," and that nothing is more politic in wise mediocrity.* Surely this was said with some purpose, especially seeing that he tells us at the outset in his philosophical works that " It is the glory of God to conceal a thing, but the glory of the King is to find it out, as if according to the innocent play of children the divine Majesty took delight to hide his work, to the end to have them found out."† " Also he hath placed the world in man's heart, yet cannot man find out the work which God worketh from the beginning to the end."‡ Following this teaching, he has set us a similar puzzle, saying, as he so frequently does, that Time with his scythe reveals all things, even though they be hidden in the very bosom of the earth. Which sentiment he further illustrates so beautifully in the frontispiece of his own " New Atlantis," as well as on works of Gascoigne, Lyly, and Weaver. To all things he ever gave Time his due, and so, resigning earthly glory, he wrote from his concealment:

> " Let fame, that all hunt after in their lives,
> Live registered upon our brazen tombs,
> And then grace us in the disgrace of *death*,"§ etc.

He continued in the same vein in the sonnets. There, after telling us in " Romeo and Juliet " that he hated

* " De Aug.," Book VIII., chap. ii.; J. M. Robertson, " Philosophical Works of Francis Bacon," p. 600.

† Bacon, " Valerius Terminus "; J. M. Robertson, " Philosophical Works of Francis Bacon," p. 187.

‡ Bacon, " Advancement of Learning "; J. M. Robertson, " Philosophical Works of Francis Bacon," p. 44.

§ Shakespeare, " Love's Labour's Lost," Act I., sc. i.

his name (*i.e.*, Bacon), he addresses his muse as his
" rose " (which by any other name would smell as
sweet), and lets us plainly know that he has often
wandered in disguise, presumably under other names:

> " Alas ! 'tis true I have gone here and there
> And made myself a *motley* to the view."
>
> (Sonnet CX.)

Finally, in " As You Like It," as Jacques, after
similarly railing against fortune and exclaiming—

> " Motley's the only wear. . . . It is my only suit."
>
> (" As You Like It," Act II., sc. vii.)

He concludes:

> " Invest me in my motley; give me leave
> To speak my mind, and I will through and through
> Cleanse the foul body of th' infected world,
> If they will patiently receive my *medicine*."*

But this is the very declared aim of Bacon, who in
his famous letter to Lord Burghley at the age of thirty-
one, after saying that he has taken all knowledge to
be his province, declares his desire to " purge it of two
sorts of rovers " and "bring in industrious observation, grounded conclusions, and profitable invention
and discovery." This, this, is his medicine ! To call
man to a strict account as to his passions. This is
how man is to be helped and cured ! It is the marriage

---

* Shakespeare, " As You Like It," Act II., sc. vii.

" The calling of a man's self to a strict account, is a *medicine*
sometimes too piercing and corrosive " (Bacon, " Essay of
Friendship ").

" I have played myself the inquisitor, and find nothing to
my understanding in them (*i.e.*, the essays) contrarie or in-
fectious to the state of religion, or manners, but rather
medicinable." (Dedication to the " Essays " by Bacon himself,
thus regarding them as his medicine). In " Euphues " we

of science and art, of the rational and empirical faculty: " Out of which marriage it is to be hoped will spring helps for man, and a line and race of inventions which may in some degree subdue and overcome the necessities and misery of humanity."*

It is perhaps, however, in " A Winter's Tale " that Shakespeare makes almost the clearest revelation concerning his identity with Bacon. Here, moreover, our delightful and perfectly impartial French Shakespearean critic, M. Jusserand, comes to our aid unconsciously, in a quite startling manner. He shows in considerable detail how Shakespeare adapted this play of " A Winter's Tale " from Greene's history of ' Pandosto," and this in so interesting a manner that I venture to transcribe a brief extract verbatim. He says:

" Greene (in ' Pandosto ') had in truth only modelled the clay; Shakespeare used it, adding the soul. Greene simply states his facts and takes little trouble about explaining them; the reader must rest satisfied with the author's bare word. There is no attempt *at the study of passions;* his heroes change their minds all of a sudden, with a stiff, sharp, improbable action of puppets in a show. Pandosto loves and hates and becomes jealous, and repents always in the same brusque wire and wood manner; the warmth of his (Leontes') passions, so great and terrible in Shakespeare, is here simply absent. . . . In Greene

---

read again: " Come to me all ye lovers that have been deceived by fancy, . . . be as earnest to seek a *medicine* as you were ready to run into a mischief." And says M. Jusserand, his intention is to give them remedies which shall cure them of loving (J. J. Jusserand, " The English Novel in the Time of Shakespeare ").

* Bacon, " Plan of Great Instauration."

18

the exquisite figure of Perdita appears as a very rough sketch under the name of Fawnia. . . . To add life and poetry was very well, but by no means necessary. Shakespeare did so because he could not do otherwise. . . ."

Now, as a matter of fact, it would be difficult to find better words to amplify the deliberate method according to which the plays were conceived and written by Shakespeare-Bacon as " natural histories," as described in Aphorism 127 of the " Novum Organum."* There Bacon says that he means his method of writing natural histories, by induction, to apply to all sciences, including logic, ethics, and politics—in fact, embracing everything. Then follows these ominous words: " For I form a history† and tables of discovery of *anger, fear, shame,* and the like . . . not less than for heat and cold or light or vegetation, or the like. . . . My method of interpretation, after the *history* has been prepared and duly arranged " regards " the working and discourse of the mind " as well as " the nature of things. . . ." " I *supply the mind with such rules and guidance that it may in every case apply itself aptly to the nature of things.*"§

Here we have given to us, in so many words, both Shakespeare-Bacon's method of writing his plays deliberately as natural histories and his aim in aiding man with examples and rules of action, to guide his mind according to the nature of things; as, for example

* This was first pointed out by Colonel Ward (see above).

† *E.g.,* Pandosto.

‡ To be found in " A Winter's Tale."

§ Bacon, " Novum Organum," Aphorism 127; J. M. Robertson, " Philosophical Works of Francis Bacon," p. 299.

n " Othello," wherein we are shown nature free and
noble, and nature erring,* in one and the same scene,
under the terrible influence of the passions of jealousy
and suspicion. "A Winter's Tale" is, however, in
some respects a yet more notable example, for here
" Pandosto" is admittedly the history "prepared and
duly arranged" and then cast upon the waters under
the name of "Greene" for people to discuss. Shakespeare listened. He heard the story discussed, possibly
shared in the discussion, and made his table of discovery
of the human passions—anger, fear, shame—all of
which not only occur frequently in "A Winter's Tale,"
but, that there may be no mistake, they occur all three
in close juxtaposition in Act II. at the end of scene ii.
and beginning of scene iii.:

AULINA: You need not *fear* it, Sir:
            The child was prisoner to the womb, and is
            By law and process of great nature thence
            Freed and enfranchised; not a party to
            The *anger* of the King, nor guilty of,
            If any be, the trespass of the Queen.

AOLER: I do believe it.

AULINA: Do not you *fear* : upon mine honour, I
            Will stand betwixt you and danger.

                        ("A Winter's Tale," Act II., sc. ii.)

Who but a great lawyer and natural philosopher
would use such terms as those of Paulina? and Shakespeare-Bacon was both. A few lines further down we

* Shakespeare, "Othello," Act III., sc. iii:
    Line 199: I would not have your *free and noble nature*
                Out of self-bounty be abused.
    Line 227: And yet, how *nature erring* from itself—
                Ay, there's the point.

read how Leontes received the news of the death o
Mamillius:

LEONTES: To see his nobleness !
        Conceiving the dishonour of his mother,
        He straight declined, drooped, took it deeply,
        Fasten'd and fix'd the *shame* on't in himself,
        Threw off his spirit, his appetite, his sleep,
        And downright languished.*

Thus beautifully from the bare history of " Pan
dosto " does Shakespeare discover the human an
natural passions of anger, fear, and shame, and transf
them to " A Winter's Tale " exactly according to tl
method described by M. Jusserand and planned b
Bacon. Nor is it difficult to see that this particul:
play is also, according to Bacon's method, a parab
Leontes being Henry VIII., and Hermione An
Boleyn, the grandfather and wronged grandmother
our most illustrious Prince-poet. It is thus doubly
natural history.

Indeed, if any man still doubts that Shakespea
Bacon meant the term " natural history "† to app
also to his plays, let him read, mark, and count t
passages in which the words " nature," " natural," a
" unnatural " occur in such plays as " Hamle
" King Lear," " Macbeth,"‡ " Julius Cæsar," " Othel
and others. In " A Winter's Tale," too, the wc
" nature " occurs no less than seven times in ten lin
in that most beautiful of passages, in which those v
flowers, so beloved by Bacon, are discussed, and in wh

* Shakespeare, " A Winter's Tale," Act II., sc. iii.
† Bacon, " Novum Organum," Aphorism 127.
‡ " Unnatural deeds do breed unnatural troubles."

                              (" Macbeth," Act IV., sc. i.

Shakespeare gives the same definition of art as Bacon—namely, that "Art itself is Nature "—nature, that is, with man to help. Hark! It is the great master's voice at his best—and note that the antithesis of nature and custom is as conspicuous in Shakespeare, especially "Hamlet," as it is in Bacon's "De Augmentis," custom and use being but forms of man's art.

PERDITA: For I have heard it said
There is an art which in its piedness shares
With great creating *nature*.

POL.:   Say there be;
Yet *nature* is made better by no mean
But *nature* makes that mean: so, over that art
Which you say adds to *nature*, is an art
That *nature* makes. You see, sweet maid, we marry
A gentler scion to the wildest stock,
And make conceive a bark of baser kind
By bud of nobler race; this is an art
Which does mend *nature, change it rather*, but
The art itself is nature."*

This very same argument about art not only helping but changing nature is used by Bacon, who says: "A subtle error has crept into the human mind—namely, that of considering art as merely an assistant to nature, having the power indeed to finish what nature has begun, but by no means to *change* . . . or fundamentally alter nature."† He then goes on to say that "It is nature which governs everything; but under nature are included these three, the course of nature, the wanderings of nature, and *art or nature with man to help.*"

* Shakespeare, " A Winter's Tale," Act IV., sc. iii.
† Bacon, " De Aug.," Book II., chap. ii.; J. M. Robertson's " Philosophical Works of Francis Bacon," p. 427.

So that here we have the same matter delightfully and skilfully expressed, both as Shakespeare in verse and as Bacon in prose, illustrating the contention both of Sidney and Shakespeare that poetry and prose are merely differences of style. The same matter may be expressed in either.

In short, Bacon-Shakespeare makes it, very plainly, a part of his " Plan of the Great Instauration," to write not only histories of the nature of things, but histories of the nature of the working of the mind, all of which he calls " natural histories," and says that " by such a natural history, then, as I have described, I conceive that a safe and convenient approach may be made to nature, and *matter* supplied of good quality and well prepared for the understanding to work upon." Such a history was " Pandosto," on which, when " prepared and duly arranged," Shakespeare brought his marvellous powers of utterance and knowledge of the working of the human mind and passions to bear, and so set it forth to the wide world as drama before men's very eyes, for them to see as in a mirror, and note by way of example. For, as he explains, "the first thing is *to set forth examples* of enquiry and invention according to my method, exhibited by anticipation in some particular subjects; choosing such subjects as are at once the most noble in themselves, amongst those under enquiry, and most different one from another, that there may be an example of every kind."* No subjects are more noble—Shakespeare repeats the word markedly— nowhere is there greater variety than those which form the foundation of the plays, and they are, moreover

* Bacon, " Plan of the Great Instauration "; J. M. Robertson's " Philosophical Works of Francis Bacon," p. 253.

exactly such as he goes on to describe as his aim. "I mean actual types and models, by which the entire process of the mind and the whole fabric and order of invention from beginning to the end, in certain subjects and those various and remarkable, should be set as it were before the eyes."

Again, the history of Hamlet * is sketched out, after Bandello, and of Pericles, in the "Apollonius of Tyre" by Barnabe Riche, whose observations on art in the "Travels of Simonides" reveal exactly Shakespeare-Bacon's application of the word "use" and his interpretation of art in the line:

"For *use* almost can change the stamp of nature,"

and in the passage from which it comes as follows: "Betwixt Nature and Art then let us put an intermediate, which is *Use*. Nature first frameth, Art teacheth, *Use* maketh perfect. Art was sought out first by natural man, and Art at first confirmed natural man: yet there was a framer of the one and an inspirer of the other. Some are born eloquent, yet art confirmeth them in their eloquence (by use?). Some valiant, yet Art compasseth their exploits. What secret soever Art found out, Nature ministereth, and whatsoever Nature hath in her bowels included, Art hath found out." All this is the very same argument used by Shakespeare and Bacon.

To sum up, the nature of Shakespeare's mind has hitherto been grossly misunderstood and misinterpreted

* The "Historie of Hamlet," by Bandello, was first translated into French by Boisteau and Belleforest, but not into English till 1608, *after* the play of "Hamlet" had made its appearance in 1603.

in certain respects. He was no mere *lusus naturæ*, but while possessed of the highest genius, his industry, learning, judgment, and perseverance were no less. So far from being humbly born, he was from the highest of that noblest and distinguished class of whose deeds he sings with such Homeric grandeur. To natural and inborn inspiration he added a minute and painstaking study of nature, gathering knowledge—like those most industrious honey bees of which he talks*— wheresoever he could, now from books, now from observation, but perhaps, above all, from his own experience. He has told us the sad and painful nature of that experience—against which his hopeful spirit helped him to struggle so bravely on—in a variety of works carefully worked out, with immense patience, and culminating in " Hamlet," which is no mere inspiration, but a natural history of true tragic life founded on matter of good quality carefully prepared with the highest skill, to swell the air like the " thunder " of a " deep and dreadful organ-pipe "† in the depth and variety of its display of human passions, noble and ignoble, human and divine, elevating and degrading. His genius as a whole, inborn and acquired, may be summed up as compounded of native talent, industry observation, and experience, coupled with profound judgment and the most perfect power of utterance yet known to man. For he was not only the acme of our language, but surpassed all—Homer, perhaps, alone

* See Preface to translation of " Historie of Hamlet," 1608 on p. 223. This is a very notable *example* of his method of types and models, showing the whole process of the mind in certain subjects—*e.g.*, Anger, Shame, Fear, Revenge, Jealousy Suspicion.

† " The Tempest," Act III., sc. iii.

excepted. Feeling from earliest youth endowed with powers more than extraordinary, he spared no pains to improve and fortify and polish them in every direction. Devoting his early days and endeavours first to his instrument of expression and utterance, the English tongue, he was able as experience ripened to dress up his plays adorned with such inconceivable delicacy, in terms of such inexpressible sweetness, exquisite judgment, and good taste, that, to borrow from Shelley—apart from their delightful rhythm, and the play of passions they stir and set before our eyes—they give a complete, perfect, unquestionable, and almost divine sense of satisfaction to the *mind*—*i.e.*, apart from the ear. Collaterally, his study of the natural history of things enabled him to foresee the coming achievements of science, and his own vivid imagination enabled him to prophesy them with absolute conviction and certainty. For he knew that the unity effected by science and art working together as a whole—the reason with the imagination—must open and indicate the way, which Aristotle had almost conceived but just missed,* to new powers which, rightly guided by philosophy and religion, to keep man in the right way to the right place, must be of untold benefit to aid the future generations of mankind. Such was Shakespeare, the great student of nature—that is, of the nature of the human mind and of the nature of things, of art and science, of the imagination and reason—the modern Solomon, England's sweet-voiced throstle, the Orpheus of Gorhambury and St. Albans,

* Since Aristotle failed to recognise the power of custom over nature, and of the mind to discover and indicate right direction by scientific method.

who, crossing the Channel, wandered forth into Europe in search of his Eurydice, his muse, and became the great masterly and musical Apollo of the world. According to the notes at my disposal the education and nurture of this lovely child of wonder were most carefully superintended by Queen Elizabeth herself—his Bath-sheba—and took place under the eyes of Sir Nicholas Bacon, the disciple of Quintilian and Plutarch and Calvin, and of the gentle and pious Lady Bacon, his foster-parents, to whom he owed much of that sweet reasonableness and transcendent nobility of temperament and character which, whatever his failures, helped him to weather the storms of a life of severe trial, ending in a turbulent attack from his enemies and rivals. It was this which enabled him to rise aloft above the world's perturbations, in spirit, looking down like Prospero as from "a hill, not to be commanded, and where the air is always clear and serene, upon the errors and wanderings of man amid the mists and TEMPESTS,* in the vale below,"† which he sought to teach man to avoid and control,‡ through the new powers to be conferred upon him by science—Ariel: *Aërei mellis cælestia dona* ("The heavenly gift of ethereal honey").

He, Bacon-Shakespeare, I believe, was the lad of twelve years old who acted in the masque concerning the Montacutes and Capels to be found in the works of Gascoigne. We obtain the next graphic glimpse of him as the witty, garrulous, and gay Laneham, so beloved of the Court ladies and Lady Sidney at the

* Shakespeare, "The Tempest."
† Bacon, "Essay on Truth" and "De Augmentis."
‡ Cervantes, "Don Quixote."

age of fourteen. That same year he wrote the play of "The Hermit" at famous Woodstock, and after two years more at Cambridge, suddenly left the University, and, again under the auspices of the Queen, proceeded from Gorhambury, under arrangements made by the Privy Council, to France with the embassy of Sir Amyas Paulet. There he fell madly in love with the renowned, beautiful, and accomplished Margaret de Valois, Princess of France, Queen and wife of the "matchless Navarre" of "Love's Labour's Lost." On his return we hear of him again as Euphues, the maker of the new English, the delight still of the ladies of the Court, who love his company and all read his book and speak in euphuisms, whilst as Immerito* he appeared before the world as "the new poet," a young "courtier" frequenting the palaces of princes. There he sang to the glory of Queen Elizabeth and the Earl of Leicester, and the adoration of his lost love, his Rosalinde, or Daiselorn, his lovely Marguerite. Nor was he forgetful of his singular affection for Hobbinal, his dear friend Gabriel Harvey, whose correspondence with him is of such deep interest, and carefully read tells so much of his method. Sir Nicholas Bacon had died. He left Francis without a living, and Lord Burghley, the Queen's other great pillar of State and Master of the Court of Wards, now became his guardian. He had been enrolled with Anthony Bacon as a student of law at Gray's Inn when still a boy. Much to his distaste he had now

* Laneham, Euphues, and Immerito are quite unmistakably the same witty, merry, wise, and mirthfully exuberant youth, ever ready to delight the ladies and delighting in them.

to go into residence there, but begged first a favour in the nature of some service to the Queen. This being apparently granted he disappeared from England for nearly two years on some secret mission,* travelling abroad in France, Germany, Austria, Italy, Spain. He saw there those places he has since rendered idyllic in the eyes of all the world—Venice, Padua, Verona, Rome, Florence, and many more. His senses all alive, where-ever he went he reaped and registered ever more knowledge of men and things, making his mind a store-house from which on his return he set to work to enrich the world. His progress was gradual. His beginnings were simple. He never attempted too much, never climbed too high for his powers, but as he improved and embellished his native tongue, and gained knowledge of men and character, he simul-taneously developed the drama. Nothing could be more naïve than the plays of John Lyly, as which he wrote " Alexander and Campaspe," " Galatea," " Sappho and Phao," " Endymion," and the like. Moreover, it is easy for any man who will carefully consider it to see that the plays of Greene, Peele, and Marlowe are but phases in the mind of the same man having the same aim as he advanced stage by stage to greater perfection. When Marlowe died, 1593, Shakespeare at once came into existence, and took up the drama at the very point where Marlowe left it, as no new-born author could. Thus Marlowe's " Edward II." is already a natural

* See p. 197 above.

" Did he not draw a sort of English priest
From Douay to the seminary at Rheims ?"

(MARLOWE: " The Massacre of Paris.")

history after Shakespeare-Bacon's model, in which we read:

> " My lord, why do you thus incense your peers
> That *naturally* would love and honour you ?"
> > (Marlowe's " Edward II.," Act I., sc. i.)
>
> " For with my *nature* war doth best agree."
> > (Marlowe's " Edward II.," Act I., sc. iv.)
>
> " Thou seest by *nature* he is mild and calm."
> > (Marlowe's " Edward II.," Act I., sc. iv.)
>
> " *Unnatural* wars, where subjects brave their King."
> > (Marlowe's " Edward II.," Act III., sc. i.)
>
> " *Unnatural* King ! to slaughter noble men
> And cherish flatterers."
> > (Marlowe's " Edward II.," Act IV., sc. i.)
>
> " This *unnatural* revolt."
> > (Marlowe's " Edward II.," Act IV., sc. v.)
>
> " And that *unnatural* Queen, false Isabel."

This is an excellent example of a natural history, a type and model—according to Bacon's method, as explained in the " Plan of the Great Instauration " and Aphorism 127 of the " Novum Organum "—setting before our eyes the errors arising from self-indulgence and favouritism, and the passions they arouse: an unnatural King incensing his peers and giving rise to unnatural revolts, unnatural wars, and an unnatural Queen. Compare it, moreover, with " Hamlet," in which the words "native," " nature," " natural," " unnatural," occur forty-three times, the last occasion, at the end of the play, being particularly illuminating:

> " So shall you hear
> Of carnal, bloody and *unnatural* acts, . . .
> > *   *   *   *   *
> Fallen on the inventors' heads."
> > (" Hamlet," last scene.)

The play of " Edward II." exemplifies just such unnatural acts of the King bringing vengeance upon
the King himself, and in " Hamlet " we see the
struggle between nature and custom* at its full
height.

Shakespeare-Bacon, as we have seen, rose gradually,
step by step, from comedy to tragedy, before he
publicly scaled the heights to attack Aristotle and excel
him in philosophy.† We know, however, also from his
letter to Fulgentio, that his scheme was in his head in
youth forty years before it saw light.‡ We see now
gradually revealed before our eyes the stages by which
he reached it. Marlowe died in 1593. A new poet
called Shakespeare appeared the same year, but instead
of working his way up, started in " Love's Labour's
Lost " (1594) at the very point where Marlowe left it,
continuing in the very same method of writing natural
history, even asking " What is the end of study ? " and
giving answer that the end of study is knowledge of
nature, not plodding over books.§ " Why that to
know, which else we should not know "—that is, for
example, nature and the beauties of nature as we see

* " Custom, which is a kind of law " (" De Aug."; " Philosophical Works of Francis Bacon," ed. by J. M. Robertson,
p. 616).
" Custom, which claims equal authority with the law "
(J. Barclay's " Argenis ": To the understanding reader).

† " Manes Verulamanii." See p. 179.

‡ " This was a kind of embryo of the Instauration " (The
Temporis Partus Maximus, or Masculus ?)—Archbishop
Tenison, 1670. See p. 41, " Francis Bacon," by Walter
Steeves. See p. xv, " Philosophical Works of Francis Bacon,"
ed. by J. M. Robertson.

§ " Ye marvel perchance to see me so bookish " (Laneham's
letter).

them in a woman's eyes, and by deep-searching.* In
" Edward II." notably, and generally in Marlowe's
plays, there is a sameness in the secondary characters
which disappears in Shakespeare in a manner not
possible in a young and new poet just trying his wings.
In fact, as I have shown, Bacon did not adopt the name
of Shakespeare till he had as nearly reached perfection
as he could expect. Gradually lengthening his stride
as the power of utterance, the sweetness of his voice
and his knowledge of character grew, he rose step by
step, under a succession of pseudonyms, till in Marlowe
we recognise the true student of nature. Then, cutting
the painter, he came forward at last as Shakespeare,
the master of all knowledge and the wonder of all men,
collecting all the best of his work in the Great Folio
of 1623.

Queen Elizabeth on her accession herself gave the
first impetus to the drama, aided by the Earl of
Leicester; and, under their eye the young Shakespeare
as Francis Bacon grew up to love it. Queen Elizabeth
herself was not indeed so much enamoured of literature
as that she loved knowledge and learning and culture
for practical purposes, power, and enjoyment. She
showed very conspicuously in her oration at Cambridge
in 1564 not only that she had a noble ambition, but
that she loved the drama as an educational instrument
and incentive to culture. She there already took
Alexander the Great, the patron of Aristotle, as her
hero and example, and we find him perpetually extolled
by Bacon, and hardly less by both Marlowe and
Shakespeare. As great Alexander's ambition was to
hellenise the world and make culture universal, so

* " Love's Labour's Lost," Act I., sc. i.

this lofty aim was breathed into Shakespeare-Bacon by his mother and became his own.   Thus in the 1604 quarto edition of Marlowe's "Dr. Faustus," the German Emperor is made to say:

> " Amongst which Kings is Alexander the Great,
> Chief spectacle of the world's pre-eminence,
> The bright shining of whose glorious acts
> Lightens the world with his reflecting beams,
> As when I hear but motion made of him
> It grieves my soul I never saw the man."*

Even so Laneham links together Alexander and the German Emperor: " What may these greatnesses bode, but only as great honour, fame, and renown, for these parts here away, as ever was to those two noble Greats: the Macedonian ' Alexander ' in Emathia or Greece, or to Romane Charles in Germany or Italy."†

And so again Shakespeare in " A Winter's Tale ":

> " Care not for issue,
> The crown will find an heir: Great Alexander
> Left his to the worthiest, so his successor
> Was like to be the best."‡

This is ominous as spoken to Leontes—*i.e.*, Henry VIII., whose heir—as his grandson—Shakespeare was, on our assumption.

This aim of Queen Elizabeth, her love of culture, her desire to emulate Alexander and so hellenise the whole

---

* " Dr. Faustus," 1604, quarto.   It is noteworthy that these words are not in earlier editions, and that his play was not printed during Marlowe's life.

† Nashe similarly admires Charles V.

‡ " A Winter's Tale," Act V., sc. i.   There is also much play on Alexander in " Hamlet," Act V., sc. i.   " He sits in his state as a thing made for Alexander " (" Coriolanus," Act V. sc. iv.).

wide world, was, so to speak, the mantle of the great Queen which fell upon her son, Shakespeare. It was she who inspired in him that untiring industry and faith in his own powers, with which he devoted himself to humanity and the study of nature in its interests; and it was, we feel absolutely convinced, the great Queen herself who at lovely Woodstock gave the young author of "The Hermit," then aged fourteen, the sage advice:

"Knight, prosecute thy purpose, it is noble, learning by me not to fear, and of thyself to take pains, remembering nothing notable is won without difficulty. Hercules had by his labour his reward, his ruin by love."*

It was with truly Herculean labour that he, remaining true to his great aim from beginning to end, applied himself to the study alike of the nature of man and of things, to art and to science, and to the marriage of the two, in the hope of, in some degree, alleviating human misery and providing it with new powers and delights. "Men," he says, "have hitherto used the faculty of reason but little, and the office of art not at all, for the discovery of inventions." He shone in both, and, thanks mainly to him, as the bellringer, to-day invention is triumphant everywhere. The Great Plays and the "Great Instauration" bear the same emblem. He taught not only the crea-

* It will be seen how consistent this sentiment is with Bacon's "Essay of Love"; also Ascham, quoting Aristotle, says: "Pleasure allureth love, love hath lust to labour, labour always obtaineth his purpose." So that the young should be taught to take pleasure in learning, as Shakespeare was taught ("Ascham's Works," J. Bennet, p. 265).

tion, but right use of power, by creation meaning always the direction of nature into new channels by man.

All Englishmen owe a great debt to Mr. J. M. Robertson for his eloquent tribute to Bacon in the introduction to "The Philosophical Works of Sir Francis Bacon." It must, however, be borne in mind in reading him that when the stolid philosopher has said that two and two make four, he is often fully satisfied. To him that ends it. He has nothing more to say. He sees no interest beyond. But the man gifted with a larger imagination coming along perceives that out of several separate units he can create an infinite variety of forms. Natural history, in short, leads to the belief that the instinct of the ostrich is not infrequently discernible in the most learned, who are sometimes observed likewise to shut their eyes to what they do not wish to see. Nevertheless it is manifest that the following beautiful and just panegyric on Bacon by Mr. Robertson, taken as a whole, is as accurately descriptive of Shakespeare's gifts as of Bacon's. He says:*

" To Bacon belonged in the very highest degree two faculties, *that of utterance or statement, and that of insight into human character.*† He has truly written of himself, addressing the King (in the ' De Augmentis, p. 606) that he was a man naturally fitted rather for literature than for anything else, and *borne by some destiny*‡ against the inclination of his genius into active

* J. M. Robertson, " Philosophical Works of Francis Bacon," p. xiii. Published by George Routledge and Sons, Ltd.

† Italicised by present author, as particularly applicabl to Shakespeare.

‡ What was the nature of that " destiny "?

life. In rightly recognising the predominance of his literary gift, he has implicitly undervalued his gift for public life, which was only less great, his moral sagacity being so keen that only his chronic failure to reck his own rede—the disparity between his insight and force of will—put him at any disadvantage as a man of action. And it is in virtue of his combination of the *gifts of speech* and of *moral insight that he is so memorable* and so convincing in his demonstration of the *why* of most men's failure to think rightly. *It is between his commanding and irrefutable censure of the vices of normal mental habit,* and his thrilling prediction of the great things to be done when those vices are amended,* that he holds still the admiration which he had conquered within a generation of his death."

Mr. Robertson seems to recognise the drift of his words, and the sense in which they might be taken, for in concluding he finds it necessary to say that "Bacon's fame is relatively undiminished, having survived even the attempt of some of his worshippers to prove that he wrote the plays of Shakespeare and a whole library besides." For this reason Mr. Robertson seems vague, and to fall short in penetration. Whilst he dwells on the admitted fact that Bacon did not discover induction but was, as he himself said, only the bellringer calling others to hear, he does not bring into sufficient prominence in a concrete form this highest aim of Bacon, which more than all proclaims him Shakespeare—namely, that he was seeking above all with all his might to find *a definite art of direction and indication* to prevent man from "wander-

---

* Italicised by present author, as particularly applicable to Shakespeare.

ing in the way, *by rounding up and down*";* thereby
" setting themselves in the right way to the wrong
place,"† to the abuse, not really the right use of
man's powers or knowledge, "which is the benefit
and relief of the state and society of man." It is
of this that Don Quixote and Dr. Faustus and
Julius Cæsar are such specific and marvellous yet
different examples, types, and models—Faustus going
straight to the wrong place—*i.e.*, hell—and Don
Quixote wandering "up and down" (words so
often recurring in Part II.) possessed by a devil—
that is, mad—Cæsar's ambitious motives terminating
in murder and assassination. Nevertheless, Cæsar
" was without dispute a man of a great and noble
soul, though rather bent upon procuring his own
private advantages, than good to the public: for
he referred all things to himself and was the truest
centre of his own actions." Thus Don Quixote,
Dr. Faustus, and Cæsar, etc., notwithstanding the
great good in many, are " types and models . . .
various and remarkable" of men rounding up and
down, well meaning, but missing the true end, which
is not self but mankind.

Finally, if for Bacon we substitute " Shakespeare "
in the verses by Cowley which Mr. Robertson quotes,
what do we see but an absolutely ideal picture of
Shakespeare as Prospero in " The Tempest " watching
the " *errors and wanderings up and down* " and the
possibilities of man, just as also described in Bacon's
" Essay of Truth " by a quotation from Lucretius,

* " Valerius Terminus," chap. ix.; J. M. Robertson, " Philosophical Works of Francis Bacon," p. 194.
    † *Ibid.*, p. 188.

and still more forcibly repeated in the "Advancement of Learning." The verses of Cowley are:

" (Shakespeare or) Bacon, like Moses, led us forth at last;
          The barren Wilderness he past;
          Did on the very border stand
          Of the blest promised land;
          And from the Mountain Top of his Exalted Wit
          Saw it himself, and show'd us it."
                                 (COWLEY.)

It would be difficult to describe the motif of Shakespeare's "Tempest" more eloquently, unless it be in the words of Lucretius as translated by Bacon: "It is a view of delight to stand and walk upon the shore, and to see a ship tossed with *Tempest* upon the sea and . . . behold . . . the wanderings '*up and down*' of other men "* as Prospero did. "But no pleasure is comparable to the standing upon the vantage ground of Truth (a hill not to be commanded and where the Ayre is alwaies cleare and serene); and to see the errors and wanderings, and Mists and *Tempests*, in the vale below;—So alwaies that this prospect be with Pitty."†

" I appeal to all humanity
To look upon this picture and on this,
And judge which is more natural and *likely*."

Examination of events in the sixteenth century shows that circumstances contrived a wonderful literary fraud, of which Gul: Shakspere of Stratford was the decoy or gull. The unity of ideas contained in the First Folio of the plays by Shakespeare, and in the

* "Advancement of Learning"; J. M. Robertson, "Philosophical Works of Francis Bacon," p. 93.
† Bacon, " Essay of Truth."

" Great Instauration of the Sciences " by Bacon, reveals that they come from the pen of one man, who wrote and lived under the cloak of many motleys, of which the chief were Shakespeare and Bacon. The two works together symbolise that marriage of science with art which, he foretold, was to make the mind of man a match for the nature of things—the one by endowing him with new discoveries and powers, the other by setting before his eyes, as in a mirror, noble examples of a remarkable kind, illustrating the effect of man's passions on his actions in the right and wrong use of those discoveries and powers, and so to guide him on the right way to the right place: " the benefit and relief of the state and society of man," and the alleviation " of the necessities and miseries of humanity."

The power of the mind behind nature far exceeds the power of the mind of man, so that foreseeing and forestalling the arrangements man would make, it works, what seems to us, like miracles. For custom is strong but nature is mighty, and, intervening often when least expected, triumphs mysteriously over man, spurning his customs and his artifices.

My story may not be correct at all points. Yet this my view presents at least a logical ladder of experience, whereby the Shaker of the Spear of Pallas, the Goddess of Invention, may well have ascended to the exalted throne of Prince of poetic invention. I reject the view that his genius was empirical, that the man whose master mind conceived the beautiful plays was an actor, country-bred, but well known in London, who remained unrecognised at Court, unrewarded by Queen Elizabeth, and unfamiliar with the great men of his age; and above all, that the moneymaking

Stratford Shakspere left sixteen brilliant plays un-published though complete, and unsold. Their great author, as all will agree, had a divine soul. But it was imprisoned in a human body, condemned to lead an unnatural life, witness and even play a part in unnatural acts, at a Court where dissimulation and licence had become a habit and custom, a Court which he spurned, from which he held aloof so far as possible, and when he tripped, cut himself off altogether. I believe all this to be discernible in the literature of his time, and that the mystery is capable of being easily unravelled by anyone who honestly attempts it, from an unbiassed point of view, with a little perseverance.

> " Shrouded in mist was gentle Shakespeare born;
> Sent, as it were, like Mercury from Heaven
> To bring a message to mankind from God:
> First of all, to endow men with new power;
> Then set before their eyes as in a mirror
> The merciful and righteous use of it . . .
> First the Creation, then the End of Power.*
> The sovereignty of reason over passion,
> Envy, hatred, jealousy, revenge;
> And the huge army of the world's desires."

" The empire of man over things depends wholly on the arts and sciences. For we cannot command nature except by obeying her " ("Novum Organum," Book I., Aphorism 129).†

* " Valerius Terminus."

† Sir David Bruce was able to show that the applications of scientific discovery to the medical art had relieved untold suffering, saved countless lives, removed some of the worst terrors from war, made possible such engineering feats as the completion of the Panama Canal, and opened up the Tropics to white men. It is an encouraging narrative of achievement and of promise, and the President of the British Association will have fulfilled the high duties of his office if his words resound through the Empire.—*Times*, August 7, 1924.

The above was written before I had read through
the cipher story, and was entirely evolved from books
written, or believed to have been written, in part or
wholly, by Francis Bacon. I have since, for the first
time, read the later portions of the cipher as evolved
by Mrs. Gallup, more especially that deciphered from
the " Silva Silvarum," where I find the following:

" One must give as great a portion o' time as seven
days in the weeke can furnish, and must *not use many
houres for recreation*, would he leave aught o' any value
to men, for life is so short. It is for this cause that
I use my time so miserlike, never spending a moment
idly, when in health. Oft my table seems to be as
a study, and I too frequently invite my friends when
my minde seemes more upon my worke than my
guests; yet do I account my reputation as an host
not of the worse, insomuch as I do converse with great
ease, and (as hath been said) with so much spirit and
wit that none know or imagine my absorption. Many
times have I thus made the plot of a story in mind,
while great lords sat at the table, follow'd many of
my experimentes to undisputable conclusions, or contrived a new cipher."

Thus the nature of this great and singular man's
character, as remarkable, above all, for his superhuman
industry and earnestness, is exactly as I have evolved
it from the study of his endeavours as it can be traced
in books. He himself bears witness to it, in a cipher
letter written in a manner such as Shakespeare himself,
or Bacon, both one, a man of the most divine sweetness
and light, only could indite.

It shows how keenly in his youth he took to heart
the wise counsel which I have traced to his Queen-
mother, to prosecute his noble purpose, learning from

her not to fear, and of himself to take pains. Thus must his Herculean industry bring him some day his reward. The day is at hand. He cast his bread upon the waters. It is about to bring him the fame he foresaw must be his—a "kingdom of immortal glory among men from generation unto coming generations: an unending fame far better worth, in any true thinking mind, than many a crowne which Kings do have set on with show and ceremony."*

Finally, then, taking Marlowe as a conspicuous instance of Baconian pseudonyms, I contend that no man of judgment can carefully examine his "Dr. Faustus" and Shakespeare's "Tempest" without perceiving that both are examples of Bacon's "Valerius Terminus," which, rightly interpreted, clearly signifies "the healthy end" or "true and lawful goal" of science, or, indeed, of life. Faustus uses his knowledge and power wrongly —*i.e.*, for selfish ends. Prospero uses it with judgment and charity, showing mercy to his enemies. By this light a comparison of the stage directions is conclusive in the two passages already quoted above; thus:

DR. FAUSTUS: I'll burn my books. (*Thunder, lightning, and exeunt devils with* FAUSTUS.)
(MARLOWE.)

PROSPERO: I'll drown my book. (*Solemn music.*)
(SHAKESPEARE: "The Tempest," Act V., sc. i.)

Indeed, Prospero invokes "heavenly" music.

So clearly is Dr. Faustus an example of what Bacon in his "Valerius Terminus" calls men "on the right way to the wrong place"†—*i.e.*, hell—whereas he speaks

* See "The Biliteral Cipher of Sir Francis Bacon," by Mrs. Elizabeth Wells Gallup, pp. 343 and 346.
† "Valerius Terminus," chap. ix., p. 194 (J. M. Robertson).

of charity such as Prospero showed as the "bond of perfection."*

In like manner the Great War may be instanced as a wrong use of knowledge and power. In short, Napoleon in our fathers' time, and still more the German Emperor in our own time, are similarly examples of what Bacon says of Cæsar—*i.e.*, they were men who erred through "the not rightly fixing their ends."† They, too, were men on the right way to the wrong place: Moscow and St. Helena; Verdun, Ypres, and imprisonment. They were overbold, seeking self-glory and admiration in excess, tilting at windmills like Don Quixote with his *Shaky Spear*, forgetting too much the Christian lesson of humility and the true welfare of their kind; whereas the life and sacrifice of Christ are the supreme example of knowledge and power used with judgment and charity, leading to Heaven.

Thus judgment and charity, which include sacrifice and goodwill, are, as it were, the wings on which a man may fly to paradise, being the essential elements of Unity or One-hood.

NE QUID NIMIS.
FORGET THYSELF. HIDE THY LIFE.‡
A CITY SET UPON A HILL CANNOT BE HID.

---

* "De Augmentis," Book VII., chap. iii., p. 577 (J. M. Robertson).

† "Imagines Civiles. Julii Cæsaris," p. 110 (G. W. Steeve's "Francis Bacon"). See also Montaigne's Essay, "Of the Inconstancie of our Actions."

‡ Montaigne's Essay, "Of Glory."

PALLAS ATHENE

Athenæum Club, London.

Facing p. 299.

MINERVA BRITANNA

" PALLAS, thou hast a second champion bred,
  As great in Artes, as was stout DIOMED
  In Armes; that 'gainst enraged MARS could stand, . . .
  Like power thou hast into this brain inspired;
  Thy champion too, whose Artes are fam'd as farre
  As was TYDIDES for his deeds of warre,
  We know thou art MINERVA that alike
  Hold'st Artes and Armes; canst speak, as well as
      strike."

THOMAS HEYWOOD.

The above lines are from the " Minerva Britanna," printed
in 1612 by Henry Peacham,* an alleged pseudonym of Francis
Bacon. On its thirty-third page is shown a hand shaking a
spear, while on the opposite page (34) is a named figure of Sir
Francis Bacon pointing to it.

The frontispiece shows Parnassus; The Sun (Apollo); the
Laurel; and the hand of a " Concealed Poet " coming from
behind a theatre curtain and writing *Mente Videbor* (By the
mind I shall be seen).   The author has endeavoured to follow
this injunction, and set forth Bacon's mind clearly to the
reader as revealed in various works. See Epilogue, " The
Ulysses of Literature."

---

* He calls himself also Peamach Ryhen, an unmistakable
pseudonym.

EPILOGUE

THE ULYSSES OF LITERATURE

By HAROLD SHAFTER HOWARD

THIS book places before the public material which I have not seen presented so amply, and elucidated so clearly in any of the books of the Tudor-Baconian persuasion; I mean by that those books which regard Francis Bacon as the elder of two sons of Queen Elizabeth, Robert Essex being the younger son. Those who have seen the name of the latter carved in the Beauchamp Tower, in the Tower of London, will remember that it is written " Robart Tidir," which is, of course, " Tudor."

In view of the Francis Bacon Tercentenary of 1926, the English author has expressed to the American writer of this book's Epilogue his desire to have English and American opinion represented. Upon receiving a copy of Mr. C. Y. C. Dawbarn's book entitled " Uncrowned," General Hickson, in thanking the present writer for it, pointed out that that interesting summary of the cipher narrative is corroborated and supplemented by his book, which is drawn entirely from history and literature of the Elizabethan period. Since reading his book, I think it is remarkable that he should have found, without the ciphers, much the same information as they contain.

General Hickson has accepted for the " Prince of Poets " the pictures of Pallas Athene among other illustrations collected by the present writer in Paris and London. He has called my attention to a passage

---

* Mr. Howard has been furthering the archæological researches of the late Dr. Owen for the last five years.—*Publisher*

301

in a book named after the Priestess of Pallas, "The Argenis." He believes, what the cipher reveals as a matter of fact, that Barclay's "Argenis" was written by Bacon, as an allegory of the latter's early life. In it, as he says, Pallas is described as holding 'a golden spear, which was so brilliant that the people thought the goddess was shaking it at them.' That is more subtle than Jonson's interpretation that the author of "Shake-speare" 'seemed to break a lance in the face of ignorance.' The "Argenis" quotation is only one of many classical allusions, in the works attributed by the ciphers to Bacon, including Rawley's "Resurrectio Divi Quirini," sometimes written "Resuscitatio Divi Quirini," meaning the Divine Spear Shaker, or Pallas, revived. These allusions imply that the name Shake-speare, hyphenated as it usually appears on the Plays, refers to Bacon and not to the actor William Shaksper.

To find the origin of a thing is to explain it. The author of this book, without conscious aid of the ciphers, has, by imaginative sympathy in the study of Bacon's early masked writings such as Laneham's "Letter," revealed to us the early life, environment, and personality of the real author of Shakespeare, 'The greatest and noblest prince o' the world' ("Antony and Cleopatra," IV., xv., 54). It is a book that will save time to many a reader who might otherwise waste time in the by-paths of the labyrinth of old-style Baconian books.

The time is ripe, 1926 being the 300th anniversary of the death of Francis Bacon, as recorded in history. (The ciphers say that he lived longer than that.)* The present writer recently discovered that if you add the single numerals of the figures 1626 and 1926 you

* Cf. p. 312.

From
NEW ATLANTIS
· 1627 ·
And other
contemporary
works.
In three of
these works

Truth will be
found still
further raised
from her hiding
place showing
the advance
of
Time.

In some the hidden truth shall be revealed

Facing p. 302.

get 33—that is, Bacon's name number in the alphabet cipher. The name number is calculated (counting *i* and *j* as one letter) as follows: A=1, B=2, C=3, N=13, O=14, total 33. A remarkable coincidence.

That Francis Bacon was regarded by contemporaries as having used the sobriquet of the goddess Pallas Athene, the Spear Shaker, changed to "Shake-speare," as his pen name, is indicated by the following instances:

A verse by Jean de la Jessée, written in 1595 or 1596, when Bacon was thirty-five years of age, and addressed "A Monsieur François Bacon," contains the following line:

"Bien que *vostre Pallas* me rende mieu instruit."

Quotations from the "Manes Verulamiani":—These verses were first translated from the Latin by a Stratfordian of my acquaintance, at the request of a friend, who let him place his orthodox interpretations in the footnotes without correcting him. (I understand that a new translation has since been made by Fra. Sutton of Dublin, author of "The Shakespeare Enigma.") First let me quote verse VI. of these Latin poems in honor of Francis Bacon.

VI.

On the Death of the Most Honoured Sir Francis Bacon, of late High Chancellor of England, etc.

"Thou bold exemplar of how far the human mind may rise; thou talented deliverer of thine age; the while thou dost happily repair the meagre arts, and ease and set free the necks of their ancient yoke, how shall thy funeral be mourned that now cometh?"

Here is a quotation from verse V. that seems to answer that question:

V.

"No dweller of earth abounds in greater gifts of genius than he, nor does any of surviving men with equal skill combine

Themis* AND PALLAS moved by such talents; while he yet flourished, the sacred choir of Aonides (*i.e.*, the Muses) poured all their eloquence forth in his praise, and nought hath left for tears !"

WILLIAM BOSWELL.

The seventh verse, by T. Vincent of Trinity College, reads in part as follows:

VII.

" Thy renown neither clings to graven columns nor does thy tomb read ' Traveller, stay thy course.' If any offspring should recall his parent, 'tis not that of his body, but such as MINERVA, sprung from the brain of Jove . . ." (which last reads in the original as follows:

" Si qua patrem proles referat non corporis illa est,
Sed quasi de cerebro nata Minerva Jovis.")

" R. C. of Trinity College" writes " A Threnody on the Death of Sir Francis," which reads in part:

" The noble Bacon, Ah, how can I extol thee, greatest Bacon, in my lay ! or how those glorious monuments of all ages, chiselled by *thy genius*, by *Minerva*."

Here is a paragraph from another of these verses:

XVIII.

" THE DAY STAR OF THE MUSES hath fallen ere his time !

" Fallen, Ah me, is the very care and sorrow of the CLARION God (Phœbus Apollo), thy darling, Nature, and the world's— Bacon; aye, passing strange—the grief of very Death. What privilege did not cruel Destiny claim ? Death would fain spare, and yet she would it not. Melpomene (the Muse of Tragedy) chiding would not suffer it, and spake these words to the stern Goddess: ' Never was Atropos† truly heartless before now; keep thou all the world only give me my PHŒBUS back. Ah me, alas, nor Heaven, nor Death, nor Muse, Oh Bacon, nor my prayers could bar the Fates.' "

---

* Themis, Goddess of Justice, as Pallas was of Wisdom and of War.

† Atropos was one of the three Fates—" The Inevitable."

POET ON PEGASUS

By Alex Falguière, Paris.

Gabriel Harvey to Immerito

Whom gentle *mistress Rosalinde* once reported to have all the intelligences at commaundement, and, another time christened her

"Segnior Pegaso"

Facing p. 304.

Bacon is spoken of in another verse as the favorite of Melpomene. That seems to fit the author of the "Romeo and Juliet" line:

"Is there no pity sitting in the clouds that sees into the bottom of my grief?"

And of the line:

"Sweet are the uses of adversity."

The quotation below, from "Timon of Athens," also accords with the characterization of our great poet, Bacon, as a favorite of The Muse of Tragedy:

"He's truly valiant, that can wisely suffer the worst that man can breathe;
And make his wrongs, his outsides, to wear them like his raiment carelessly;
And ne'er prefer his injuries to his heart, to bring it into danger."

The following verse is by Thomas Randolph of Trinity College, and contains another reference to Bacon as Apollo, the god of the Muses, and to Minerva, the Shaker of the Spear (or, as Ben Jonson phrased it, "Breaker of the Lance, in the face of Ignorance").

XXXII.

". . . When he saw the arts were held by no root and languishing like seeds scattered on top of the soil, he taught the Pegasian Arts to grow even as the *spear of Romulus* grew, and in short time was a bay. So since he taught the Heliconian goddesses to grow, no ages will lessen his renown. Nor could the fires of a well-born breast bear further, DIVINE MINERVA, men's neglect of thee. His heavenly reed (*i.e.*, pen) restored thy wonted honour; a second Apollo routed thy clouds—aye even now PALLAS steps forth clad in new robe."

Bacon may be regarded as having applied his "new method," under the Shakespeare pen-name and other

20

pseudonyms such as Chapman and Samuel Daniel, who, in "An Apologie For Ryme," writes: 'Poetry and Philosophy are nothing, unless we bring the discerning light of right concepts with us to apply it to use. It is not books, but only that great book of the world, and the all-overspreading grace of heaven that makes men truly judicial.' That calls to mind the Shakespeare lines:*

> "From women's eyes this doctrine I derive:
> They sparkle still the right Promethean fire;
> They are the books, the arts, the academies,
> That show, contain, and nourish all the world:
> Else nought at all in aught proves excellent."

The provenances of Bacon's genius are revealed to the discerning in many works under other vizards. Bacon wrote: ' A new method must be devised by which to glide gradually into the human mind in this universal insanity.' He regards humanity as a prey to the "idols of the mind," and says that " every hollow idol is dethroned by skill, insinuation, and gradual approach." So well has he succeeded in concealing his identity as the greatest of world poets, that we have to go to mythology to find an analogy for such "prodigious wit" and strategy.

As Ulysses captured Troy by hiding his men in a wooden Pegasus, so Bacon, the Ulysses of Literature, succeeded in outwitting his enemies by concealing his drama and poetry behind the nom-de-plume derived from the sobriquet of the Greek goddess, Pallas Athene.

It has recently been affirmed by a popular ecclesiastic that the failure of scholasticism† to hold the world's attention is the cause of its present chaos. Bacon long ago saw that the inductive method of reasoning was

* *Cf.* p. 286.

† See Life, Diary, and Letters of O. L. Shafter, p. 257.

needed in its stead if the people were to be freed from autocratic control and given full opportunity for self-government. He was as opposed, as Dean Church points out in Morley's " English Men of Letters " Series, to the tyrannies of Puritanism as to the coercions of scholasticism. The remedy for both is to be found in supplanting rule-of-thumb methods by the ideals and inspirations of the great prophets, seers, and philosophical poets, among whom Francis Tudor stands, under the names "Bacon" and " Shakespeare," as the summits, Mounts Everest and Gaurisankar, in the Himalayas tower above all mountains; (the two are frequently identified with each other). It is for want of such vision, understanding of human nature and right direction to right ends, that, to quote the poet Young:

> " Millions are shipwrecked on life's stormy coast,
> With all their charts on board, and powerful aid,
> Because their lofty pride disdained to learn
> The instructions of a pilot, and a God."

" A rarer spirit " than Francis Bacon " never did steer humanity" ("Antony and Cleopatra," V., i., 32).

Dean Church says that Bacon was " obsequious to the tyranny of power, but he was never inclined to bow to the tyranny of opinion; and the tyranny of Puritan infallibility was the last thing to which he was likely to submit."

There is evidence to show that the alleged "obsequiousness " was due to the fact that as the representative of the Crown, whatever he might think and advise, he was obliged after a set time to enforce the Crown's decision. Dean Church has indeed judged our great philosophical poet, to use the Dean's own words, ' from partial and imperfect knowledge," judging by the evidence of Thomas Bushel's letters. With regard to the charge of bribery brought against Bacon, his own comment is that he " was the justest judge that was in England these fifty years. But it was the justest censure in Parliament that was these two hundred years." Bacon did not approve of the practice of taking gifts, but he never took bribes, which is not the case with some of his accusers. The inequitable censure was apparently due to his failure to dismiss his servant, Thomas Bushel, for accepting gifts in his name, if we are to judge only by Bushel's letter to John Eliot,* confessing that he and other servants were the cause of the bribery charges, having taken presents unknown to their master. This is of a piece with the " Henry VIII." lines where Bohun, Duke of Buckingham, says,

" both
Fell by our servants, by those men we loved most."

But there is another letter of Bushel's which reveals that Archbishop Williams proposed the scheme to the King and Prince Charles to save Buckingham by making Bacon his scapegoat. Bacon under coercion confessed guilt though innocent of the serious charges, and it is indicative that the enemies whom he is related in the cipher to have concealed his poetic works under other names to deceive were behind his shameful mistreatment. Church says, " Sir John Bennett, who had been condemned as a corrupt judge by the same Parliament and between whose case and Bacon's there was as much difference as between black and grey, got his full pardon, but Bacon's plea for pardon was rejected.' Because of this undeserved disgrace many conside

* Cf. " The Greatest of Literary Problems," by James Phinney Baxter, p. 336.

Bacon as unworthy to have written the plays. But he alone had the calibre, character, motives and genius requisite to have composed the great dramas. It is certain that 'without the passion for truth, without the passionate desire to understand the universe, without, too, the missionary passion to save souls by communicating their own uplifting and fortifying faith,' Bacon like "Dante and Lucretius, would have been less occasionally tedious, doubtless, but also would have missed some of those heights in poetry which they, in fact, achieved."* Let us bear those words of Dr. Herford's in mind when we hear the remark made that "it makes no difference whether Bacon or Shakespeare wrote the plays." It is interesting to read in one of Bushel's books these words: "The Lord St. Albans' 'Atlantis' is a magazine of compendious (but sublime) documents to enrich a commonwealth with universal notions as far above a vulgar capacity as the imperial Heavens are the earth." That reveals Bacon's calibre. What have the Stratfordians got to show that William Shakespeare was of like calibre and capacity?

No one but a Ulysses in ability to dissimulate or camouflage could have acted the part of a guilty person so uncomplainingly though innocent. Bacon was made a scapegoat because his magnanimity† was such that he could conceal his innocence, but the subsequent Shakespeare line tells, I think, his point of view about it. "Who steals my good name, steals that which not enriches him, and makes me poor indeed."

* "Shakespeare's Treatment of Love and Marriage," by C. H. Herford.

† "Magnanimity owes no account to prudence of its motives," Marquis de Vauvenargues, "Words of the Wise"; "Treasure Trove," by John o' London.

In " Antony and Cleopatra " our great poet says:

> " The loyalty well held to fools does make
> Our faith mere folly: yet he that can endure
> To follow with allegiance a fall'n lord
> Does conquer him that did his master conquer,
> And earns a place i' the story."
>
> (Act III., sc. xiii., l. 41.)

And in Act V., sc. ii., l. 177, he says:

> " Be it known, that we, the greatest, are misthought
> For things that others do; and, when we fall,
> We answer others' (de) merits in our names,
> Are therefore to be pitied."

Tobie Matthew wrote to this Master in Motley, Francis Shake-speare Bacon, these well known but too seldom comprehended words: " The most prodigious wit that I ever knew of my nation, and of this side of the sea, is of your Lordship's name, *though he be known by another.*"*

Bacon realised that he was ahead of his time as a reformer,† therefore he employed many masks, and so made it appear that all the literary world thought the same, as Ulysses used the fabulous Horse of Troy to conceal his soldiers under. He wrote to his friend and Fra. Sarpi's (the Friar Laurence compositely with Bacon's friend Lawrence Washington, in " Romeo and Juliet," some think), Fra. Fulgentio, as follows:

" I work for posterity, and the next generations, it requires ages for accomplishment." Let us see to it, accordingly, in this Tercentenary Year of Bacon's " Departure " (whether it was for the continent, as the cipher says, or the next world), that he is 'given leave

* The italics are mine.
† He left his good name " to foreign nations " in his will.

to speak his mind,' remembering his words to Tobie Matthew: "And since I lost much time with this age, I would be glad if God would give me leave to recover it with posterity."

Alexander Pope, in Epistle I., Bk. II., of " The Imitations of Horace," wrote the familiar lines which apply to the actor Shaksper rather than to " The Great Unknown " (Francis Tudor Dudley):

> " Shakespeare (whom your every Play-house bill
> Styles the Divine, the matchless, what you will),
> For gain, not glory, wing'd his roving flight,
> And grew immortal in his own despight."

Contrast that with Bacon's statement that he " wrote for the glory of the Creator, and the relief of man's estate." Would you expect such great works from a selfish character regardless of the question of Shaksper's education and knowledge of Europe and the *haute monde* generally ? Victor Hugo's words that " after God Shakespeare is the greatest creator," hardly apply to such a character as the Rosicrucian, Alexander Pope, depicts. Pope's words about Bacon being " the wisest, brightest, meanest of mankind " are cryptic, and very probably the last adjective refers to his " meanness " in deceiving us as to the authorship, to say nothing of the other definition of the word, namely, " self-effacing."

The contemporary writers at the universities who wrote the thirty-two poems in Latin at the time of Bacon's " departure," " To the Memory of the Most Eminent Man, Francis Bacon, Baron Verulam, Viscount St. Albans," (from which I have already cited the references to Pallas Athene), have the following lines:

XV.

" Who greater-souled than he unbarred Nature and the Arts?
Why should I speak of each in turn when many writings of great
fame abound?

" *A part of them lies buried;** that a part should see the light
Rawley, faithful Achates unto Francis, hath achieved."

ROBERT ASCHAM OF THE MIDDLE TEMPLE.

I.

" Every Age methinks will adorn and amplify this structure:
then to what age it is vouchsafed to set the finishing hand—
this is known only to God and to the Fates."

G. RAWLEY.

XXIX.

" Thou who couldst immortalise the Muses,
    Couldst thou, thyself, O Bacon, die?"

XXII.

" Yet shall thy writings, Bacon, live and reach thy descendants late in time even in spite of death."

In one of his emblems, a picture of which you will
find on page 415 of my late friend James Phinney
Baxter's " The Greatest of Literary Problems," Bacon
has a picture of Father Time helping a figure representing Truth out of a cave, and around it are written these
words: " Tempore patet occulta veritas " (" In time
the hidden truth shall be revealed ").† To paraphrase
the words of Cæsar's friend, Agrippa, in " Antony and
Cleopatra," it is not too much to prophesy that
eventually—

' Truths shall be tales, where now half tales are truths.'

The question whether Francis Bacon outlived his
alleged death date of April 9 (Easter Sunday), 1626, is

* The italics are mine.
† Refer to p. 415, Baxter, "The Greatest of Literary
Problems."

opened by a line in the " Manes Verulamiani," which reads as follows:

" He has gone—I said not, He is dead."

In a book by Bacon's Major-domo Thomas Bushel, called " Mr. Bushel's Abridgment of the Lord Chancellor Bacon's Philosophical Theory in Mineral Prosecutions," the alleged author tells of his travels in China and Japan, with his "heroic master." Bushel, whose occupation is mentioned on the title-page as " Farmer of the King's Mines in Wales," has a verse in that book headed, "The Hermit's Contemplations Upon A Rock," in which the hermit says, " This my prophetic soul foretells shall be," which, of course, recalls Hamlet's exclamation, " Oh, my prophetic soul, my uncle." The palace where Queen Elizabeth spent a great deal of time in her youth was first used as a Court Palace by Henry III. Bacon is so composite in his sources for trick names that, in addition to Amleth of the original story, one wonders if poetic license led him to think of Eltham Palace (Eltham, Kent)* as a derivation for the name Hamlet also. If Bacon survived until 1637 or 1668, as various ciphers respectively claim, he had ample time to do the " Posthumous " work attributed to him by the more advanced Baconians. The original spelling of the name Bushel is with one l; it is not fantastic to suppose that Bacon hid his light under a Bushel.

General Hickson has said that Ariel is derived from the Latin quotation in " De Augmentis Scientiarum," Book V., chap. ii.: " The Celestial Gift of Ariel (*aërei mellis cælestia dona*), the heavenly honey that we call science." As Bacon " took all knowledge for his

* Elsinore is suggested by Eltham and Windsor conjointly.

province," it is possible that the twenty-ninth chapter of Isaiah may also have been in his mind in that regard.

In the Century Bible, edited by Owen C. Whitehouse, Ariel is defined as a problematic word, one of the meanings being "God's lion." In his essay of "The Greatness of Kingdoms," Bacon speaks of "the lion's whelp," Judah, so-called by his father Isaac when he prophesied that "The sceptre should not pass from him." In "Cymbeline," you remember the quotation in the last act: "When as a lion's whelp shall to himself unknown without seeking find . . . and when from a stately cedar shall be lopped branches which being dead many years, shall after revive, be jointed to the old stock, and freshly grow; then shall Posthumus Leonatus end his miseries, Britain be fortunate and flourish in peace and plenty." The meaning seems to be that when the various names under which Francis Bacon wrote in the sixteenth and seventeenth centuries are revealed as his masks, he will come into his own as the greatest genius the world has known.

In conclusion, let me cite a verse in the twenty-ninth chapter of Isaiah, which begins, "Ho, Ariel, the city where David encamped." "And thou shalt speak out of the ground, and thy speech shall be low out of the dust; and thy voice shall be as one that hath a familiar spirit, out of the ground, and thy speech shall whisper out of the dust. . . ."

In view of the present progress of archæological research in line with the late Dr. Owen's directions I venture to hope that the above prophecy of Isaiah may prove virtually true in the case of the Prince of Poets and Ulysses of Literature.

LONDON,
January 15, 1926.

VIEW OF ELTHAM PALACE PRIOR TO CROMWELL

From Gregory's "Royal Eltham.

Facing p. 314.

INDEX

315

21